Online Searching

ONLINE SEARCHING
A DICTIONARY and BIBLIOGRAPHIC GUIDE

GREG BYERLY

LIBRARIES UNLIMITED, INC.
Littleton, Colorado
1983

LIBRARIES UNLIMITED, INC.
P.O. Box 263
Littleton, Colorado 80160-0263

Library of Congress Cataloging in Publication Data

Byerly, Greg, 1949-
    Online searching.

    Bibliography: p. 123
    Includes index.
    1. On-line bibliographic searching--Bibliography.
2. On-line bibliographic searching--Dictionaries.
I. Title.
Z699.2.B9 1983   025'.04   83-853
ISBN 0-87287-381-1

Libraries Unlimited books are bound with Type II nonwoven material that meets
and exceeds National Association of State Textbook Administrators' Type II
nonwoven material specifications Class A through E.

TABLE OF CONTENTS

DICTIONARY

BIBLIOGRAPHY

JOURNAL ARTICLES: Part I
General Overview of Online Searching (cont'd)

JOURNAL ARTICLES: Part II
Specialized Subject Areas and Databases of Online Searching

INTRODUCTION

Online searching is rapidly becoming an integral part of reference service in many libraries. More and more professional librarians are actively involved in either conducting searches or using the results of such searches to provide information to patrons. It is, furthermore, increasingly difficult to read an article in a professional journal about reference work without being exposed to online searching concepts and terminology. Both librarians and library administrators need basic information to guide them in setting up and managing an online search service. In a similar fashion, online search analysts also find it increasingly difficult to keep up with the tremendous number of articles published on search techniques and strategies.

This dictionary and bibliographic guide to online searching provides easy access to concise and understandable definitions of online searching terminology and also presents a selective annotated bibliography of journal articles, arranged by specific topics, which are readily accessible to most librarians. In addition, representative books, directories, bibliographies, annuals and proceedings, and journals are identified.

This work is not designed to deal with the entire spectrum of library automation or information retrieval, but only with online searching. Online searching is further restricted to those computerized applications commonly available from the three major commercial search services (Bibliographic Retrieval Service [BRS], DIALOG Information Retrieval Service [DIALOG], and System Development Corporation [SDC]). Other applications (e.g., electronic mail) and other systems (e.g., National Library of Medicine's MEDLARS) are briefly covered both in the dictionary section and the bibliography, but emphasis is on online searching as exemplified by the three general search services.

Over 1,200 terms are included in the dictionary section. Definitions are purposely short and concise. As in any dictionary, the intent is not to explain in detail, but simply to identify basic meanings and to indicate through cross-references how a specific word is related to other terms. The main criterion used in selecting a term was whether it is used in the field of online searching. This is not a dictionary of computer science or library automation. Computer terminology is kept to a minimum and identified as "COMPUTER SCIENCE USAGE." The majority of the terms included deal directly with online searching. Examples are given where appropriate, and many "see" and "see also" references are included.

In addition, certain terms are typed in **boldface** to indicate that that term is defined in the dictionary and to suggest that it might also be consulted. However, some terms (e.g., "online" and "computer") are used so frequently that they are boldfaced only when a basic comprehension of the term is essential to understanding the definition in which it is used. As a general rule, acronyms and names of databases are capitalized.

System specific terms for BRS, DIALOG, and SDC are also defined. Over 150 such definitions, representing system commands, messages, abbreviations, and other unique terms, are included and noted as "BRS USAGE," "DIALOG USAGE," and "SDC USAGE." In a similar fashion, over 200 databases available from these three commercial search services and the MEDLARS files are identified. These databases and their file names are listed not as a directory of available databases, but simply as an easy means to identify databases commonly referred to in the articles included in the bibliography. For each database the general subject coverage is summarized, its availability is noted, and the file name or number is given, e.g., "Available on BRS (CAIN file), DIALOG (Files 10 and 110), and SDC (AGRICOLA file)." Common online messages from the communications networks are also included, e.g., "TYMNET USAGE" or "TELENET USAGE."

The bibliography section consists primarily of annotated journal articles, although significant books, directories, bibliographies, journals, annuals, and proceedings are also identified and briefly annotated in "Sources of Additional Information." Material beyond the scope of this bibliography includes: individual papers presented at conferences and meetings; ERIC documents; user manuals and other publications of commercial search services and database producers; search aids, including thesauri, and user manuals in general; and newsletters and other non-journal serial publications.

The 722 annotated journal articles in the bibliography are grouped into two major divisions. Part I has 32 subdivisions which provide a general overview of online searching and are designed to aid in the establishment of an online search service. Topics range from the "Design and Theory of Online Searching" to "User Evaluation and Attitudes." Part II includes articles for the experienced searcher, detailing how to perform searches in specific subject areas. Ten general subject areas and their representative databases are also included.

The annotations are descriptive, not critical, in nature. However, over 1,200 articles were specifically considered for inclusion and all of those included are judged to be of particular value. An extensive subject index is provided, as well as a periodicals cited index and an author index. In general, only items published since 1970 were selected. Coverage includes items available as of June 1982. Articles also had to be in English and, in part I, all were from readily accessible journals. Certain exceptions were made in part II (Specialized Subject Areas and Databases) and some items from more specialized journals or journals in a particular discipline were included.

Articles were selected from a wide variety of journals, but certain journals were extensively covered. All articles from *Database, Online*, and *Online Review* were included. A *de visu* examination of an additional 17 journals (noted with an asterisk in the Periodicals Cited Index) was conducted for the period January 1970 through June 1982 and relevant items selected and annotated. Entries from 49 other journals were retrieved through both manual and online searches of appropriate indexes and databases.

Each section of this book can be used to complement the other. For example, online terminology or databases mentioned in the article abstracts are defined and identified in the dictionary section. Similarly, persons using the dictionary to identify an unfamiliar database can also use the subject index to discover additional journal articles which deal with that database. This book should provide librarians, library administrators, online searchers, library students, and other interested laypersons with a concise guide to the terminology of online searching and easy access to the research in the field.

Dictionary

ABI/INFORM (Database)
Bibliographic database covering all areas of business management and administration. Available on BRS (INFO File), DIALOG (File 15), and SDC (INFORM file).

ABSTRACT
Brief summary of the main points of a **document**. Abstracts are typically available either **online** or **offline** when conducting a search. However, due to their length, they are generally cheaper if printed offline. Not all **files** have abstracts.

ABSTRACT NUMBER
Number given to an **abstract** of a **document** to uniquely identify it. Generally known as an **accession number**.

ACCESS
To "have access" to a system or **file** implies permission and ability to use it. To "access" a system or file means to communicate with it in order to retrieve or manipulate the **data** contained in it.

ACCESS POINTS
Any part of a **record** that is directly searchable and can be used to retrieve a specific item. For example, besides assigned **descriptors** and words or phrases in the title or **abstract**, access points also frequently include other **searchable fields** such as author, date of publication, language, or **document type**. The greater number of access points is one of the major advantages of **online searching**. See also: **FIELD**.

ACCESS TIME
Technically, the length of time it takes to receive a response once a **command** is **executed**. In some cases, however, it simply refers to the amount of time needed to **logon** to a given system.

ACCESSION NUMBER
Number sequentially assigned to an item when it is entered into a **file**. Consequently, it can often be used to retrieve items chronologically, e.g., the most recent items entered into a file. In some cases, the accession number is equivalent to the number assigned to the item in a corresponding printed index. For example, the accession numbers in the **ERIC** file are identical to the "ED" and "EJ" numbers used in the printed versions.

ACCOUNTANTS (Database)
Bibliographic database covering accounting literature and related topics. Available on SDC (ACCOUNTANTS file).

ACCT (Database)

BRS USAGE: BRS database which provides a total online accounting system known as AMIS. A BRS user can obtain detailed usage statistics and modify certain parts of the master record, e.g., assign privacy passwords or change the **default format** for any database.

ACCURACY

Freedom from error. **COMPUTER SCIENCE USAGE:** Computer scientists contrast accuracy with **precision.** Accuracy concerns the quality of the results, while precision indicates the quantity of detail used in displaying the results. For example, a computation to two significant decimal points is more precise than a calculation rounded to the nearest whole number, but if it contains an error, it is less accurate. See also: **RECALL.**

ACOUSTIC COUPLER

A type of **modem** which is used with a telephone to connect a **terminal** with the **computer** of a specific **commercial search service.** It converts the electrical signals of the terminal into audio signals which can then be transmitted over ordinary telephone lines to a computer not physically connected to the terminal.

ACTIVE FILE

File which can be **accessed** and manipulated **online** and, in most cases, a file which is **updated** on a regular basis. **BRS,** for example, splits several of its larger files chronologically, and only the most recent portions are available for **online searching.** The **backfiles** are not considered active files.

ADDITIONAL INDEXES

DIALOG USAGE: All **searchable fields** that are not part of the **basic index.** These are generally nonsubject **fields** (e.g., author, journal, or date of publication) and are searched using **prefix codes,** e.g., AU = to search the author field.

ADDRESS

COMPUTER SCIENCE USAGE: A label, name, or number which identifies a specific location in **storage.** Each location in storage is uniquely identified and assigned an address.

ADJ OPERATOR

BRS USAGE: See **FREE TEXT OPERATORS. SDC USAGE:** See **PROXIMITY OPERATORS.**

ADJACENCY

Requirement that two or more terms immediately precede and follow each other in a specified order in order to be retrieved. Contrast with: **PROXIMITY.** For example, in **DIALOG** searching "sex(w)discrimination" requires the word "discrimination" to be the next word after "sex" in any of the **searchable fields.** It will not retrieve "discrimination based on sex," but only those items containing the exact phrase "sex discrimination." See also: **POSITIONAL OPERATORS.**

ADP

COMPUTER SCIENCE USAGE: Acronym for **Automatic Data Processing.** See: **AUTOMATIC DATA PROCESSING.**

ADTRACK (Database)
Bibliographic database which indexes all advertisements larger than a quarter page appearing in 148 major American magazines. Available on DIALOG (File 143).

AFTER THE FACT QUALIFICATION
See: **POST-QUALIFICATION OF SEARCH TERMS.**

AGLINE (Database)
Bibliographic database which corresponds to the Doane Information Center Indexing Service's file and covers various agricultural topics, including agribusiness. Available on SDC (AGLINE file).

AGRICOLA (Database)
Bibliographic database of the National Agricultural Library which provides comprehensive coverage of agriculture and related areas. Available on BRS (CAIN file), DIALOG (Files 10 and 110), and SDC (AGRICOLA file).

AIM/ARM (Database)
Bibliographic database covering vocational and technical education. Absorbed by **ERIC** in 1977. Available on DIALOG (File 9).

ALGEBRA, BOOLEAN
See: **BOOLEAN LOGIC.**

ALCOHOL (Database)
BRS USAGE: See **DRUGINFO/ALCOHOL (Database).**

ALL
SDC USAGE: The word "all" is placed before a **truncated** term, and all variations of the term are then retrieved. Otherwise, a display of multi-meanings will be presented.

ALL PORTS BUSY MESSAGE
TYMNET USAGE: All **ports** of the requested **commercial search service's** computers are temporarily in use.

ALPHANUMERIC
Combination of alphabetic letters, numerical digits and, in some cases, special **characters** (e.g., + or −) which are **machine readable**.

ATLA RELIGION (Database)
Bibliographic database which covers religious or theological works. Available on BRS (RELI file).

AMERICA: HISTORY AND LIFE (Database)
Bibliographic database covering American and Canadian history. Available on DIALOG (File 38).

AMERICAN MEN AND WOMEN OF SCIENCE (Database)
Directory database which includes famous American and Canadian scientists currently active. Available on BRS (MWSC file) and DIALOG (File 236).

AMERICAN SOCIETY FOR INFORMATION SCIENCE

National association which is concerned with all aspects of **information science**. Publishes two significant journals: *Bulletin of the American Society for Information Science* and *Journal of the American Society of Information Science.*

AMERICAN STANDARD CODE FOR INFORMATION INTERCHANGE
See: **ASCII CODE.**

AMERICAN STATISTICS INDEX (Database)

Bibliographic database which indexes various statistical publications from over 400 federal government agencies. Also known as ASI. Available on DIALOG (File 102).

AMIS ONLINE ACCOUNTING SYSTEM
BRS USAGE: See **ACCT (Database).**

ANCILLARY EQUIPMENT
See: **PERIPHERAL EQUIPMENT.**

AND OPERATOR

Boolean operator which requires that all terms connected with "and" be present for the item to be retrieved. Logically expressed as: A AND B is true if, and only if, A is true and B is true. For example, in **SDC** searching "library AND automation" retrieves only those items in which *both* words appear in the **searched fields**. No degree of **proximity** or **adjacency** is required. See also: **BOOLEAN LOGIC, OR OPERATOR,** and **NOT OPERATOR.**

AND NOT OPERATOR
See: **NOT OPERATOR**

ANNOTATION

Generally considered synonymous with **abstract**.

APILIT (Database)

Bibliographic database which covers the international petroleum refining literature. Available on SDC (APILIT file).

APIPAT (Database)

Nonbibliographic database providing citations to petroleum refining patents from the United States and eight other major refining countries. Available on SDC (APIPAT file).

APTIC (Database)

Air Pollution Technical Information Center. **Bibliographic database** covering all areas of air pollution. Available on DIALOG (File 45).

AQUACULTURE (Database)

Bibliographic database which covers the growth of marine, brackish, and freshwater organisms. Available on DIALOG (File 112).

AQUALINE (Database)

Bibliographic database covering all aspects of water, waste water, and the aquatic environment. Available on DIALOG (File 116).

AQUATIC SCIENCES AND FISHERIES ABSTRACTS (Database)
   Bibliographic database which covers the aquatic sciences and related areas dealing with the seas and inland waters. Available on DIALOG (File 44).

ARTBIBLIOGRAPHIES MODERN (Database)
   Bibliographic database which indexes items related to modern art and design from books, dissertations, periodicals, and exhibition catalogs. Available on DIALOG (File 56).

ASCII CODE
   COMPUTER SCIENCE USAGE: Acronym for American Standard Code for Information Interchange. Pronounced "ass-key." Seven-bit standardized code used to represent all of the different **alphanumeric characters**. Allows the exchange of data among various types of **data processing**.

ASI (Database)
   See: **AMERICAN STATISTICS INDEX (Database)**.

ASIS
   See: **AMERICAN SOCIETY FOR INFORMATION SCIENCE**.

ASSIGNED SUBJECT HEADINGS
   See: **DESCRIPTORS** and **CONTROLLED VOCABULARY**.

ASYNCHRONOUS TRANSMISSION
   COMPUTER SCIENCE USAGE: Data communications term which refers to the transmission of **data** in which the interval of time between **characters** may vary. This necessitates the use of start and stop elements for each character for proper transmission. See also: **SYNCHRONOUS TRANSMISSION**.

AUDIT COMMAND
   SDC USAGE: Command used to discover the number of **postings** for each term within a **search statement**.

AUTHORIZED FILE
   File is valid for user's **password**. Certain files have restricted **access**. For example, certain files in **DIALOG** are not searchable as part of the **classroom instruction program**. If a student attempts to enter the CHEMICAL INDUSTRY NOTES database in DIALOG, he will be told the file is **unauthorized**. See also: **UNAUTHORIZED FILE**.

AUTOMATIC CROSS – DATABASE SEARCH SYSTEM
   BRS USAGE: See **CROS (Database)**.

AUTOMATIC DATA PROCESSING
   COMPUTER SCIENCE USAGE: Data processing which is performed as much as possible by mechanical (e.g., electronic or electrical devices which attempt to minimize the need for human involvement. Usually abbreviated ADP.

AUTOMATIC LOGON
   Procedure in which a **smart terminal** can be used to **logon** to a system automatically without individually keying in the necessary **passwords** and **user numbers**.

AVAILABILITY

Percentage of time a system is operational. Contrast with: **DOWN TIME**. Most **commercial search services** have extensive **backups** and have an extremely high percentage of availability.

AUTOMATIC UPDATING

See: **SELECTIVE DISSERMINATION OF INFORMATION** and **UPDATE**.

AUTOMATION

General term used to identify a technique or system which operates automatically with little human input required. Self-operational or self-controlled. In libraries, the term is often used in conjunction with computerized operations.

AUXILIARY EQUIPMENT

See: **PERIPHERAL EQUIPMENT**.

AVLINE (Database)

Directory and **catalog database** which represents all audiovisual materials cataloged by the National Library of Medicine since 1975. AVLINE stands for AudioVisual Catalog Online. Available on MEDLARS (AVLINE file).

BACKFILE

Older segments of larger **databases** which are maintained in separate files and which may not be available for **online access**. See: **OFFLINE SEARCHING**.

BACKSPACE

To move the **cursor** or printing element back one or more spaces, erasing one **character** for each backspace. Many **terminals** do not have actual backspace keys, and different keys must be used for this function. For example, backspacing on many terminals is accomplished by holding down the **control key** and then pressing the H key once for each character that is to be erased. See also: **CONTROL-H** and **CONTROL KEY**.

BACKUP

Auxiliary equipment, procedures, or personnel which are ready to be used if the primary means of performing a task are not functioning. **Commercial search services** maintain elaborate backup systems and are rarely **down** or inoperational.

BACKUP COMMAND

SDC USAGE: Command used to eliminate either all previous **search statements** or only the last one. Used to erase unnecessary search statements before **saving a search** or to create room for additional statements to be entered before reaching the system's limit.

BACKWARD SLASH

Method of correcting **errors** during **input**. A backward slash is typed for each **character** to be changed and the correct characters are typed after the slashes. For example, "libar\\rary" corrects the mistyping to "library." Compare: **CONTROL-H**. See also: **ERROR CORRECTION**.

BANKER (Database)

Bibliographic database which indexes all articles in the *American Banker*. Available on SDC (BANKER file).

BASIC INDEX

Generally, all **searchable fields** that have subject information. The basic index of most **bibliographic databases** includes title, **descriptors, identifiers**, section headings, and note words, when they are available. These fields are individually searched by using appropriate **field operators**. The basic index is the default search field, i.e., the system automatically searches in the basic index, unless terms are qualified with one or more field indicators. Both **DIALOG** and **SDC** assign certain searchable fields to a basic index. **DIALOG USAGE**: Alphabetical list of all meaningful terms having subject information used in the database. **Fields** contained in the basic index vary for each database. **SDC USAGE**: Subject terms found in any of a database's searchable subject fields.

BATCH MODE

See: **BATCH PROCESSING**.

BATCH PROCESSING

COMPUTER SCIENCE USAGE: Performing a variety of individualized searches or **programs**, which have been grouped together ("batched"), in the same **computer** operation. **ONLINE SEARCHING USAGE**: Predecessor of **interactive online searching**. Users submitted requests, searches were then formulated, and then groups of searches were processed or **run** by the computer. The user had no direct interaction with the computer and results were often not received for two or three weeks. See also: **OFFLINE** and **ONLINE**.

BAUD

Rate of modulation of a signal. One baud equals one **bit**. Dividing the baud rate by ten gives a rough estimate of the **characters-per-second**. Specifically, a 300 baud **terminal** transmits at a rate of 30 characters-per-second. Similarly, a 1200 baud terminal produces 120 characters-per-second. Most terminals currently used in **online searching** are 300 baud.

BAUD RATE

See: **BAUD**.

BBIP (Database)

BRS USAGE: See **BOOKS IN PRINT (Database)**.

BEBA (Database)

BRS USAGE: See **BILINGUAL EDUCATION BIBLIOGRAPHIC ABSTRACTS (Database)**.

BEGIN COMMAND

DIALOG USAGE: **Command** used to enter or change **files**. This command automatically resets the elapsed time clock and the **set number** counter to zero.

BELL AND HOWELL NEWSPAPER INDEX

See: **NEWSPAPER INDEX (Database)**.

BHRA FLUID ENGINEERING (Database)

Bibliographic database which covers virtually all areas of fluid engineering. Available on DIALOG (File 96).

BIBL (Print Option)
   BRS USAGE: Dispays a predetermined **default format,** usually representing a basic **bibliographic citation.**

BIBLIOGRAPHIC CITATION
   All necessary information to uniquely identify a particular publication. Typically includes author, title, journal or publisher, date, and pages. Corresponds to the items needed to correctly cite a reference in a **bibliography.** See also: **CITATION.**

BIBLIOGRAPHIC DATABASE
   File containing items which are generally bibliographical, i.e., they refer to other primary sources for the actual information. A complete **bibliographic citation** is generally retrieved. ERIC and PSYCINFO are examples of bibliographic databases. Contrast with: **NONBIBLIOGRAPHIC DATABASE.**

BIBLIOGRAPHIC FILE
   See: **LINEAR FILE** and **BIBLIOGRAPHIC DATABASE.**

BIBLIOGRAPHIC RECORD
   See: **RECORD.**

BIBLIOGRAPHIC REFERENCE
   See: **BIBLIOGRAPHIC CITATION.**

BIBLIOGRAPHIC RETRIEVAL
   See: **INFORMATION RETRIEVAL.**

BIBLIOGRAPHIC RETRIEVAL SERVICES
   Major **commercial search service** established in 1976. Commonly known as BRS. Many BRS databases ("BRS files") and **system specific** commands ("BRS USAGE:") are identified and described in this dictionary.

BIBLIOGRAPHIC UTILITY
   Organization which provides access to a large **bibliographic database** and offers users specific services and products, e.g., the printing of catalog cards. OCLC and the Washington Library Network (WLN) are examples of bibliographic utilities.

BIBLIOGRAPHY
   List of items dealing with a particular topic or written by a specific author. Normally, each entry has a complete **bibliographic citation.** Can be annotated or unannotated. See also: **BIBLIOGRAPHIC DATABASE.**

BI/DATA FORECASTS (Database)
   Numeric database which provides detailed market forecasts on various business activities for 35 countries. Available on DIALOG (File 129).

BI/DATA TIME SERIES (Database)
   Numeric database which contains as many as 317 economic indicators for up to 131 countries represented in time series records. Available on DIALOG (File 128).

BILINGUAL EDUCATION BIBLIOGRAPHIC ABSTRACTS (Database)
Bibliographic database which covers bilingual and bicultural education and related topics. Available on BRS (BEBA file).

BINARY CODE
System in which information is represented using only two symbols, usually one (1) and zero (0), known as **binary digits**.

BINARY DIGIT
One of two symbols, generally either zero (0) or one (1), which is used to represent information in a **binary code**. Abbreviated as "bit."

BIOCODES (Database)
Dictionary database which contains **BIOSIS** Category (Concept) Codes and Taxonomic (Biosystematic) Codes. Used in conjunction with the BIOSIS database.

BIOETHICS (Database)
Bibliographic database which deals with bioethics and bioethical issues in health care or biomedical research. Available on MEDLARS (BIOETHICS file).

BIOGRAPHICAL DATABASE
Nonbibliographical database which contains biographical information, e.g., **AMERICAN MEN AND WOMEN OF SCIENCE database**.

BIOGRAPHY MASTER INDEX (Database)
Bibliographical and **biographical database** which provides biographical information and references for persons found in more than six hundred standard reference publications. Available on DIALOG (File 88).

BIOL (Database)
BRS USAGE: See **BIOSIS PREVIEWS (Database)**.

BIOSIS PREVIEWS (Database)
Bibliographic database which covers all areas of the life sciences as indexed in *Biological Abstracts* and *Biological Abstracts/RRM*. Available on BRS (BIOL file), DIALOG (Files 5 and 55), and SDC (BIOSIS, BIO7479, and BIO6973 files).

BIOTECHNOLOGY (Database)
Bibliographic database which covers all technical aspects of biotechnology. Available on SDC (BIOTECHNOLOGY file).

BIT
Abbreviation of **binary digit**. **COMPUTER SCIENCE USAGE:** Usually represented by either a pulse (1) or absence of a pulse (0). **ONLINE SEARCHING USAGE:** Generally considered the smallest unit of information. Several bits make up a word or **byte**. See also: **BINARY CODE**.

BLAISE
See: **BRITISH LIBRARY AUTOMATED INFORMATION SERVICE**.

BLINKING CURSOR
See: **CURSOR.**

"BLIP"
See: **PROCESSING CUE.**

BLS CONSUMER PRICE INDEX (Database)
Numeric database which includes time series of consumer price indexes as calculated by the United States Bureau of Labor Statistics (BLS). Available on DIALOG (File 175).

BLS EMPLOYMENT, HOURS, AND EARNINGS (Database)
Numeric database which provides time series on employment, earnings, and hours of work for most industries in the United States. Available on DIALOG (File 178).

BLS LABOR FORCE (Database)
Numeric database which includes time series on American employment, unemployment, and general nonparticipation in the labor force. Available on DIALOG (File 177).

BLS PRODUCER PRICE INDEX (Database)
Numeric database which provides time series of producer price indexes as calculated by the United States Bureau of Labor Statistics (BLS). Available on DIALOG (File 176).

BLUESHEET
DIALOG USAGE: Summary sheet of **documentation** produced for each database available on DIALOG. Known as the "bluesheet" because it is published on blue paper.

BOOK (Database)
BRS USAGE: See **BOOKSINFO (Database).**

BOOK REVIEW INDEX (Database)
Bibliographic database which identifies sources of published reviews of books and periodicals appearing in over 380 journals. Available on DIALOG (File 137).

BOOKS IN PRINT (Database)
Bibliographic database which identifies books currently in print in the United States. Available on BRS (BBIP file) and DIALOG (File 470).

BOOKSINFO (Database)
Bibliographic database containing citations to English-language monographs currently available. Produced by Brodart, Inc. Available on BRS (BOOK file).

BOOLEAN ALGEBRA
See: **BOOLEAN LOGIC.**

BOOLEAN LOGIC
System of symbolic logic used to express relationships between individual concepts. One of the most valuable capabilities of **online searching**. Three basic **Boolean operators (AND, OR, NOT)** are used to link the various concepts. For example, connecting "gasoline AND price AND United States" would retrieve items concerned with the price of gasoline in the United States. See also: **BOOLEAN OPERATOR.**

BOOLEAN OPERATOR

Word or symbol that represents a logical function. Three basic operators (**AND, OR, NOT**) are commonly used in **online searching**. Also known as Boolean connector. See also: **BOOLEAN LOGIC**.

BOUND DESCRIPTOR

DIALOG USAGE: Multi-word **descriptor** or **identifier**. The entire index phrase is directly searchable, i.e., the computer does not need to search for both "library" and "automation" and combine them to retrieve items indexed under "library automation," but it can simply search directly for the phrase. The terms can, however, also be searched individually.

BREAK

To stop or interrupt the actions of the computer. On many terminals an actual **break key** is provided which is used to perform this function. The break key is typically employed to stop **online printing**, especially after the searcher has seen enough of a given result. In some systems the break key will also interrupt the processing of a **command** by the computer and, instead of completing the search, the computer will respond with a **prompt**.

BREAK KEY

Used to **break** or interrupt a system response after a **command** has been sent to the computer. See: **BREAK**.

BRITISH LIBRARY AUTOMATED INFORMATION SERVICE

Organization which functions as a **commercial search service** in the United Kingdom. Known as BLAISE. Also serves as a **bibliographic utility** and offers both a cataloging service and access to bibliographic citations for all books published in the United Kingdom since 1950 and in the United States since 1968.

BROADCAST MESSAGE

BRS USAGE: See **SYSTEM MESSAGE**.

BRS

See: **BIBLIOGRAPHIC RETRIEVAL SERVICES**.

BUFFER

COMPUTER SCIENCE USAGE: Temporary, short-term **storage** device used to equalize differences in operating speeds and the flow of **data**. For example, a buffer would be needed to compensate for the differences in operating speeds between a terminal inputting data and a computer processing it.

BUG

Any mistake or malfunction which results in inappropriate or mistaken **search results**. Generally, bugs are considered to be the problems of the **commercial search services** and **database producers**. For example, a **database** has a bug when it cannot accurately restrict searches to a given year, even though it is supposed to be able to and has been programmed to do this. The problem must be fixed, or debugged, by either the database producer or the commercial search service.

BUSY CONNECTIONS MESSAGE
TELENET MESSAGE: All **ports** of the requested **commercial search service's** computers are temporarily in use.

BUSY PASSWORD
Password is already in use in the system or has not been properly disconnected from an earlier online session. See: **PASSWORD.**

BYTE
Unit of **machine readable** data generally used to designate a single **character.** A byte is normally composed of eight **bits** and usually represents an **alphanumeric** character.

C OPERATOR
DIALOG USAGE: See **FULL TEXT OPERATORS. SDC USAGE:** See **PROXIMITY OPERATORS.**

CA CONDENSATES (Database)
BRS USAGE: See **CA SEARCH (Database).**

CA SEARCH (Database)
Bibliographic database of the Chemical Abstracts Service which offers comprehensive coverage of the chemical literature. Available on BRS (CHEM file), DIALOG (Files 308, 309, 310, 311, and 320), SDC (CAS82, CAS77, CAS72, and CAS67 files).

CA SEARCH TRAINING (Database)
BRS USAGE: Economical, royalty-free practice file for CA SEARCH. Available on BRS (CAST file).

CAB ABSTRACTS (Database)
Bibliographic database produced by the Commonwealth Agricultural Bureaux (CAB) which covers agricultural and biological information. Available on DIALOG (File 50).

CAI
Acronym for **computer assisted instruction.**

CAIN (Database)
Original name for AGRICOLA (Database). **BRS USAGE:** See **AGRICOLA (Database).**

CALIFORNIA UNION LIST OF PERIODICALS (Database)
Catalog database which also indicates location information. This file is a current listing of periodicals and serials held by over 600 libraries in California. Available on BRS (CULP file).

CANCERLINE (Database)
MEDLARS USAGE: Previous name for CANCERLIT database. See: **CANCERLIT (Database).**

CANCERLIT (Database)
Bibliographic database which covers all aspects of cancer and cancer research. Available on MEDLARS (CANCERLIT file).

CANCERPROJ (Database)
  Directory database which identifies and summarizes current cancer research projects. Available on MEDLARS (CANCERPROJ file).

CAREER PLACEMENT REGISTRY (Databases)
  Directory databases which list information on both students and experienced employees who are seeking jobs. Available on DIALOG (File 162, Experienced Personnel, and File 163, Students).

CARRIAGE RETURN KEY
  Key on a **terminal** which must be depressed to send messages to the computer. Since it is normally required after every line or **command** typed, it is usually assumed and not specifically stipulated when describing search techniques. Technically, the term is inappropriate since a terminal has no typewriter-like carriage to return. Often abbreviated (CR).

CARRIER LIGHT
  Light on a **terminal** which comes on when a proper connection has been achieved between the telephone and a **communications network.** After dialing the appropriate telephone number and hearing a high-pitched tone, the headset is inserted into the **acoustic coupler** or **modem** of the terminal and the carrier light comes on to indicate that a connection has been made. Also known as a signal light.

CAS DATABASES
  Databases produced by the Chemical Abstracts Service (CAS). These include **CA SEARCH, CHEMNAME, CHEMDEX, CASSI, CHEMSDI,** and **CHEMICAL INDUSTRY NOTES.** Different names are frequently used by the major **commercial search services** to describe similar CAS files. **SDC USAGE:** See **CA SEARCH (Database).**

CASIA (Database)
  CA Subject Alert Index. See **CA SEARCH (Database).**

CASSI (Database)
  Bibliographic and **directory database** which includes both **bibliographic citations** and library holdings information for significant primary literature dealing with the chemical sciences. Available on SDC (CASSI file).

CAST (Database)
  BRS USAGE: See **CA SEARCH TRAINING (Database).**

CATFAX: DIRECTORY OF MAIL ORDER CATALOGS (Database)
  Directory database which lists over four thousand records of mail order catalogs. Available on DIALOG (File 198).

CATALOG DATABASE
  Nonbibliographic database which contains lists or catalogs of materials available. Although **bibliographic citations** are retrieved, in many cases the purpose is to simply verify the existence of an item. Examples include **CALIFORNIA UNION LIST OF SERIALS database** and **UNIVERSAL SERIALS AND BOOK EXCHANGE database.**

CATEGORY CODES
    See: **CLASSIFICATION CODES.**

CATENATE
    See: **CONCATENATE.**

CATHODE RAY TUBE
    Type of **video display unit** which uses a cathode ray tube to display searches. Screen is similar to a television screen. See also: **VIDEO TERMINAL.**

CATLINE (Database)
    Catalog database which represents serials and monographs cataloged by the National Library of Medicine. CATLINE stands for CATALOG ONLINE. Available on MEDLARS (CATLINE file).

CENTRAL PROCESSING UNIT
    Part of a **computer** which includes the internal **memory** and the arithmetic and control units. Controls the responses to demands made on the system and allocates processing circuits to meet these demands. Abbreviated CPU.

CHAINING SEARCH COMMANDS
    See: **STACKING SEARCH COMMANDS.**

..CHANGE COMMAND
    BRS USAGE: Command which allows the user to switch from one database to another during an **online search.**

CHARACTER
    Any **alphanumeric** representations or other symbols, including spaces or punctuation marks, which are used to record **data** and which can be processed by a **computer.**

CHARACTER RESTRICTIONS
    BRS USAGE: Maximum number of **characters** that can be entered in a single **search statement.**

CHARACTER STRING
    String or group of **alphanumeric characters.** See: **STRING.**

CHARACTERS-PER-SECOND
    See: **BAUD.**

CHECK TAGS
    Categories which must be checked by an indexer. For example, MEDLINE indexers must indicate whether an article is based on animal or human experiments. Similarly, other files are broadly categorized by check tags for types of document (e.g., review article, book review, letter, etc.).

CHEMCON (Database)
    SDC USAGE: See **CA SEARCH (Database).**

CHEMDEX (Database)
Dictionary database which lists all chemical compounds cited since 1972 and gives a Registry Number and other identification information provided by the Chemical Abstracts Service (CAS). Available on SDC (CHEMDEX file).

CHEMICAL DICTIONARY DATABASES
Online lists of alternative names and unique identifiers, known as CA Registry Numbers, for chemical substances. Examples include CHEMLINE and CHEMNAME. Classified as dictionary nonbibliographical databases.

CHEMICAL ABSTRACTS SOURCE INDEX (Database)
See: CASSI (Database).

CHEMICAL INDUSTRY NOTES (Database)
Bibliographical database which indexes articles from over seventy business journals which deal with any aspect of the chemical processing industry. Available on DIALOG (File 19) and SDC (CIN file).

CHEMICAL REACTIONS DOCUMENTATION SERVICE (Database)
Bibliographic database which provides current indexing of the monthly *Journal of Synthetic Methods*. Subject area is synthetic chemistry. Available on SDC (CRDS file).

CHEMICAL REGULATIONS AND GUIDELINES SYSTEM (Database)
Directory database which serves as the authoritative index to all federal regulations covering chemical substances. Available on DIALOG (File 174).

CHEMLINE (Database)
Dictionary database which provides Chemical Abstracts Service Registry Numbers for substances which have appeared in various MEDLARS files. Available on MEDLARS (CHEMLINE file).

CHEMNAME (Database)
Dictionary database which lists chemical substances and provides the Chemical Abstracts Service Registry Number, molecular formula, and other identifying information. Available on DIALOG (File 301).

CHEMSEARCH (Database)
Dictionary database which lists the chemical substances which have most recently appeared in CA SEARCH. Used in conjunction with CHEMNAME. Available on DIALOG (File 30).

CHEMSDI (Database)
Bibliographic database which serves a current awareness function by reporting information cited in the last six weeks of *Chemical Abstracts*. Available on SDC (CHEMSDI file).

CHEMSIS (Database)
Dictionary database which lists any chemical substance which has appeared at least once in a Collective Index Period of *Chemical Abstracts*. Available on DIALOG (File 328, 329, 330, and 331).

CHILD ABUSE AND NEGLECT ABSTRACTS (Database)

Bibliographic and **directory database** which both lists bibliographic references and identifies current research projects and service programs in the area of child abuse. Available on DIALOG (File 64).

CHIP

COMPUTER SCIENCE USAGE: Single integrated circuit which contains many logic elements. A chip is actually a small piece of impregnated silicon onto which electrical paths are formed. The **microprocessor** which makes up a **microcomputer** is simply one or more of these silicon chips.

CHRONOLOG

Newsletter of **DIALOG**. Published monthly and sent to all DIALOG users. See also: **CHRONOLOG NEWSLETTER (Database)**.

CHRONOLOG NEWSLETTER (Database)

Full text database which corresponds to the print *CHRONOLOG* **newsletter** published by **DIALOG**. Available on DIALOG (File 410). See also: *CHRONOLOG*.

CIN (Database)

SDC USAGE: See **CHEMICAL INDUSTRY NOTES (Database)**.

CIRCUITS BUSY MESSAGE

TYMNET USAGE: **TMYNET** computer is temporarily unable to accept **logon**.

CIS (Database)

Bibliographic database produced by the Congressional Information Service (CIS) which covers virtually all congressional papers produced by the various committees and subcommittees of the House and Senate. Available on DIALOG (File 101) and SDC (CIS file).

CITATION

Complete **record** of information available in the **database**. Generally treated as synonymous with **record**. In some files it is equivalent to the **bibliographic citation**. See also: **BIBLIOGRAPHIC CITATION**.

CITATION FILE

See: **LINEAR FILE**.

CITATION INDEXING

Technique of listing all items "cited" by an author in a publication and then listing those items which subsequently "cite" that publication. The best-known citation indexes are those produced by the **Institute for Scientific Information**: *Science Citation Index* (available online as **SCISEARCH database**), *Social Science Citation Index* (available online as **SOCIAL SCISEARCH database**), and *Arts and Humanities Citation Index*.

CLAIMS/CHEM (Database)

Nonbibliographic database which lists American chemical and chemically related patents issued from 1950-1962. Available on DIALOG (File 23).

CLAIMS/CITATION (Database)
Nonbibliographic database which identifies later patents that cite an earlier patent. Available on DIALOG (Files 20, 221, and 222).

CLAIMS/CLASS (Database)
Dictionary database which lists all classes and certain subclasses of the United States Patent Classification System. Available on DIALOG (File 124).

CLAIMS/U.S. PATENTS (Database)
Nonbibliographic database which lists all patents contained in the general, chemical, electrical, and mechanical sections of the *Official Gazette* of the United States Patent Office from 1963 through 1970. Available on DIALOG (File 24).

CLAIMS/U.S. PATENT ABSTRACTS (Database)
Nonbibliographic database which lists patents from a wide variety of areas, including chemistry, engineering, and technology, issued since 1970. Available on DIALOG (File 25). Weekly updates are available on **CLAIMS/U.S. PATENTS ABSTRACTS WEEKLY database** (DIALOG, File 125).

CLAIMS/UNITERM (Database)
Nonbibliographic database which provides subject access to chemical and chemically related patents. Available on DIALOG (Files 223, 224, and 225).

CLASSROOM INSTRUCTION PROGRAM
DIALOG USAGE: Program which provides inexpensive access to most DIALOG files for students in authorized programs of study.

CLASSIFICATION CODES
Subject or category codes assigned to a **document** by a **database producer** to describe its general content. Some codes are hierarchical and can be used to retrieve a variety of closely related terms. Examples of hierarchical classification codes are found in **BIOSIS** and **MEDLINE**. See also: **HIERARCHICAL VOCABULARY**.

CLINPROJ (Database)
Directory database which includes summaries of approximately 3,000 clinical studies of recent anticancer agents and cancer treatments. Available on MEDLARS (CLINPROJ file).

CODEN
Six-character notation used to represent the titles of periodicals. Developed by the Chemical Abstract Service, it is frequently a **searchable field** and can be used to retrieve items from specific journals.

COFFEELINE (Database)
Bibliographic database which covers virtually all aspects of coffee production and marketing. Available on DIALOG (File 164).

COLD REGIONS (Database)
Bibliographic database covering all disciplines which study Antarctica, the Antarctic Ocean, and cold regions in general. Available on SDC (COLD file).

COLON SEARCHING
   DIALOG USAGE: See **RANGE SEARCHING.**

COMBINATION SEARCH LOGIC
   See: **NESTING.**

COMBINE COMMAND
   DIALOG USAGE: Used for logical operations. Previously numbered **sets** can be united using various **Boolean operators.** For example, "COMBINE 1 AND 2" groups together sets 1 and 2 in an AND relationship. This **command** works only on **set numbers** and cannot be used directly with **search terms.** See also: **SELECT COMMAND.**

COMBINING LOGICAL OPERATORS
   See: **COMBINING SEARCH TERMS.**

COMBINING SEARCH TERMS
   Using **logical operators** to combine terms and/or **sets** to form another set. For example, to find information on adolescent drug use, it is necessary to "combine" in an **AND** relationship the citations to "drugs" and "adolescents." The **commercial search services** use different **commands** to accomplish this function.

COMMAND
   Instruction given to initiate an action of the computer. See also: **COMMAND LANGUAGE.**

COMMAND LANGUAGE
   Commands, in either words or symbols, which are used to communicate with the computer. Unfortunately, all of the major **commercial search services** use different command languages. Attempts are being made, especially in Europe, to develop a common control language which would facilitate switching between commercial search services.

COMMAND STACKING
   BRS USAGE: See **STACKING COMMANDS.**

COMMAND WORD SEARCHING
   See: **LITERAL SEARCHING.**

COMMENT COMMAND
   SDC USAGE: Command used to transmit messages to the SDC Search Service Action Desk in Santa Monica. The **FETCH MAIL command** is used to retrieve any online responses sent by the Action Desk.

COMMERCIAL SEARCH SERVICES
   Organizations which offer access to one or more **databases** by providing all necessary computer operations and support services. The major general commercial search services are **BRS, DIALOG,** and **SDC.** Since these three are private companies, they are also commonly known as **vendors** or **database vendors.** These organizations are also frequently referred to as **search services.** However, because many libraries and information centers refer to their online search operations as "search services," it is helpful to call organizations such as SDC "*commercial* search services."

COMMON COMMAND LANGUAGE
See: **COMMAND LANGUAGE.**

COMMUNICATION LINK
Connection between a **terminal** and a **computer** when a **communications network** is used.

COMMUNICATIONS
Transmission of **data** regardless of its form, e.g., verbal, pictorial, symbolic, or digital. **ONLINE SEARCHING USAGE:** Transmission of digital information between a **terminal** and the **computer** of a **commercial search service** through a **communications network.** Since this typically involves the use of a telephone and regular telephone lines to connect with the communications network, these are also commonly referred to as **telecommunications** and **telecommunications networks.** Also known as **data communications.**

COMMUNICATIONS COSTS
Cost of communicating with a **commercial search service** to conduct an **online search.** Typically includes cost of telephone service and the cost of using a **communications network.**

COMMUNICATIONS NETWORK
Network designed to transmit information over communication lines. **ONLINE SEARCHING USAGE:** Network which transmits digital information to and from the computer of the **commercial search service** and the searcher's **terminal.** Commonly used communications networks include **TELENET, TYMNET, AND UNINET.**

COMP (Database)
BRS USAGE: See **COMPENDEX (Database).**

COMPENDEX (Database)
Bibliographic database which provides international coverage of engineering and technological literature. Corresponds to the printed *Engineering Index.* Available on BRS (COMP file), DIALOG (File 8), and SDC (COMPENDEX file).

COMPREHENSIVE DISSERTATION INDEX (Database)
Bibliographic database which includes virtually all American dissertations accepted at accredited institutions since 1861. Available on BRS (DISS file) and DIALOG (File 35).

COMPUSERVE
Information and entertainment service available to owners of **microcomputers.**

COMPUTER
Electronic device designed to manipulate **machine readable data** that has been **input** and placed in **storage** within it. The operations of the computer are directed by instructions contained in a **program** which is designed to produce desired results for the user. although the distinctions are rapidly diminishing, three types of computers are commonly identified: **main frame, minicomputer,** and **microcomputer.**

COMPUTER ASSISTED INSTRUCTION

Online tutorial program designed to assist in the instruction of students. Very little has been done in this area with regard to the training of online **search analysts. *MEDLEARN*** is perhaps the best example currently available. Commonly abbreviated CAI.

COMPUTER-BASED

Operations which are primarily conducted by computer processing. A "computer-based literature search service" would rely on **online searches** to retrieve as much of the information as possible, but might also conduct **manual searches.**

COMPUTER MEMORY
See: **MEMORY.**

COMPUTER PROGRAMS
See: **PROGRAMS.**

COMPUTER READABLE
See: **MACHINE READABLE.**

COMPUTER SEARCHING
See: **ONLINE SEARCHING.**

COMPUTER TERMINAL
See: **TERMINAL.**

COMPUTER-USER INTERFACE
See: **INTERFACE.**

COMPUTERIZED ENGINEERING INDEX (Database)
See: **COMPENDEX (Database).**

CONCATENATE

Technique which links together two or more **character strings** into one character string. Also known as catenate.

CONFERENCE PAPERS INDEX (Database)

Bibliographic database which indexes scientific and technical papers given at major meetings each year. Available on DIALOG (File 77).

CONGRESSIONAL RECORD ABSTRACTS (Database)

Bibliographic databases which indexes and abstracts every issue of the *Congressional Record.* Available on DIALOG (File 135) and SDC (CRECORD file).

CONJUNCTION
See: **AND OPERATOR.**

CONNECT

To establish a direct connection between a **terminal** and the **host computer.** Usually requires the completion of a **logon** procedure. See: **LOGON.**

CONNECT TIME
Amount of time spent connected to the **host computer.** Generally considered either the total time between **logon** and **logoff** or the amount of time spent searching in a given **database.** Both **communications charges** and **online charges** are determined by connect time.

CONNECTOR
Logical operator used in **Boolean logic** (e.g., **AND** or **OR**) and in **proximity** searching (e.g., **ADJ**). See also: **BOOLEAN OPERATOR.**

CONTEXT SEARCHING
See: **PROXIMITY.**

CONTROL COMMANDS
Commands used to correct **errors** or direct the actions of the computer in some manner. May involve the use of the **control key.**

CONTROL-H
Procedure for **backspacing** on most **terminals.** Simultaneously depressing the **control key** and the letter "h" results in a "backspace and delete" message being sent to the **host computer.** Works similar to the **backward slash.** See also: **CONTROL KEY** and **ERROR CORRECTION.**

CONTROL KEY
Terminal key which can be used to alter the output of the **keyboard.** The control key is always used simultaneously with another key. See also: **CONTROL-H** and **FUNCTION KEYS.**

CONTROLLED TERMS
See: **CONTROLLED VOCABULARY.**

CONTROLLED THESAURUS
See: **THESAURUS.**

CONTROLLED VOCABULARY
Standardized subject terms or headings used to index documents by subject. These controlled terms, generally known as **descriptors,** are usually listed in an established **thesaurus.** Databases with assigned controlled vocabularies can also be searched using **free text searching** techniques. A vocabulary which additionally ranks or classifies these controlled terms into related categories is known as a **hierarchical vocabulary.** Contrast with: **UNCONTROLLED VOCABULARY.**

CONTROLLED VOCABULARY DATABASE
DIALOG USAGE: Database with assigned **descriptors.** These descriptors are generally listed in a **thesaurus. Controlled vocabulary** databases may also be partially **natural language.**

CONVERSATIONAL MODE
Implies direct communication or "conversation" between the **computer** and the user. Synonymous with interactive system. See also: **ONLINE SYSTEMS.**

COORDINATOR
See: **SEARCH SERVICES COORDINATOR.**

CORPORATE SOURCE
Author or corporate author's affiliation. Often includes address. **DIALOG USAGE:** Abbreviated "/CS." **SDC USAGE:** Known as "Organizational Source" and abbreviated "/OS."

CORRECTING ERRORS
See: **ERROR CORRECTION.**

COST COMMAND
Online command to get an estimate of all costs incurred since initiating a search in a specific file. Much like looking at the meter during a taxi ride, it does not reset the accounting clock.

.COST COMMAND
DIALOG USAGE: See **COST COMMAND.**

..COST COMMAND
BRS USAGE: See **COST COMMAND.**

COST DISPLAY
DIALOG USAGE: Estimate of all charges from a specific **online search** that is provided directly by the computer with each **logoff** or change of file.

COSTS
See: **DIRECT COSTS, INDIRECT COSTS,** AND **USER FEES.**

CPS
Abbreviation for characters-per-second. See: **BAUD.**

CPU
Acronym for central processing unit. See: **CENTRAL PROCESSING UNIT.**

CR
Acronym for carriage return. See: **CARRIAGE RETURN.**

CRDS (Database)
SDC USAGE: See **CHEMICAL REACTIONS DOCUMENTATIONS SERVICE (Database).**

CRECORD (Database)
SDC USAGE: See **CONGRESSIONAL RECORD ABSTRACTS (Database).**

CRIMINAL JUSTICE PERIODICAL INDEX (Database)
Bibliographic database which covers the major journals in criminal justice and law enforcement. Available on DIALOG (File 171).

CRSD/USDA (Database)
Directory database which identifies current agriculturally related research projects. Available on DIALOG (File 60).

CROS (Database)
BRS USAGE: Master index of all searchable terms available on all BRS databases. Can be used to browse various files to determine which contain enough citations to justify actually being searched. Also known as the "Automatic Cross-Database Search System." Similar to DIALOG's DIALINDEX database and SDC's DATA BASE INDEX database.

CROSS FILE SEARCHING
See: MULTIFILE SEARCHING.

CRT
Acronym for cathode ray tube. See: CATHODE RAY TUBE. See also: VIDEO TERMINAL.

CRT TERMINAL
See: VIDEO TERMINAL.

CUE
Synonymous with prompt. See: PROMPT.

CULP (Database)
BRS USAGE: See CALIFORNIA UNION LIST OF PERIODICALS (Database).

CURRENT AWARENESS SEARCH
Any search or service which provides users the newest information on topics previously selected by them. ONLINE SEARCHING USAGE: Search of the latest update of a database to retrieve current or recently added items. Often used synonymously with selective dissemination of information, especially when the search strategy is stored and automatically executed each time the file is updated by a commercial search service.

CURSOR
Movable spot of light on a video terminal which indicates the location of the next character to be entered.

CUSTOMER NUMBER
See: USER NUMBER.

DAISY WHEEL PRINTER
Printer which has a circular print element with the characters attached at the end of individual spokes or stalks. Results in letter-quality printing and is most commonly used in word processing and not in online searching.

DATA
Basic piece of information which is processed by the computer. Information is conveyed by data and, therefore, the terms are not technically equivalent. Common usage allows "data" to be considered either singular or plural.

DATA BANK
See: **DATABANK.**

DATA BASE INDEX
SDC USAGE: Master index of the **basic index** search terms and multi-word **index terms** of all SDC databases. Can be searched to produce a ranked list of databases that contain a given term. Commonly abbreviated DBI. Similar to BRS's **CROS database** and DIALOG's **DIALINDEX.**

DATA COMMUNICATIONS
See: **COMMUNICATIONS.**

DATA COMMUNICATIONS NETWORK
See: **COMMUNICATIONS NETWORK.**

DATA ELEMENT
Specific cateogry or **field** of information. In a bibliographic **record**, the author is an example of a data element. Often used synonymously with field. See: **FIELD.**

DATA PROCESSING
COMPUTER SCIENCE USAGE: Systematic operation performed on **data** to yield information or to manipulate it. Any device which can execute such operations on data is known as a **data processor**, but is is not necessarily a **computer.** For example, a pocket calculator is an example of a data processor, but it is not a computer.

DATA SET
See: **FILE.**

DATA TRANSMISSION
Sending and receiving of **data** between the **computer** and a **terminal**, generally using a **communications network.** See also: **TRANSMISSION SPEED.**

DATABANK
COMPUTER SCIENCE USAGE: Large **database** or collection of databases. **ONLINE SEARCHING USAGE:** Synonymous with database. See: **DATABASE.**

DATABASE
Collection of data in **machine readable** form which is accessible by a **computer.** Used interchangeably with **file.** For example, references are made to either the **ERIC file** or the **ERIC database.** However, a database may technically be made up of numerous files. Databases are also commonly referred to as **databanks.** There are many kinds of databases, but most can be considered either **bibliographic** or **nonbibliographic.** Most databases are directly equivalent to a print source, but certain databases contain additional data and are considered to be "enhanced databases." See also: **BIBLIOGRAPHIC DATABASE** and **NONBIBLIOGRAPHIC DATABASE.**

DATABASE FILE STRUCTURE
See: **FILE STRUCTURE.**

DATABASE NAME
BRS USAGE: See **SEARCH LABEL.**

DATABASE PRODUCER

Organization or publisher which compiles a **database**. A print version of the database may also be published. For example, the Educational Resources Information Center which produces the **ERIC database** also publishes the print components of ERIC, *Resources in Education* and *CIJE* (*Current Index to Journals in Education*). In most cases, a database producer is also a **database supplier**, i.e., the organization that makes the database available to the **commercial search services**, but this is not necessarily the case. Database producers may be commercial organizations, government agencies, or other professional organizations.

DATABASE SPECIFIC

Commands, features, or functions that vary from database to database, even though the databases may be available from the same **commercial search service**.

DATABASE SPECIFICATIONS

Indication of the overall content and **searchable fields** of a **database**. Generally includes file description, subject coverage, file size, and producer.

DATABASE SUPPLIER

Organization that makes a **database** available to a **commercial search service**. Normally a database supplier is also a **database producer**, i.e., the originator of the actual database. However, in some cases two different organizations are involved. For example, the National Technical Information Service (NTIS) serves as the supplier for several databases which are produced by other governmental agencies. See also: **DATABASE PRODUCER**.

DATABASE VENDORS

See: **COMMERCIAL SEARCH SERVICES**.

DATAPAC

Special **communications network** used to access the major **commercial search services** from Canada through the major American communications networks.

DATAPHONE

Special type of telephone installed by the telephone company which functions as a **modem** and allows the transmission of **machine readable data**.

DATE RANGING

SDC USAGE: Allows **search results** to be limited to a specific time period. For example, "AND GREATER THAN 1979" will restrict results to those published in the 1980s. See also: **LIMITING SEARCHES**.

DBI

SDC USAGE: See **DATA BASE INDEX (Database)**.

DEDICATED LINE

COMPUTER SCIENCE USAGE: Telephone line which directly connects a **terminal** to a specific computer. No **modem** or **acoustic coupler** is required. Contrast with: **DIALUP**, the normal procedure for conducting **online searches**.

DEFAULT DATABASE
Database to which the user is automatically connected when **logging on** to a **commercial search service**. Generally it is either an inexpensive database or one that is heavily used.

DEFAULT FILE
See: **DEFAULT DATABASE**.

DEFAULT FORMAT
Format the system prints if no format is specified. For example, if no specific format is requested in DIALOG, the system typically responds with Format 2.

DELETE
To erase or eliminate. **COMPUTER SCIENCE USAGE**: To remove a **record** or group of records from a file. **ONLINE SEARCHING USAGE**: There may be a delete key on the **terminal keyboard** which performs the delete function.

DEMODULATE
See: **MODEM**.

DESCRIPTORS
Standardized **index terms,** usually listed and defined in an established **thesaurus**. May be single words or phrases. Descriptors are assigned to a document, usually by a human indexer. They may also have weighted rankings. For example, the indexer may designate some descriptors as **major,** e.g., considered as identifying a "major" point within an article, and some as **minor,** e.g., of less importance in identifying the subject content.

DESKTOP COMPUTER
See: **MICROCOMPUTER**.

DIALINDEX (Database)
DIALOG USAGE: Dictionary database which includes the file indexes for all of DIALOG's **bibliographic databases**. Available on DIALOG (File 411). Similar to BRS's **CROS database** and SDC's **DATA BASE INDEX database**.

DIALOG
Technically the computer **programs** developed by the Lockheed Corporation which are used to allow **online searching** of the system's databases. The name was initially used to emphasize the interactive, e.g., "dialog," potential of the system. Now commonly used as the name of the **DIALOG Information Retrieval Service**.

DIALOG INFORMATION RETRIEVAL SERVICE
Major **commercial search service**. Formerly known as the Lockheed Information Systems, but as of 1981, DIALOG is a wholly owned subsidiary of Lockheed Corporation. Commonly known as DIALOG. DIALOG DATABASES ("File n") and **system specific** commands ("DIALOG USAGE") are identified and described in this dictionary.

DIALOG PUBLICATIONS (Database)
DIALOG system database which allows a user to order directly any DIALOG publications while on **online**. Available on DIALOG (File 200).

DIALORDER
Online **document delivery** service offered by DIALOG for virtually all of its **bibliographic databases**.

DIALUP
Use of a telephone to connect temporarily with any **host computer** in order to conduct a search of the system's databases. Contrast with: **DEDICATED LINE**, which requires permanent and direct connection between the **terminal** and a specific computer.

DICTIONARY DATABASE
Nonbibliographic database which produces a list of definitions, vocabulary terms, chemical compounds, etc. Examples include **CHEMNAME database** and **BIOCODES database**.

DICTIONARY FILE
COMPUTER SCIENCE USAGE: See **INVERTED FILE**. **BRS USAGE:** Alphabetical listing of all searchable terms in a given database. **Postings** are included for each term listed.

DIRECT ACCESS
See: **RANDOM ACCESS**.

DIRECT COSTS
Charges which can be directly attributed to a specific **online search**. Typically comprised of **online connect time** charges, **communications costs**, and any online or offline **print charges**.

DIRECT DIAL
Method of connecting with a **host computer** without using a **communications network**. The **commercial search service** is dialed directly using regular telephone connections. Normally, this is not a cost-effective alternative to using a communications network, but all of the major systems offer this option.

DIRECT RECORD ACCESS
DIALOG USAGE: Using the DIALOG **accession number** for a specific item to either directly **display** or **print** the record.

DIRECTLY EQUIVALENT DATABASE
See: **DATABASE**.

DIRECTORY DATABASE
Nonbibliographic database which lists organizations, associations, institutions, research projects, contracts awarded, etc. Examples include **ENCYCLOPEDIA OF ASSOCIATIONS database** and **ELECTRONIC YELLOW PAGES database**.

DISC, MAGNETIC
See: **MAGNETIC DISC**.

DISCLOSURE II (Database)
Nonbibliographic database which provides extracts from various reports filed by publicly owned companies with the United States Securities and Exchange Commission. Available on DIALOG (File 100).

DISCONNECT

To sever or break the direct connection between a **terminal** and the **host computer**. Can occur because of mechanical problems, but is normally accomplished through the completion of a **logoff** procedure. See: **LOGOFF**.

DISCONNECTED MESSAGE

TELENET USAGE: When preceded by a **commercial search service's** computer number, e.g., "415 20 DISCONNECTED," this indicates a system failure or unexpected disconnection from the system. See: **DISCONNECT**.

DISK STORAGE OVERFLOW MESSAGE

DIALOG USAGE: Online message received when search **storage** capacity has been exceeded. Search must be repeated after a **BEGIN command** and an attempt must be made to avoid highly posted or nonspecific terms. Not a frequent occurrence as storage capacity is 1,000,000 **citations**.

DISPLAY

Technically, the presentation of a search in a visual fashion, usually using a **cathode ray tube**. However, it is also common to refer to **results** being "displayed" **online** on a **print terminal**. Contrast with: **PRINT**.

DISPLAY COMMAND

DIALOG USAGE: Command for **online display** of **records** on a **video terminal**. See also: **DISPLAY**.

..DISPLAY COMMAND

BRS USAGE: Provides a listing of all previously entered **search strategies** and their results. Used to review complicated search strategies, especially when using a **video terminal**. Similar to SDC's **HISTORY command** and DIALOG's **DISPLAY SETS command**.

DISPLAY SCREEN

See: **VISUAL DISPLAY UNIT**.

DISPLAY SETS COMMAND

DIALOG USAGE: Provides a summary of an ongoing **search strategy** at any time during an **online search**. Used primarily when a search is being performed on a **video terminal**. Similar to SDC's **HISTORY command** and BRS's **..DISPLAY command**.

DISPLAYING RESULTS

See: **DISPLAY**.

DISS (Database)

BRS USAGE: See **COMPREHENSIVE DISSERTATION INDEX (Database)**.

DJNR (Database)

See: **DOW JONES NEWS (Database)**.

DOCUMENT

Record which contains **information**. Can refer both to the data and the form or medium it is recorded on. A document is most commonly considered to be produced on paper. See also: **RECORD. BRS USAGE: Bibliographic citation** and **abstract**, if one is available.

DOCUMENT DELIVERY
Process of providing actual documents of items retrieved through an **online search.** Online searches can readily identify relevant items, but economical delivery of them is a significant problem. However, the major **commercial search services** do provide, to varying degrees, online ordering capabilities. For example, DIALOG's **DIALORDER** allows direct online ordering of documents retrieved from any of its **bibliographic databases.**

DOCUMENT REQUEST
BRS USAGE: Indication by the searcher of which retrieved documents are to be **displayed** or **printed.** BRS uses the "doc = " prefix and allows various options, e.g., "doc = all" results in *all* documents being displayed or printed. Must be used with the appropriate **print commands.** Not to be confused with **document delivery.**

DOCUMENT RETRIEVAL
See: **INFORMATION RETRIEVAL.**

DOCUMENT TYPE
Searchable field in many databases which distinguishes between the types of materials, e.g., books, dissertations, conference proceedings, journal articles, etc., included in the database's coverage.

DOCUMENTATION
COMPUTER SCIENCE USAGE: Any documents which describe or explain the design and operation of a search system or **program. ONLINE SEARCHING USAGE:** Loosely, refers to all available **search aids** or **user manuals.**

DOE ENERGY (Database)
Bibliographic database prepared by the United States Department of Energy which covers energy and related areas. Available on BRS (ENERGY file), DIALOG (File 103), and SDC (EDB file).

DOED (Database)
BRS USAGE: See **DOE ENERGY (Database).**

DOLLAR SIGN
Used for **truncation** on some systems. **SDC USAGE:** Key used on some **terminals** to erase an entire typed line before it is transmitted to the **computer.** See also: **ERROR CORRECTION** and **LINE DELETION.**

DOT MATRIX PRINTER
See: **THERMAL PRINTER.**

DOUBLE-CHARACTER RESPONSE
Occurs when the **duplex** switch on a **terminal** and/or **modem** is incorrectly set. If the system responds with double letters, e.g., SSEELLEECCTT, it is generally possible to correct this by setting the duplex switch at "half." See also: **DUPLEX.**

DOUBLE POSTINGS
BRS USAGE: Search process available for most BRS databases which eliminates the need to make two entires to retrieve both **controlled** and **uncontrolled vocabulary** uses of the same term. Involves the use of the **ADJ operator**. For example, "library ADJ automation" will retrieve both the **descriptor** "Library Automation" and any use of that phrase in any of the **searchable** fields.

DOW JONES NEWS (Database)
Bibliographic database covering general business and financial news as reported in the *Wall Street Journal, Barron's,* and on the Dow Jones News Wire Service. Available from BRS (DOWJ file) and the Dow Jones News/Retrieval (DJNR) Service.

DOWJ (Database)
BRS USAGE: See **DOW JONES NEWS (Database).**

DOWN
COMPUTER SCIENCE USAGE: A **computer** is "down" when it is not available for use. See also: **DOWN TIME.**

DOWN TIME
Period during which a **computer** system is inoperable, usually because of unexpected problems. The major **commercial search services** have extensive **backup** systems and down time is seldom a problem.

DROPPED BY HOST SYSTEM MESSAGE
TYMNET USAGE: Indicates a **system failure** or unexpected **disconnect** from the system.

DRSC (Database)
BRS USAGE: See **DRUGINFO/ALCOHOL (Database).**

DRUG (Database)
BRS USAGE: See **DRUGINFO/ALCOHOL (Database).**

DRUGINFO/ALCOHOL (Database)
Bibliographic database covering all aspects of alcohol and drug use and abuse. Actually two separate **files,** DRUGINFO and ALCOHOL, which can be searched separately or together. Available on BRS (DRUG file, both files; DRSC file, DRUGINFO only; and HAZE file, ALCOHOL only). The HAZE file is produced by the Hazelden Foundation.

DS
See: **DISPLAY SETS COMMAND.**

DUMB TERMINAL
Terminal that lacks a **microprocessor** and can only be used to transmit and receive **data.** Contrast with: **SMART TERMINAL.** See also: **TERMINAL.**

DUN'S MARKET IDENTIFIERS 10+ (Database)
Directory database which provides detailed information on more than one million American companies which have 10 or more employees. Available on DIALOG (File 516).

DUPLEX
Mode of **data transmission** through **communications networks**. Synonymous with **full duplex,** a method of data communication which allows simultaneous transmission and receipt of messages. See: **FULL DUPLEX.** See also: **HALF DUPLEX.**

E REFERENCE NUMBER
DIALOG USAGE: Number assigned to each term displayed as a result of an **EXPAND command.**

EBIB (Database)
Bibliographic database which indexes the energy literature contained in the Texas A & M Library collection and corresponds to the *Energy Bibliography and Index.* Available on SDC (EBIB file).

ECER (Database)
BRS USAGE: See **EXCEPTIONAL CHILD EDUCATION RESOURCES (Database).**

ECONOMIC ABSTRACTS INTERNATIONAL (Database)
Bibliographic database which provides international coverage of economics and market information for various countries. Available on DIALOG (File 90).

EDB (Database)
SDC USAGE: See **DOE ENERGY (Database).**

..EDIT COMMAND
BRS USAGE: **Command** used to modify or update an established **selective dissemination of information** search.

EDUCATION
General term used to distinguish between the **training** of **search analysts** in the actual mechanics of performing **online searches** and the need to educate all staff members about the potential applications of online searching.

EICI (Database)
BRS USAGE: See **ENERGYLINE (Database).**

EIMET (Database)
Bibliographic database which indexes significant papers from engineering conferences and meetings. Acronym stands for Engineering Index Engineering Meetings. Serves as a companion file to **COMPENDEX database.** Available on SDC (EIMET file).

EIS DIGEST OF ENVIRONMENTAL IMPACT STATEMENTS (Database)
Directory database which provides abstracts of the indexes to environmental impact statements required by federal agencies. Available on BRS (EIST file).

EIS INDUSTRIAL PLANTS (Database)
Directory database which provides current information on over 150,000 American establishments which have sales of more than $500,000. Available on DIALOG (File 22).

EIS NONMANUFACTURING ESTABLISHMENTS (Database)
Directory database that includes current information for over 250,000 American nonmanufacturing establishments which employ over 20 persons. Available on DIALOG (File 92).

EIST (Database)
BRS USAGE: See **EIS DIGEST OF ENVIRONMENTAL IMPACT STATEMENTS (Database)**.

EITHER-OR OPERATOR
See: **OR OPERATOR**.

EIVI (Database)
BRS USAGE: See **ENVIROLINE (Database)**.

ELAPSED TIME
Total amount of time to complete all or part of an operation. **ONLINE SEARCHING USAGE**: Synonymous with **CONNECT TIME**.

ELCOM (Database)
Bibliographic database which covers electronics and communications, especially computer applications. Available on SDC (ELCOM file).

ELECTRIC POWER (Database)
Directory database which includes project summaries and research developments of interest to the electric power industry. Available on DIALOG (File 241).

ELECTRIC POWER INDUSTRY ABSTRACTS (Database)
Bibliographic database covering electric power plants and related facilities. Available on SDC (EPIA file).

ELECTRICAL COUPLERS
See: **ACOUSTIC COUPLER**.

ELECTRONIC MAIL
Generic term describing relatively new area of electronic transmission of messages. The major **commercial search services** offer basic electronic mail capabilities, to varying degrees, which allow them to communicate with their users and for users to send messages to them: For example, the BRS **MSGS database** allows users to send and receive messages not only with BRS, but also with anyone else using the BRS system.

ELECTRONIC MAILDROP® SERVICE
Online **document delivery** service offered by SDC.

ELECTRONIC YELLOW PAGES (Databases)
Directory databases which provide online access to yellow-page listings from current telephone directories for every part of the United States. Files are grouped by broad classifications and are available on DIALOG, e.g., Financial Services Directory (File 501), Professionals Directory (File 502), Retailers Directory (Files 504, 505, and 506), and Wholesalers Directory (File 503).

ELHILL
Computer **software programs** that control the **online searching** capabilities of the **MEDLARS** system. ELHILL is a contraction of the name of Senator Lister Hill, for whom the Lister Hill National Center for Biomedical Communications was named. ELHILL is very similar to SDC's **ORBIT** search language and is also used by **BLAISE** in the United Kingdom.

EMBEDDED CHARACTER TRUNCATION
See: **INTERNAL TRUNCATION.**

EMBEDDED STRING
See: **STRING SEARCHING.**

EMULATOR
COMPUTER SCIENCE USAGE: Hardware device or combination of hardware and **software** which allows the **programs** written for one **computer** to be used on another. **ONLINE SEARCHING USAGE: In-house** computer system which imitates or "emulates" the search features available on a larger **commercial search service**. Used for inexpensive training. The **TRAINER** program at the School of Library and Information Science, University of Pittsburgh, is an example of an emulator system.

ENCYCLOPEDIA OF ASSOCIATIONS (Database)
Directory database which lists information on over 15,000 trade associations, professional organizations, labor unions, and other groups. Available on DIALOG (File 114).

END/SAVE COMMAND
DIALOG USAGE: Command given to store all set-producing commands since the last **BEGIN command**. Used as part of DIALOG's **SEARCH*SAVE** feature.

END USER
Person who actually uses the information retrieved in an **online search**. In many cases, the **search analyst** functions as an **intermediary** between the information and the eventual user of it.

ENERGY (Database)
BRS USAGE: See **DOE ENERGY (Database).**

ENERGYLINE (Database)
Bibliographic database which covers all areas of energy and energy research. Available on BRS (EICI file), DIALOG (File 69), and SDC (ENERGYLINE file).

ENERGYNET (Database)
Directory database which lists current organizations and people in energy-related areas. Available on DIALOG (File 169).

ENHANCED DATABASE
See: **DATABASE.**

ENTER
Process which inputs a **command** or **request** to the computer. Normally accomplished by depressing the **carriage return key**. Synonymous with SEND.

ENVIROLINE (Database)
Bibliographic database which covers all aspects of environmental information on an international basis. Available on BRS (EIVI file), DIALOG (File 40), and SDC (ENVIROLINE file).

ENVIRONMENTAL BIBLIOGRAPHY (Database)
Bibliographic database which covers environmental research, human ecology, water and land resources, and energy. Available on DIALOG (File 68).

EPIA (Database)
SDC USAGE: See **ELECTRIC POWER INDUSTRY ABSTRACTS (Database)**.

EPILEPSY (Database)
Bibliographic database which covers all aspects of epilepsy. Available on MEDLARS (EPILEPSY file).

ERASE
See: **DELETE**.

ERASEALL COMMAND
SDC USAGE: **Command** used to **delete** all **search statements** and begin a new search in the same database with search statement number one.

ERIC (Database)
Bibliographic database which covers all aspects of educational research and materials produced by the Educational Resources Information Center. Available on BRS (ERIC file), DIALOG (File 1), and SDC (ERIC file).

ERROR
General term for mistake, miskeying, incorrect entry, inappropriate **command**, or any unintentional action which results in poor **search results**. **COMPUTER SCIENCE USAGE:** Any deviation from correct results due to an identifiable and logical cause. Contrast with: **MISTAKE**, which results from human failings.

ERROR CORRECTION
Established methods of correcting **errors** during **input**. The actual procedure varies depending on the **terminal** being used, the **commercial search service** being accessed, and the type of error. See also: **BACKWARD SLASH, CONTROL-H, DOLLAR SIGN KEY,** and **ESCAPE KEY**.

ERROR MESSAGE
See: **SYSTEM MESSAGE**.

ERSLL COMMAND
SDC USAGE: See **ERASEALL COMMAND**.

ESA-IRS
European Space Agency — Information Retrieval Service. Functions as a **commercial search service** in Europe.

ESCAPE KEY

   DIALOG USAGE: Key used on most terminals to cancel or **delete** a whole line before transmitting it to the computer. See also: **ERROR CORRECTION** and **LINE DELETION**.

EURONET

   Major **communications** network in Europe.

EXCEPTIONAL CHILD EDUCATION RESOURCES (Database)

   Bibliographic database which includes materials relevant to the education of both handicapped and gifted children. Available on BRS (ECER file) and DIALOG (File 54).

EXCERPTA MEDICA (Database)

   Bibliographic database which provides extensive coverage of biomedical literature. Available on DIALOG (Files 72, 73, and 172).

EXCLUDE (PRINT OPTION)

   SDC USAGE: Print command which can be used to exclude one or more **fields** from any **print format**. Can be used in either **online** or **offline print** commands. For example, a user can stipulate that a full online **record** without index terms (IT) be displayed by entering: "PRINT FULL *EXCLUDE* IT." See also: **INCLUDE (PRINT OPTION)** and **PRINT FORMAT.**

EXCLUSIVE OR LOGIC

   SDC USAGE: Logical strategy that retrieves a **set** from which a combination of two or more terms has been eliminated. For example, a user might want any records that mention "acquisitions" or "cataloging," but *not* both words. The **search statement** would be: "(acquisitions OR cataloging) NOT (acquisitions AND cataloging)." Also known as NAND logic.

..EXEC COMMAND

   BRS USAGE: Command used to execute a previously **saved search.**

EXECUTE

   To perform or cause a given **command** or instruction to be carried out. To "execute" a search means to perform the entire search online.

.EXECUTE COMMAND

   DIALOG USAGE: Command given to ask the system to perform a **saved search,** either in the same database or in another database. The .EXECUTE STEPS command is used to retrieve the saved search so that each step of the search is assigned a **set number.** The period preceding the command must be used to distinguish it from the **EXPAND command.** This command is used as part of DIALOG's **SEARCH*SAVE** feature.

EXPAND COMMAND

   DIALOG USAGE: Command used to **display** a list of alphabetically related **search terms** contained in a particular database. In some cases, an EXPAND command can also be used to provide a display of specific subject-related terms. An **E Reference Number** is assigned to each term displayed as a result of an EXPAND command for alphabetically related terms, and an **R Reference Number** is given to each subject-related term which results from an additional EXPAND command. Similar to BRS's **ROOT command** and SDC's **NEIGHBOR command.**

EXPLAIN COMMAND

Synonymous with **HELP command. SDC USAGE: Command** used to retrieve online information and assistance concerning SDC services, features, commands, and databases.

EXPLICIT NESTING

See: **NESTING.**

F OPERATOR

DIALOG USAGE: See **FULL TEXT OPERATOR. SDC USAGE:** See **PROXIMITY OPERATOR.**

FALSE DROPS

Items retrieved that are irrelevant to the search topic, even though they match the requirements of the **search strategy.** Contrast with: **HITS.** May be caused by a variety of factors, e.g., line **noise,** inaccurate selection of **search terms,** or poor **indexing** by the **database producer.** Sometimes also referred to as **garbage.**

FAMILY RESOURCES (Database)

Bibliographic database which covers all types of family-related literature. Available on BRS (NCFR file).

FD COMMAND

SDC USAGE: See **FIND COMMAND.**

FEDE (Database)

BRS USAGE: See **FEDERAL ENERGY DATA INDEX (Database).**

FEDERAL ENERGY DATA INDEX (Database)

Bibliographic database which contains citations to all statistical data publications produced by the United States Department of Energy's Energy Information Administration. Available on BRS (FEDE file).

FEDERAL INDEX (Database)

Bibliographic and **directory database** which covers federal actions on such things as proposed rules and regulations, roll-call votes, executive orders, hearings, and articles in publications which deal with governmental actions. Available on DIALOG (File 29) and SDC (FEDEX file).

FEDERAL REGISTER ABSTRACTS (Database)

Bibliographic database which indexes the items related to federal regulatory actions that are published in the *Federal Register.* Available on DIALOG (File 136) and SDC (FEDREG file).

FEDEX (Database)

SDC USAGE: See **FEDERAL ENERGY DATA INDEX (Database).**

FEDREG DATABASE

SDC USAGE: See **FEDERAL REGISTER ABSTRACTS (Database).**

FEE-BASED SERVICES
Search service which charges a **user fee**. Fees may vary depending on the relationship of the requester to the search service.

FEES
See: **USER FEES.**

FETCH MAIL COMMAND
SDC USAGE: Command used to receive any online messages sent by the SDC Search Service Action Desk to an individual user. A user can send messages to the Action Desk by using the **COMMENT command.** See also: **ELECTRONIC MAIL.**

FIELD
Portion of a **record** containing a specific unit of information. The author field contains the author's name. The abstract field contains the abstract. Often used snynonymously with **data elements**.

FIELD INDICATOR
DIALOG USAGE: Prefix or **suffix codes** comprised of two letters which stand for a specific **field**, e.g., "/DE" for the **descriptor** field or "AU =" for the author field. See: **FIELD.**

FIELD QUALIFIER
An indicator which designates a specific **field**. See also: **FIELD INDICATOR** (DIALOG usage) and **FIELD TAG** (SDC usage).

FIELD TAG
SDC USAGE: Standardized names and two-letter mnemonic abbreviations, e.g., "TI" for title and "AU" for author, for the various **fields** in a database.

FILE
Collection of related **records** which are treated as a unit by the computer. **ONLINE SEARCHING USAGE:** Technically, a **database** is made up of various files, but common usage has made the terms practically interchangeable. For example, references are made to either the **BIOSIS** file or the BIOSIS database. However, in discussing **file structure**, a distinction is made between **inverted file** and the **linear file** contained within one database.

FILE COMMAND
SDC USAGE: Command used to enter a specific **database**. The name of the desired database is given after the file command, e.g., "FILE **ERIC.**"

FILE (Database)
Directory database which provides online descriptions of all BRS databases. Meant to be used as a database selection tool and as a companion to **CROS database**. Databases can be identified based on subject area, intended audience, file type, publication types, and country of origin. Available on BRS (FILE file).

FILE DOCUMENTATION
See: **DOCUMENTATION.**

FILE MAINTENANCE
Process of changing or **updating** files to add, delete, or alter **data**. Files are updated on a regular basis, but most **bibliographic databases** do not ordinarily delete or remove records.

FILE NAME
See: **DATABASE NAME.**

FILE SEGMENT
SDC USAGE: Subfiles of large databases. These often represent specific portions of the database, e.g., individual abstract journals (*Biological Abstracts* and *Bioresearch Index* in the **BIOSIS database**) or major subject divisions (Food and Nutrition [FNC] in **AGRICOLA database**). File segments are searched with the "/FS" qualifier.

FILE STRUCTURE
Organization of the **data elements** within each **record** and arrangement of these records in the database. Two types of files are generally identified within the file structure: 1) **Inverted File**, an **alphanumeric** list of all **searchable terms** within a given field and 2) **Linear File**, a sequential listing, usually by **accession number,** of the full **bibliographic citations** for all records in the database. The inverted files are searched by the computer to identify relevant citations in the linear file, which can then be displayed.

FIND COMMAND
SDC USAGE: Command which may be used to enter **search terms** or **search statements**. Normally not necessary as the system automatically searches for any terms that are not commands.

FIND/SVP REPORTS AND STUDIES INDEX (Database)
Bibliographic database which identifies and abstracts industry and market research reports and studies produced by over 300 American and international publishers. Available on DIALOG (File 196).

FINTEL COMPANY NEWSBASE (Database)
Bibliographic database which indexes and abstracts all articles published by the *Financial Times* in both the London and Frankfurt editions. Available on BRS (FNTL file).

FNTL (Database)
BRS USAGE: See **FINTEL COMPANY NEWSBASE (Database).**

FIXED FIELD
Field with a predefined and specific length. For example, in some databases the publication year (PY) field is limited or "fixed" to two digits, e.g., PY = 83. See also: **VARIABLE FIELD.**

"FLICKER"
See: **PROCESSING QUE.**

FLOPPY DISC
COMPUTER SCIENCE USAGE: Type of **magnetic disc** used as a **storage** device for microcomputers. See: **MEMORY.**

FOOD SCIENCE AND TECHNOLOGY ABSTRACTS (Database)

Bibliographic database which covers all aspects of food science and technology. Available on DIALOG (File 51) and SDC (FSTA file).

FOODS ADLIBA (Database)

Bibliographic database which provides current information on food technology and packaging. Available on DIALOG (File 79).

FOREIGN TRADERS INDEX (Database)

Directory database which lists manufacturers, retailers, wholesalers, distributors, and other groups in 130 foreign countries which either currently import American goods or wish to represent U.S. firms. Available on DIALOG (File 105).

FOREST PRODUCTS (Database)

Bibliographic database which provides coverage of the entire wood products industry. Available on SDC (FOREST file).

FORGIVING SYSTEM

See: **USER FRIENDLY.**

FORMAT

Arrangement of **data.** See: **PRINT FORMAT.**

FORMAT OPTIONS

See: **PRINT FORMAT.**

FOUNDATION DIRECTORY (Database)

Directory database which includes descriptions of over 3,500 foundations which have over $1 million in assets or which annually make grants of $100,000 or more. Available on DIALOG (File 26).

FOUNDATION GRANTS INDEX (Database)

Directory database describing grants which have been awarded by more than 400 major American philanthropic foundations. Available on DIALOG (File 27).

FREE TEXT OPERATORS

BRS USAGE: Special operators which allow users to specify a certain relationship between two or more **search terms.** See also: **ADJACENCY, POSITIONAL OPERATORS,** and **PROXIMITY.** Free text operators available on BRS include:

ADJ	Requires terms to be directly adjacent in the specified order.
SAME	Requires terms to be in the same **paragraph** or **fields.**
WITH	Requires terms to be in the same **sentence.**

FREE TEXT SEARCHING

Type of searching required when **no controlled vocabulary** has been used to **index** the documents in the database. All **fields** with subject-content, e.g., title, **abstract,** note, and **identifier** fields, can be directly searched. The most significant aspect of free text searching is the ability to search each word of the abstract for relevant terms.

FROST & SULLIVAN DM^2 (Database)

Directory database which reports the announcements of various federal contract awards, request-for-proposals, and other governmental projects. Available on DIALOG (File 59).

FULL (PRINT OPTION)

SDC USAGE: See **PRINT FULL COMMAND**.

FULL CITATION

Complete **record** of information in the database. Generally synonymous with **CITATION**.

FSTA (Database)

SDC USAGE: See **FOOD SCIENCE AND TECHNOLOGY ABSTRACTS (Database)**.

FULL DUPLEX

Method of **data** communication which allows simultaneous transmission and receipt of messages. Also known as simply DUPLEX. See also: **HALF DUPLEX**.

FULL TEXT DATABASE

Database which includes the complete text of the document or item retrieved. Since the entire document is produced, a full text database is generally considered a **nonbibliographic database**. Many types of nonbibliographic databases are truly full text, but in most cases, only those files which have lengthy documents readily available online are considered full text. For example, most **directory databases** are directly equivalent to their print versions and could be referred to as full text databases, but they are not. An example of a full text database is the **HARVARD BUSINESS REVIEW/ONLINE database,** which includes the full text of all articles from the *Harvard Business Review,* starting in 1982.

FULL TEXT OPERATORS

DIALOG USAGE: Single letter inserted in parentheses between two words to specify a certain relationship between the terms as part of **full text searching**. See also: **ADJACENCY, POSITIONAL OPERATORS,** and **PROXIMITY**. Full text operators available on DIALOG include:

C Operator	Requires terms to be in the same citation or **record.**
F Operator	Requires terms to be in the same field, but in any order.
L Operator	Requires hierarchical relationship of terms in the **descriptor field.**
W Operator	Requires terms to be directly adjacent in specified order.
nW Operator	Requires n or fewer words between the terms in the specified order.
X Operator	Requires terms to be exactly alike and adjacent.

FULL TEXT SEARCHING

Often used synonymously with **free text searching,** but has specific and different meanings for the three major **commercial search services**. DIALOG USAGE: Ability to search for multi-word **search terms** in any of the database's **searchable fields**. This may involve **adjacency** or **proximity** searching. SDC USAGE: Ability to use **strings of** characters to search any printable part of a **record**. **BRS USAGE**: Ability to search for any term from any **field** in a record.

FUNCTION KEYS

Terminal keys, normally separate from the main **keyboard**, which have been designated to correspond to frequently used **commands** or functions. For example, one function key could be wired to serve as the **SELECT command**. This would allow the user to simply hit this key each time that command was needed.

GARBAGE

COMPUTER SCIENCE USAGE: Useless and irrelevant **data** which is stored in the computer's **memory** and can be retrieved. Often used in the phrase, "Garbage in, garbage out" (commonly abbreviated GIGO). This emphasizes that, if the **input** is bad ("Garbage in"), any data retrieved will also be bad ("Garbage out"). **ONLINE SEARCHING USAGE**: Generally used as synonymous with **false drops**. See: **FALSE DROPS**.

GEOARCHIVE (Database)

Bibliographic database which covers all aspects of geoscience and related disciplines. Available on DIALOG (File 58).

GEOREF (Database)

Bibliographic database which covers geology and such related topics as geochemistry and geophysics, petrology, seismology, and mineralogy. Available on DIALOG (File 89) and SDC (GEOREF file).

GIGO

Acronym for "Garbage In, Garbage Out." See: **GARBAGE**.

GLOBE AND MAIL (Database)

Full text database which includes the complete text of Toronto's *Globe and Mail* newspaper. Available from the Globe and Mail.

GPO MONTHLY CATALOG (Database)

Bibliographic database which is the online equivalent of the printed *Monthly Catalog of United States Government Publications*. Available on BRS (GPOM file), DIALOG (File 66), and SDC (GPO file).

GPO PUBLICATIONS REFERENCE FILE (Database)

Bibliographic database which lists government documents currently available from the United States Government Printing Office. Available on DIALOG (File 166).

GPOM (Database)

BRS USAGE: See **GPO MONTHLY CATALOG (Database)**.

GRANTS (Database)

Directory database which lists more than 1,500 grant programs currently available from governmental agencies, commercial organizations, or private foundations. Available on DIALOG (File 85).

HALF DUPLEX

Method of **data communications** which allows both transmission and receipt of data, but only in one direction at a time. See also: **FULL DUPLEX**.

HANDSHAKE
COMPUTER SCIENCE USAGE: Process which establishes a direct connection between a **terminal** and a **host computer**. Involves the exchange of predetermined signals, which establishes synchronization and allows for proper communication. See also: **LOGON**.

HANDS-ON
Training experience that allows actual use and interaction with the system.

HARD COPY
Printed copy of an item, as opposed to its momentary display on a **video display unit**. **ONLINE SEARCHING USAGE**: **Printout** of an **online search**.

HARDWARE
Physical equipment in a **computer** or **data processing** system. This includes the computer and **terminals** used to access it. Contrast with: **SOFTWARE**.

HARDWIRED TERMINAL
Terminal that is permanently connected to a specific computer. See also: **DEDICATED LINE**.

HARF (Database)
BRS USAGE: See **HARFAX INDUSTRY DATA SOURCES (Database)**.

HARFAX INDUSTRY DATA SOURCES (Database)
Bibliographic database which provides sources of statistical and directory information on 65 major industries. Available on BRS (HARF file) and DIALOG (File 189).

HARVARD BUSINESS REVIEW/ONLINE (Database)
Bibliographic and **full text database** which indexes and abstracts the *Harvard Business Review*. The full text of all articles is included, starting in 1982. Available on BRS (HBRO file).

HAZE (Database)
BRS USAGE: See **DRUGINFO/ALCOHOL (Database)**.

HBRO (Database)
BRS USAGE: See **HARVARD BUSINESS REVIEW/ONLINE (Database)**.

HEALTH (Database)
MEDLARS USAGE: See **HEALTH PLANNING AND ADMINISTRATION (Database)**.

HEALTH PLANNING AND ADMINISTRATION (Database)
Bibliographic database which covers nonclinical literature related to health care and health planning. Available on BRS (HLTH file), DIALOG (File 151), and MEDLARS (HEALTH file).

HEDGE
Prepared list of synonyms on a specific topic that can be used as a concept in another search. For example, both **EXCERPTA MEDICA** and **MEDLINE databases** employ standardized hedges for particular medical concepts.

HELP COMMAND
Command which provides online information about commands, databases, or system messages. Designed to provide immediate assistance when conducting an **online search**. Also known as online assistance, explain command, or tutorial features. **SDC USAGE:** Command which provides a brief explanation of SDC search procedures and alerts the user to other **EXPLAIN commands** which are available online.

HIERARCHICAL VOCABULARY
Controlled vocabulary which additionally ranks or classifies these controlled terms into related catagories. See also: **TREE.**

HIGH SPEED
ONLINE SEARCHING USAGE: Transmission speed of 120 characters-per-second (cps). Currently not as commonly used as 30 cps **terminals**. Limited accessibility to 120 cps **nodes** through the **communications networks,** and the frequently more expensive equipment required are barriers to its use. The biggest advantage is the cost-effectiveness of **printing** citations **online.** Contrast with: **LOW SPEED.** See also: **TRANSMISSION SPEED** and **TERMINAL.**

HISTLINE (Database)
Bibliographic database which covers the history of medicine and related sciences. Available on MEDLARS (HISTLINE file).

HISTORICAL ABSTRACTS (Database)
Bibliographic database which covers all aspects of world history, except for American and Canadian history (See: **AMERICA: HISTORY AND LIFE [Database]**). Available on DIALOG (File 39).

HISTORY COMMAND
See: **SEARCH HISTORY. SDC USAGE: Command** which displays previously entered **search statements** during an **online search** in a database. Allows the user to review the complete **search strategy** since beginning in the database. Similar to BRS's **..DISPLAY command** and DIALOG's **DISPLAY SETS command.**

HIT
Retrieved item that matches the search strategy. Commonly also referred to as an **item** or a **posting,** although there are technical differences. See: **ITEM** and **POSTING.**

HLTH (Database)
BRS USAGE: See **HEALTH PLANNING AND ADMINISTRATION (Database).**

HOME
Starting point for a **cursor** on the screen of a **video terminal.** Usually in the upper-left corner.

HOME COMPUTER
See: **PERSONAL COMPUTER.**

HOST
Occasionally used synonymously with **commercial search service.** See also: **HOST COMPUTER.**

HOST COMPUTER
   Computer of the **commercial search service** to which a user's **terminal** is connected via a **communications network**.

HOST DOWN
   TYMNET USAGE: The requested **commercial search service's** computer is temporarily not working. May be due to **system failure** or schedule **down time**.

HOST NOT RESPONDING MESSAGE
   TYMNET USAGE: System problem with the TYMNET computer.

HOST OUT OF PORTS MESSAGE
   TYMNET USAGE: See **ALL PORTS BUSY**.

HS COMMAND
   SDC USAGE: See **HISTORY COMMAND**.

IDENTIFIERS
   Words or phrases assigned to a **document** by an indexer, but which are not **descriptors** because they are not included in the **controlled vocabulary**. Generally used to identify a significant aspect of a document which cannot be indexed using established descriptors. May be synonymous with **index terms**.

IHSP (Database)
   BRS USAGE: See **STATE PUBLICATIONS INDEX (Database)**.

ILLEGAL ADDRESS MESSAGE
   TELENET USAGE: No system exists with the address entered by the user. Generally the result of a typing **error**.

IMPACT PRINTER
   Printer which imprints by striking the paper with some type of raised type or print element. Similar to a typewriter. Generally heavier and noisier than **thermal printers**. Contrast with: **THERMAL PRINTER**.

IMPLICIT NESTING
   See: **NESTING**.

INCLUDE (PRINT OPTION)
   SDC USAGE: **Print command** which can be used to include one or more **fields** in any **print format**. Can be used in either **online** or **offline printing**. For example, a user can ask that index terms (IT) be included in the standard print format by entering: "PRINT *INCLUDE* IT." See also: **EXCLUDE (PRINT OPTION)** and **PRINT FORMAT**.

INDENTED (PRINT OPTION)
   SDC USAGE: **Print command** that provides the full name of each **field** of the **record** in the **printout**. Each field is clearly labeled and indented so that the information is easy to identify.

INDEX
   1) List of the contents of a **document** or **file**. 2) To establish such a list. See also: **INDEXING**.

INDEX FILE
See: **INVERTED FILE.**

INDEX TERMS
Words or phrases that are chosen to represent the subject content of a **document**. If they are a part of the **controlled vocabulary**, they are also known as **descriptors**. Otherwise, they may be considered synonymous with **identifiers**. Index terms can also have weighted rankings. For example, the indexer may designate some descriptors as **major**, e.g., considered as identifying a "major" point within an article, and others as **minor**, e.g., of less importance.

INDEX WORDS
See: **INDEX TERMS.**

INDEXING
Process of assigning **descriptors** from a **controlled vocabulary** to documents in order to indicate their subject content and to allow subsequent retrieval of the document. See also: **INDEX** and **INDEX TERMS.**

INDEXING TERMS
See: **INDEX TERMS.**

INDIRECT COSTS
Charges involved in conducting an **online search** which cannot easily be directly attributed to a specific search. Indirect costs include monthly telephone expenses, clerical services, and the time spent by the **search analyst** in preparing and conducting the search.

INDUSTRY AND INTERNATIONAL STANDARDS (Database)
Directory database which lists voluntary industrial and engineering standards. Available on BRS (STDS file). Is also combined with **MILITARY SPECIFICATIONS AND STANDARDS database** to form **INDUSTRY STANDARDS AND MILITARY SPECIFICATIONS database.**

INFO (Database)
BRS USAGE: See **ABI/INFORM (Database).**

INFORMATION
Meaning assigned to **data** in a standardized fashion. For example, 5 is a data element, but common conventions allow it to represent the month of May, the fifth month of the year. The 5 then becomes information. The computer processes data to produce recognizable and understandable information. However, the distinction between **data** and **information** is no longer clearly defined and the terms are commonly used synonymously.

INFORMATION BANK
See: **NEW YORK TIMES INFORMATION BANK.**

INFORMATION BROKER
Person or agency which provides information, often retrieved using **online searching**, for a fee.

INFORMATION CENTER
See: **INFORMATION RETRIEVAL CENTER.**

INFORMATION ON DEMAND ORGANIZATIONS
See: **INFORMATION BROKERS.**

INFORMATION PROCESSING
See: **DATA PROCESSING.**

INFORMATION STORAGE AND RETRIEVAL
See: **INFORMATION RETRIEVAL.**

INFORMATION RETRIEVAL
Process of identifying desired information. Used frequently to describe the use of a computer to produce a bibliography, often annotated, on a particular subject. However, information retrieval properly refers to the recovery of a specific item from any collection of information, regardless of its form (e.g., print index or database).

INFORMATION RETRIEVAL CENTER
Organization that specializes in retrieving information. If **online searching** is used, the center may also be known as a **search service.**

INFORMATION SCIENCE
Study of the creation, use, transfer, and communication of **information.** Term is commonly used to refer to computerized applications, but any study of how people use and communicate information, regardless of its format, can be considered information science. Expert in the field is known as an information scientist.

INFORMATION SCIENTIST
See: **INFORMATION SCIENCE.**

INFORMATION SPECIALISTS
ONLINE SEARCHING USAGE: See **SEARCH ANALYSTS.**

INFORMATION THEORY
See: **INFORMATION SCIENCE.**

INFORMATION UTILITIES
ONLINE SEARCHING USAGE: Generally considered synonymous with **commercial search service.**

INFORMATIONAL INTERVIEW
See: **PRESEARCH INTERVIEW** and **POST-SEARCH INTERVIEW.**

IN-HOUSE
Operation or system carried on within an organization. Generally self-contained and not directly connected to or dependent on outside sources. An **emulator** is an example of an in-house training system. In some cases, **online searches** performed within a library to answer specific ready reference questions are referred to as "in-house searches."

INPADOC (Database)
   Nonbibliographic database which identifies current (most recent six weeks) patents assigned by about 45 major countries. Available on DIALOG (File 123).

INPUT
   COMPUTER SCIENCE USAGE: 1) **Data** to be **processed**. 2) To enter data into a **computer** to be processed. Technically correct to state, "I'm going to input the input." **ONLINE SEARCHING USAGE**: Generally, to perform an **online search** by entering the **search strategy**.

INPUT ERROR CORRECTION
   See: **ERROR CORRECTION**.

INPUT I/O ERROR MESSAGE
   DIALOG USAGE: Indicates momentary **hardware** problem.

INPUT/OUTPUT
   COMPUTER SCIENCE USAGE: Combination of equipment, **communications**, techniques, and **data** used to achieve a man-machine **interface**. Total process of entering data into a computer and, after processing, retrieving the manipulated data and making it available for further use.

INQUIRY
   See: **SEARCH REQUESTS**.

INSP (Database)
   BRS USAGE: See **INSPEC (Database)**.

INSPEC (Database)
   Bibliographic database which covers the areas of physics, electrotechnology, computers, and control. Available on BRS (INSP file), DIALOG (Files 12 and 13), and SDC (INSPEC and INSP6976 files).

INSTITUTE FOR SCIENTIFIC INFORMATION
   Major database producer. Produces two **citation indexes** readily available online: **SCISEARCH database** and **SOCIAL SCISEARCH database**.

ISI
   See: **INSTITUTE FOR SCIENTIFIC INFORMATION**.

INSTRUCTION
   See: **COMMAND**.

INSTRUCTIONAL RESOURCES INFORMATION SYSTEM (Database)
   Directory database which identifies educational and instructional materials dealing with water resources and water quality. Commonly abbreviated IRIS. Available on DIALOG (File 53).

INSURANCE ABSTRACTS (Database)
   Bibliographic database which indexes articles concerned with life, property, or liability insurance. Available on DIALOG (File 168).

INTELLIGENT TERMINAL
See: **SMART TERMINAL.**

INTERACTIVE SYSTEM
Online system which allows direct interaction or "dialogue" between the computer and the user. The major **commercial search services** are interactive systems. Each entry requires a response and each response invites further **input.** Also known as conversational mode. See also: **ONLINE SYSTEMS** and **REAL TIME.**

INTERFACE
Technically a shared boundary. The point of connection between two systems or devices. A piece of **hardware** may serve as an interface between two different systems to allow them to interact. Also, it is common to refer to the need for an efficient interface between people and equipment; known as the man-machine interface, computer-user interface, or user-computer interface.

INTERFERENCE
See: **NOISE.**

INTERMEDIARY
Search analyst who performs an **online search** for other people who will be the **end users** of the **data** retrieved. Difficulties in successfully functioning as the middleman between a **requester** and the information contained in a database are frequently cited by both researchers and search analysts.

INTERNAL TRUNCATION
Truncation which retrieves words with various embedded **characters.** For example, in DIALOG "m?n" will retrieve both "m*a*n" and "m*e*n." Also known as embedded character truncation.

INTERNATIONAL PHARMACEUTICAL ABSTRACTS (Database)
Bibliographic database which covers the clinical, practical, and theoretical aspects of pharmaceutical practice. Available on DIALOG (File 72).

INTERNATIONAL SOFTWARE DIRECTORY (Database)
Directory database which lists commercially available **software** for both **microcomputers** and **minicomputers.** Available on DIALOG (File 232).

INTERRUPT
See: **BREAK.**

INTERVIEW
See: **PRESEARCH INTERVIEW** and **POSTSEARCH INTERVIEW.**

INVALID MESSAGE
Generally indicates user **error,** e.g., **password** has been incorrectly entered and the response is "Invalid Password."

INVERTED FILE
Alphanumeric list of all **searchable items** within a given **field** in a database. The inverted files are searched to retrieve relevant items from the **linear file** which can then be displayed. See: **FILE STRUCTURE.**

I/O
 Abbreviation for **input/output**. See: **INPUT/OUTPUT**.

IRIS (Database)
 See: **INSTRUCTIONAL RESOURCES INFORMATION SYSTEM (Database)**.

ISCI (Database)
 BRS USAGE: See **SCISEARCH (Database)**.

ISMS (Database)
 BRS USAGE: See **INDUSTRY STANDARDS AND MILITARY SPECIFICATIONS (Database)**.

ISMEC (Database)
 Bibliographic database which covers mechanical engineering, engineering management, and production engineering. ISMEC stands for Information Service in Mechanical Engineering. Available on DIALOG (File 14).

ITEM
 1) A complete **record** in a **database**. Synonymous with record. 2) Synonym for **hit** or **posting**. See also: **HIT** or **POSTING**.

JARGON
 Technical terminology associated with a particular profession or business. **Online searching** is heavily jargonistic.

JOURNAL OF THE SOCIETY OF ARCHITECTURAL HISTORIANS (Database)
 Bibliographic database which covers the specific area of architectural history. Available on BRS (JSAH file).

JASH (Database)
 BRS USAGE: See **JOURNAL OF THE SOCIETY OF ARCHITECTURAL HISTORIANS (Database)**.

K
 COMPUTER SCIENCE USAGE: Abbreviation for the number 1024 (2^{10}). Used to indicate the size of a **computer's memory**.

K COMMAND
 DIALOG USAGE: See **KEEP COMMAND**.

KEEP COMMAND
 DIALOG USAGE: **Command** used to edit or selectively group records together and create a new set of these selected records. This new set is numbered and referred to as **set 99**. The KEEP command is primarily used with **DIALORDER**, DIALOG's **online document delivery** service. SDC USAGE: Command used to keep certain **search statements** and to eliminate others when the limit of 60 search statements is being approached.

KEYBOARD

Group of keys on a **terminal** which operate like the keys on a typewriter. They are used to produce both a **machine readable** version and a print copy of the **data** being transmitted to the computer.

KEYBOARDING

Process of converting **data** into **machine readable** form and inputting it into a **computer** by using a typewriter-like console on a **terminal** which is connected to the computer.

KEYWORD IN CONTEXT

Use of **keywords** to **index** an item. See: **KEYWORDS**.

KEYWORDS

Words or phrases that describe the subject content of a document. A distinction is made between keywords, which are generally found in a title and/or abstract and are not assigned by an indexer, and **index terms**, which are selected and assigned by the indexer of the document and may or may not be included in the actual citation.

KNOWLEDGE INDEX (Database)

DIALOG USAGE: New service available from DIALOG which provides online access to various DIALOG databases for users of **personal computers**. Most DIALOG search techniques can be used, but hours of access and databases available are restricted.

KWIC

See: **KEYWORD IN CONTEXT**.

L OPERATOR

DIALOG USAGE: See **FULL TEXT OPERATORS**. **SDC USAGE:** See **PROXIMITY OPERATORS**.

LABELING OUTPUT

Technique of assigning a brief title or an identifying notation to an **online search** so that when the **offline prints** are received they can be easily identified and sorted.

LABORDOC (Database)

Bibliographic database which provides international coverage in the fields of labor and industrial relations. Available on SDC (LABORDOC file).

LANGUAGE

Set of established rules and conventions which are used to communicate **information** through symbols, representations, and **characters**. See also: **MACHINE LANGUAGE** and **NATURAL LANGUAGE**.

LANGUAGE AND LANGUAGE BEHAVIOR ABSTRACTS (Database)

Bibliographic database which covers the use of language and various aspects of language behavior. Available on DIALOG (File 36).

LANGUAGE, MACHINE

See: **MACHINE LANGUAGE**.

LANGUAGE, NATURAL
See: **NATURAL LANGUAGE.**

LEFT TRUNCATION
Truncation used to allow for various prefixes before a specified **word stem**. For example, a search of the left truncated word "history" would retrieve not only "history," but also "*pre*history" and "*post*history."

LEGAL RESOURCES INDEX (Database)
Bibliographic database which indexes over 660 major law journals and other legal publications. Available on DIALOG (File 150).

LENGTH
See: **FIXED FIELD** and **VARIABLE FIELD.**

LETTER
Character of the alphabet which can be combined with other letters to form **words.**

LETTER-BY-LETTER FILING
Alphabetical filing procedure in which words are arranged letter by letter, ignoring all spaces and punctuation. For example, in letter-by-letter filing, the following words would be filed in this order: Newberry, New Data, Newsweek, and New Technology. See also: **WORD** and **WORD-BY-WORD FILING.**

LEXIS (Database)
Major legal **full text database** which offers searching of legal texts and decisions. Based on a prototype system (OBAR/LEXIS) established in Ohio. Produced and made available by Mead Data Control.

LIBCON (Database)
Bibliographic database which includes the monographic publications, serials, maps, manuscripts, and other materials cataloged by the Library of Congress. Available on SDC (LIBCON file).

LIBRARY AND INFORMATION SCIENCE ABSTRACTS (Database)
Bibliographic database which covers library and information science materials. Available on DIALOG (File 61) and SDC (LISA file).

LIBRARY AND INFORMATION TECHNOLOGY ASSOCIATION
Division of the American Library Association which is concerned with all aspects of library and information technology. Publishes *Information Technology and Libraries* (formerly the *Journal of Library Automation*).

LIFE SCIENCES COLLECTION (Database)
Bibliographic database which covers a wide range of life sciences, including biochemistry, ecology, genetics, toxicology, and virology. Available on DIALOG (File 76).

LIMIT COMMAND
DIALOG USAGE: Command which is used to narrow or restrict **search results.** See: **LIMITING SEARCHES.**

..LIMIT COMMAND

BRS USAGE: Command used to refine a search by restricting results to certain categories, e.g., language or **document type**. See: **LIMITING SEARCHES**.

LIMITING SEARCHES

Ability to narrow or restrict **search results**. Many **bibliographic databases** allow results to be limited by date of publication, **document type**, or language. In some cases, a specific LIMIT command is used, e.g., "LIMIT 1/ENG" limits results to the English language in many DIALOG databases, but in other databases, normal **Boolean logic** is used to restrict results, e.g., "LIBRARIES AND PY = 1983" retrieves only documents mentioning "libraries" published in 1983.

LINE DELETION

Method of **error correction** which deletes an entire line of **input** before it is transmitted to the computer. The major **commercial search services** use slightly different techniques to delete lines: DIALOG uses the **escape key**, SDC requires a **dollar sign**, and BRS uses a **question mark**. See: **ERROR CORRECTION**.

LINE NOISE

See: **NOISE**.

LINE NUMBER

See: **SET NUMBER**.

LINE PRINTER

Type of **printer** commonly used in **online searching** and which **displays** the results one line at a time.

LINEAR FILE

Sequential listing, usually by **accession number**, of the complete **citations** for all of the **records** in a database. Access to the linear file is gained through the **inverted file**. Also known as the Print File. See: **FILE STRUCTURE**.

LINK OPERATOR

SDC USAGE: Operator used with databases which have multiple-part **records**. Two terms combined with LINK are either in the same main record, the same subrecord, or in the main record and one subrecord. The LINK command is more precise than the **AND operator**. A LINK NOT command is also available. The LINK command is **database specific**, and the appropriate user manual should be consulted. See also: **PROXIMITY OPERATORS**.

LISA (Database)

See: **LIBRARY AND INFORMATION SCIENCE ABSTRACTS (Database)**.

LITA

See: **LIBRARY AND INFORMATION TECHNOLOGY ASSOCIATION**.

LITERAL SEARCHING

Technique for searching for words that are also system **commands, Boolean operators**, or **stop words**. The different **commercial search services** handle this slightly differently. For example, this is accomplished on SDC by using apostrophes or single quotation marks to enclose the term, but DIALOG uses double quotation marks. Also known as "command word searching."

LITERATURE SEARCHING

Process of identifying specific items which satisfy a request for information. If a computer search is performed to retrieve the desired information, the process is also known as **online searching**.

LLBA (Database)

See: **LANGUAGE AND LANGUAGE BEHAVIOR ABSTRACTS (Database)**.

LOAD

To place **information** into the **storage** of a **computer**. When a **commercial search service** "loads" a file, it enters all of the **machine readable** information contained in that file into the **memory** of the service's **host computer**.

LOCAL MODE

Setting on a **terminal** which causes it to function basically as an electric typewriter. **Characters** are printed, but not transmitted to the computer. Contrast with: **REMOTE MODE**. See also: **MODE**.

LOCKHEED DIALOG INFORMATION RETRIEVAL SERVICE

Early name for the **DIALOG Information Retrieval Service**. See: **DIALOG INFORMATION RETRIEVAL SERVICE**.

LOG

See: **SEARCH LOG**.

LOGGING OFF

See: **LOGOFF**.

LOGGING ON

See: **LOGON**.

LOGIC

Study of the formal theories of reasoning and thought. **COMPUTER SCIENCE USAGE**: Principles of the interconnection between logical elements when processed by a computer. **ONLINE SEARCHING USAGE**: Commonly used synonymously with **Boolean logic**. See also: **BOOLEAN LOGIC**.

LOGIC, SYMBOLIC

See: **BOOLEAN LOGIC**.

LOGICAL OPERATORS

See: **BOOLEAN OPERATORS**. See also: **BOOLEAN LOGIC**.

LOGICAL PRODUCT

See: **AND OPERATOR**.

LOGICAL SUM

See: **OR OPERATOR**.

LOGOFF

Process used to **disconnect** a **terminal** from a **host computer**. Procedures vary depending on which **commercial search service** is used, but in general a command is simply given to the computer (e.g., "END" in BRS) and the search session is finished.

LOGOFF COMMAND

DIALOG USAGE: Command used to **logoff** from the DIALOG system. See: **LOGOFF**.

LOGOFF HOLD COMMAND

DIALOG USAGE: Command which allows a user to temporarily **disconnect** from the system for up to 10 minutes and then reconnect and continue the search from the same point.

LOGON

Process used to connect a **terminal** with a **host computer** so an **online search** can be performed. Procedures vary depending on which **commercial search service** is used, but in general the following steps are required: 1) telephone number of a **communications network** is dialed; 2) high-pitched tone is heard; 3) headset is placed in the **acoustic coupler** or **modem** of the terminal; 4) the **carrier light** comes on; and 5) **system specific** procedures required by the particular service are completed to establish a direct connection with the host computer.

LOGON MESSAGE

Brief message provided by the **commercial search service** immediately after the user has **logged on**; announces new databases or features of the system, schedule changes, etc.

LOW SPEED

ONLINE SEARCHING USAGE: Transmission speed of either 10, 15, or 30 characters-per-second (cps). Most online searching is currently being done using 30 cps **terminals**. The lower speeds are too slow for cost-effective searching. Contrast with: **HIGH SPEED**. See also: **TRANSMISSION SPEED**.

MACHINE ASSISTED REFERENCE SECTION

See: **MARS**.

MACHINE LANGUAGE

Language or code used directly by a **computer**. All communications are in a **machine readable** form and typically are not actual words of speech understood by humans. See also: **LANGUAGE** and **NATURAL LANGUAGE**.

MACHINE READABLE

Information which is in the form a machine, normally a computer, can read and process. The information is conveyed by **data** and is usually represented in digital form. All of the data contained in a **database** is machine readable.

MACHINE SEARCHABLE

Machine readable data accessible through a **database** which can be searched to retrieve specific pieces of desired information. Normally considered synonymous with **machine readable**.

MAGAZINE INDEX (Database)
Bibliographic database which indexes over 370 popular magazines. Available on DIALOG (File 47).

MAGNETIC DISC
Storage medium which consists of a coated disc on which **data** can be recorded and stored. See: **MEMORY**.

MAGNETIC TAPE
Storage medium which consists of a tape with a magnetic surface on which **data** can be recorded and stored. See: **MEMORY**.

MAIN FRAME
COMPUTER SCIENCE USAGE: 1) Synonymous with **central processing unit**. 2) Commonly used to refer to any large **computer** to distinguish it from **minicomputers** and **microcomputers**.

MAJOR DESCRIPTORS
Descriptors considered by an **indexer** to identify a "major" point within an item. Contrast with: **MINOR DESCRIPTOR**. See also: **DESCRIPTOR** and **INDEX TERMS**.

MANAGEMENT CONTENTS (Database)
Bibliographic database which indexes a wide variety of business, financial, and management journals. Available on BRS (MGMT file), DIALOG (File 75), and SDC (MANAGEMENT file).

MAN-MACHINE INTERFACE
See: **INTERFACE**.

MANUAL SEARCHING
Information retrieval which does not involve any mechanized or computerized assistance. Using a card catalog or a printed index are common examples of manual searching. Contrast with: **ONLINE SEARCHING**.

MANUALS
See: **USER MANUALS**.

MARC (Database)
Bibliographic database which contains **bibliographic citations** for all books cataloged by the Library of Congress since 1968. Available on DIALOG (File 426).

MARKET ANALYSIS
Ascertaining the need, identifying potential users, and estimating their ability to support a service or product. Typically done before initiating a **search service** in a library or information center.

MARS
Acronym for Machine-Assisted Reference Section of the Reference and Adult Services Division (RASD) of the American Library Association. Concentrates on the public service and reference applications of various automated library systems, with particular emphasis on **online searching**.

MATCH
Generally used synonymously with **hit**. Technically, "match" is a verb, i.e., to check for an item that corresponds to the **search strategy**, and "hit" a noun, i.e., the item that "matches" the search strategy. If items are found to match, they are labeled as hits. See also: **HIT**.

MATH (Database)
BRS USAGE: See **MATHFILE (Database)**.

MATHFILE (Database)
Bibliographic database which provides international coverage of mathematical research. Available on BRS (MATH file) and DIALOG (File 239).

MATRIX PRINTER
See: **DOT MATRIX PRINTER**.

MDOC (Database)
BRS USAGE: See **MEDICAL DOCUMENTS (Database)**.

MEAD DATA GENERAL COMPANY
Database producer (**LEXIS** and **NEXIS** files) which also functions as a **commercial search service** and makes these databases available to online users.

MECHANICAL LITERATURE SEARCHING
See: **MECHANIZED INFORMATION RETRIEVAL**.

MECHANIZED INFORMATION RETRIEVAL
Early version of automated **information retrieval** or **data processing** which generally used mechanical machines, as opposed to programmable **computers**.

MEDICAL DOCUMENTS (Database)
Bibliographic database which covers United States government documents in the health sciences. Available on BRS (MDOC file).

MEDLARS
Refers to the entire National Library of Medicine system (NLM). Stands for Medical Literature Analysis and Retrieval. Includes not only the **MEDLINE database**, but also all other files available from NLM, e.g., **CATLINE** or **EPILEPSY** files. Major MEDLARS databases (MEDLARS "file") are identified and briefly described in this dictionary.

MEDLEARN
Computer assisted instruction program designed to train users in searching the **MEDLINE database**. Available on MEDLARS (*MEDLEARN* file).

MEDLINE (Database)
Bibliographic database which provides coverage of virtually all areas of biomedical literature. MEDLINE (MEDLARS ONLINE) is produced by the National Library of Medicine (NLM). Available on BRS (MESH files), DIALOG (Files 152, 153, and 154), and MEDLARS (MEDLINE and MED **backfiles**).

MEMORY

Storage of **machine readable** information which can be manipulated and retrieved by a **computer**. Generally considered synonymous with storage. **Data** can be stored on **magnetic discs** or **magnetic tape**. The latter lacks direct access and generally is used only to provide copies of a database to a **commercial search service** or for certain types of **offline** processing. Magnetic discs, which allow rapid and direct access, are generally used for most large online systems. **COMPUTER SCIENCE USAGE**: Internal or "core" storage of a computer. See also: **STORAGE**.

MENTAL HEALTH ABSTRACTS (Database)

See: **NIHM (Database)**.

MENU

COMPUTER SCIENCE USAGE: Set of options which can be selected by the user of a system. The major **commercial search services** are typically not menu-driven.

MERGE

COMPUTER SCIENCE USAGE: Operation which creates a single file from two or more **sets** of **records**. ONLINE SEARCHING USAGE: See also **..MERGE COMMAND**.

..MERGE COMMAND

BRS USAGE: **Command** which combines the results of different **offline print** requests from various databases into a single, "merged" **printout**. Although duplicate citations cannot be eliminated, this merged result readily identifies them to the **end user**.

MESH

Acronym for *MEdical Subject Headings*, the thesaurus of **controlled vocabulary** terms used to search **MEDLINE** and many **MEDLARS** files.

MESH (Database)

BRS USAGE: See **MEDLINE (Database)**.

MESSAGE LENGTH MESSAGE

SDC USAGE: **Command** which can be used to change the length of system **prompts** and messages to aid less experienced searchers.

MESSAGE SWITCHING

See: **PACKET SWITCHING**.

MESSAGE SWITCHING SYSTEM

BRS USAGE: See **MSGS (Database)**.

MESSAGES

See: **SYSTEM MESSAGE**.

METADEX (Database)

See: **METALS ABSTRACTS/ALLOYS INDEX (Database)**.

METALS ABSTRACTS/ALLOYS INDEX (Database)

Bibliographic database which indexes materials relevant to the science and practice of metallurgy. Available on DIALOG (File 32) and SDC (METADEX file).

METALS INFORMATION DESIGNATIONS AND SPECIFICATIONS (Database)
Directory database which provides designation and specification numbers for ferrous and nonferrous metals and alloys. Available on SDC (MIDAS file).

METEOROLOGICAL AND GEOASTROPHYSICAL ABSTRACTS (Database)
Bibliographic database which offers international coverage of meteorological and geoastrophysical research. Available on DIALOG (File 29).

MGMT (Database)
BRS USAGE: See **MANAGEMENT CONTENTS (Database)**.

MICROCOMPUTER
Small **computer** which has a **microprocessor** as its **central processing unit**. The distinction between a microcomputer and a **minicomputer** is rapidly diminishing, but the latter is generally larger, both in **storage** capacity and computing power. See also: **PERSONAL COMPUTER**.

MICROCOMPUTER INDEX (Database)
Bibliographic database which indexes over 20 popular **microcomputer** journals. Available on DIALOG (File 233).

MICROPROCESSOR
Central processing unit that is contained on one or a few **chips** and used in a **microcomputer**. Commonly considered synonymous with microcomputer.

MIDAS (Database)
SDC USAGE: See **METALS INFORMATION DESIGNATIONS AND SPECIFICATIONS (Database)**.

MIGRATION FROM PRINTED RESOURCES
The cancellation of subscriptions to **print indexes** when their corresponding **databases** become available **online** from one of the major **commercial search services**. Can also simply refer to changes in research styles brought about by the availability of **online searching**.

MILITARY SPECIFICATIONS AND STANDARDS DATABASE
Bibliographic database which indexes military and federal specifications and standards as reported in government documents. Available on BRS (MLSS file). Is also combined with **INDUSTRY AND INTERNATIONAL STANDARDS database** to form **INDUSTRY STANDARDS AND MILITARY SPECIFICATIONS database**.

MILLION DOLLAR DIRECTORY (Database)
Directory database which lists information on 121,000 American companies for the *Million Dollar Directory Series*. Available on DIALOG (File 517).

MILLISECOND
One thousandth of a second.

MINICOMPUTER
Small **computer**, larger in **storage** capacity and computing power than a **microcomputer**, but smaller than a **main frame**. The distinction, especially between minicomputers and microcomputers, is rapidly diminishing.

MINOR DESCRIPTORS

Descriptors assigned by an **indexer**, but considered to identify only "minor" points within an item. Contrast with: **MAJOR DESCRIPTORS**. See also: **DESCRIPTORS** and **INDEX TERMS**.

MISKEYING

See: **ERROR**.

MISTAKE

Generally synonymous with **error**. COMPUTER SCIENCE USAGE: Unintended and incorrect results produced by human failings. See also: **ERROR**.

MISTAKE IN KEYING

See: **ERROR**.

MLA BIBLIOGRAPHY (Database)

Bibliographic database which covers published books and articles dealing with literature, modern language, and linguistics. Available on BRS (MLAB file) and DIALOG (File 71).

MLAB (Database)

BRS USAGE: See **MLA BIBLIOGRAPHY (Database)**.

MLSS (Database)

BRS USAGE: See **MILITARY SPECIFICATIONS AND STANDARDS (Database)**.

MODE

Different ways a piece of equipment, e.g., a **terminal**, can function. See also: **LOCAL MODE** and **REMOTE MODE. BRS USAGE:** Major operations and processes within the system, e.g., **print mode** or **search mode**. User must be in the proper mode. For example, no searching can be done while in the print mode.

MODEM

Acronym for mo̲dulator-de̲modulator. Device connected to a **terminal** which converts **machine readable** data into signals which can be transmitted over communications lines. Digital signals from the terminal are converted ("modulated") into signals which can be transmitted over regular telephone lines and then reconverted ("demodulated") when **input** into the **computer**. Process also works in reverse, i.e., from computer to terminal. An **acoustic coupler** is a type of modem. See also: **DATAPHONE**.

MODULATE

See: **MODEM**.

MONITOR

1) **Cathode ray tube** used to **display online searches**. Frequently used with a **video terminal** to display searches to larger groups during **online demonstrations**. 2) **COMPUTER SCIENCE USAGE: Hardware** or **software** which supervises and controls the overall operations of a system.

MONITOR (Database)
Bibliographic database which indexes all articles and many columns in the *Christian Science Monitor.* Available on SDC (MONITOR file).

MORE MESSAGE
DIALOG USAGE: Indicates that a listing provided is not complete. The searcher can view additional items by using the **PAGE command.**

MSGS (Database)
BRS USAGE: BRS file which functions as an **electronic mail** system. See: **ELECTRONIC MAIL.**

MULTIDISCIPLINARY DATABASES
Databases which cover a wide range of subject areas. Examples include **COMPREHENSIVE DISSERTATIONS INDEX database** and **NTIS database.**

MULTIFILE SEARCHING
See: **MULTIPLE FILE SEARCHING.**

MULTIPLE FILE SEARCHING
Process of executing the same **search strategy** on different databases, often involves **saving searches.** See also: **SAVING SEARCHES.**

MULTI-WORD TERMS
See: **BOUND DESCRIPTORS.**

MWSC (Database)
BRS USAGE: See **AMERICAN MEN AND WOMEN OF SCIENCE (Database).**

NAND LOGIC
See: **EXCLUSIVE OR LOGIC.**

NANOSECOND
One billionth of a second. One thousand millionth of a second.

NARROWING SEARCHES
See: **LIMITING SEARCHES.**

NATIONAL CRIMINAL JUSTICE REFERENCE SERVICE (Database)
Bibliographic database which indexes materials related to criminal justice and law enforcement. Available on DIALOG (File 21).

NATIONAL FOUNDATIONS (Database)
Directory database which lists all 21,800 American foundations which annually award grants. Available on DIALOG (File 78).

NATIONAL INFORMATION CENTER FOR EDUCATIONAL MEDIA (Database)
See: **NICEM (Database).**

NATIONAL INFORMATION SOURCES ON THE HANDICAPPED (Database)
Directory database which describes organizations that make available information on handicapped and disabled individuals. Available on BRS (NISH file).

NATIONAL LIBRARY OF MEDICINE
ONLINE SEARCHING USAGE: Commercial search service which also functions as a **database producer.** Generally abbreviated NLM. The online databases produced by NLM are known as **MEDLARS. MEDLINE** is the best known MEDLARS database produced by NLM. See also: **MEDLARS.**

NATIONAL NEWSPAPER INDEX (Database)
Bibliographic database which indexes the *Christian Science Monitor*, the *New York Times*, and the *Wall Street Journal.* Available on DIALOG (File 111).

NATIONAL REHABILITATION INFORMATION CENTER (Database)
Bibliographic database which covers the rehabilitation of the physically and mentally disabled. Available on BRS (NRIC file).

NATURAL LANGUAGE
Human language. Also commonly refers to the process of communicating with a computer by using actual words of speech instead of symbols. See also: **LANGUAGE** and **MACHINE LANGUAGE.**

NATURAL LANGUAGE DATABASE
Database which does not have assigned **descriptors** or **index terms.** Such databases are searchable only by using **free text searching** techniques.

NBR COMMAND
SDC USAGE: See **NEIGHBOR COMMAND.**

NCFR (Database)
BRS USAGE: See **FAMILY RESOURCES (Database).**

NCJRS (Database)
See: **NATIONAL CRIMINAL JUSTICE REFERENCE SERVICE (Database).**

NCMH (Database)
BRS USAGE: See **NIMH (Database).**

NDEX (Database)
SDC USAGE: See **NEWSPAPER INDEX (Database).**

NEGATIVE LOGIC
See: **NOT OPERATOR.**

NEIGHBOR COMMAND
SDC USAGE: Command used to list alphabetically or numerically related terms and give their individual **posting.** Similar to BRS's **ROOT command** and DIALOG's **EXPAND command.**

NESTED STATEMENTS
See: **NESTING.**

NESTING
Use of **parentheses** with a **search statement**, normally to specify the **priority of execution**. This is technically "explicit nesting." The order of execution followed when no parentheses are used is actually "internal nesting."

NETWORKS
COMPUTER SCIENCE USAGE: System of **computers** and **terminals** interconnected through **communications networks**. **ONLINE SEARCHING USAGE**: See **COMMUNICATIONS NETWORKS**.

NEW YORK TIMES INFORMATION BANK
Bibliographic database which indexes the articles in the *New York Times* and many other newspapers and magazines. Available on BRS (NYTS file) and from the New York Times Information Service.

NEW YORK TIMES INFORMATION SERVICE
Database producer which produces the **NEW YORK TIMES INFORMATION BANK (Database)**. Also functions as a **commercial search service** and makes this database directly available to subscribers.

NEWS
See: **LOGON MESSAGE**.

NEWS COMMAND
SDC USAGE: **Command** used to obtain current system news while **online**.

NEWS (Database)
BRS USAGE: BRS file which briefly reports system news and other important news items concerning databases, training schedules, and pricing changes.

NEWSLETTERS
Publications which keep online users up to date about all aspects of searching. Newsletters are distributed both by the major **commercial search services**, e.g., DIALOG's *CHRONOLOG*, and **database producers**, e.g., BIOSIS' *Preview Memo*.

NEWSEARCH (Database)
Bibliographic database which represents the daily updates of five other databases produced by Information Access Corporation: **LEGAL RESOURCES INDEX, MAGAZINE INDEX, MANAGEMENT CONTENTS, NATIONAL NEWSPAPER INDEX**, and **TRADE AND INDUSTRY INDEX**.

NEWSPAPER INDEX (Database)
Bibliographic database which indexes nine major regional American newspapers and 10 black newspapers. Available on SDC (NDEX file).

NEXIS (Database)
Full text database produced and made available by **Mead Data General**, which offers access to the full text of wire services, magazines, and newspapers.

NICEM (Database)
Directory database which identifies all types of educational media and nonprint materials that can be used at all educational levels. Available on DIALOG (File 46).

NICSEM/NIMIS (Database)
Directory database which identifies and describes all types of media and educational equipment that can be used with handicapped children. Available on DIALOG (File 70).

NIMH (Database)
Bibliographic database which covers the area of mental health. Available on BRS (NCMH file).

NIMI (Database)
BRS USAGE: See NICSEM/NIMIS (Database).

NIMIS (Database)
BRS USAGE: See NICSEM/NIMIS (Database).

NISH (Database)
BRS USAGE: See NATIONAL INFORMATION SOURCES ON THE HANDICAPPED (Database).

NLM
Abbreviation for the National Library of Medicine. See also: MEDLARS and NATIONAL LIBRARY OF MEDICINE.

NO CORE AVAILABLE MESSAGE
DIALOG USAGE: Indicates momentary system task switch.

NODE
Point or location in a communications network at which terminals can gain access and be connected to the network. Reference is made to the local "node," e.g., the point in the system reached by the local telephone number which then connects the user, through the communications network, with the commercial search service requested.

NOISE
1) Unwanted signals that are caused by disturbances in a data transmission line. Its appearance is beyond the control of the user, but it can result in errors or the retrieval of irrelevant items. Consequently, it is frequently considered synonymous with false drops. However, false drops are not necessarily the result of line noise and, similarly, line noise does not automatically generate false drops. Synonymous with line noise and interference. See also: FALSE DROPS. 2) Loudness level of the operation of the terminal. An important factor in the selection of a terminal for online searching.

NONBIBLIOGRAPHIC DATABASE
Database which holds data that is generally self-contained, e.g., it is not necessary to consult further references for the desired information. Contrast with: BIBLIOGRAPHIC DATABASE. There are many different categories of nonbibliographic databases, and the differences between them are often confusing. Examples of types of nonbibliographic databases include: Catalog database, dictionary databases, directory databases, and numeric databases.

NONFERROUS METALS ABSTRACTS (Database)
Bibliographic database which covers all areas of nonferrous metallurgy and related technology. Available on DIALOG (File 118).

NOT OPERATOR

Boolean operator which negates or eliminates certain items. Logically expressed as "A is true if and only if B is not true." For example, in SDC searching "library NOT automation" retrieves all mentions of "library" that do *not* also include the term "automation." No degree of **proximity** or **adjacency** is required. See also: **BOOLEAN LOGIC** and **BOOLEAN OPERATOR**.

NOT AVAILABLE MESSAGE

TELENET USAGE: The requested **commercial search service's** computer is not working. May be due to **system failure** or scheduled **down time**.

NOT OPERATING MESSAGE

TELENET USAGE: See **NOT AVAILABLE MESSAGE**.

NOT REACHABLE

TELENET USAGE: System problem with the TELENET computer.

NOT RESPONDING MESSAGE

TELENET USAGE: See **NOT AVAILABLE MESSAGE**.

NRIC DATABASE

BRS USAGE: See **NATIONAL REHABILITATION INFORMATION CENTER (Database)**.

NTIS (Database)

Bibliographic database produced by the National Technical Information Service (NTIS) and which covers a wide variety of governmental publications dealing with government-sponsored research and other scientific or engineering projects. Available on BRS (NTIS file), DIALOG (File 6), and SDC (NTIS and NTIS/6469 file).

NUC/CODES (Database)

Directory database which lists the names, addresses, and National Union Catalog codes for all libraries cited in the **CASSI (database)**. Available on SDC (NUC/CODES file).

NUMERIC DATABASE

Nonbibliographical database which consists primarily of statistical and numeric **data**. Examples include **DISCLOSURE database** and **BLS CONSUMER PRICE INDEX database**.

NYTS (Database)

BRS USAGE: See **NEW YORK TIMES INFORMATION BANK (Database)**.

OBAR/LEXIS (Database)

See: **LEXIS (Database)**.

OCEANIC ABSTRACTS (Database)

Bibliographic database which provides international coverage of a wide variety of marine-related subject areas. Available on DIALOG (File 28).

..OFF COMMAND
BRS USAGE: Command used to **logoff** from the system.

..OFF CONTINUE COMMAND
BRS USAGE: Command which allows a user to temporarily **disconnect** from the system and then **reconnect** any time during the same day.

OFFLINE
Processing which occurs after the user is no longer directly connected to the **computer,** e.g., the user is "off" the telephone "line" which had served to connect the **terminal** and the computer. Contrast with: **ONLINE.** See also: **OFFLINE PRINTING.**

OFFLINE PRINT CHARGES
Fees assessed for each **citation** or reference which is **printed offline** and sent to the user. Prices vary depending on the **print format** chosen. See also: **ONLINE PRINT CHARGES.**

OFFLINE PRINTING
Delayed printing of **search results** after an **online search** has been completed and the connection with the **commercial search service's** computer has been broken. Results are typically mailed to the user and received within five to seven days. Contrast with: **ONLINE PRINTING.** See also: **PRINT COMMANDS.**

OFFLINE SEARCHING
Technique in which certain **backfiles** are not available for **online** access. A search is performed in the online portion of the database and a special **command,** e.g., **..SEARCHOFF** in BRS, is used to instruct the computer to save the search and execute it against the offline files later the same day.

ONLINE
Direct, interactive communication between a user and the computer, e.g., the user is "on" the telephone "line," which serves to connect the computer and the user. Contrast with: **OFFLINE.** See: **INTERACTIVE SYSTEM.** See also: **ONLINE PRINTING.**

ONLINE ASSISTANCE
See: **HELP COMMAND.**

ONLINE BIBLIOGRAPHIC REFERENCE SERVICE
See: **SEARCH SERVICE.**

ONLINE CHARGES
Costs incurred during the time a search is actually being performed online. Normally composed of the **commercial search service's** charges for **connect time, communications costs** assessed, and any **online print** fees.

ONLINE CHRONICLE (Database)
Full text database which presents the latest news and information relevant to **online searching.** Represents an expanded version of the "News" columns in *Online* and *Database.* Available on DIALOG (File 170).

ONLINE CONNECT TIME
See: **CONNECT TIME.**

ONLINE CURRENT AWARENESS
See: **CURRENT AWARENESS SEARCH.**

ONLINE DEMONSTRATION
Presentation to explain **online searching** which involves the actual conducting of a search for the audience.

ONLINE EXPLANATIONS
See: **HELP COMMANDS.**

ONLINE PRINT CHARGES
Fees assessed for individual **citations** or references which are **printed online.** Prices may vary depending on **print format** chosen. See also: **OFFLINE PRINT CHARGES.**

ONLINE PRINTING
Immediate presentation of **search results** while conducting an **online search.** Frequently known as **displaying** results, as opposed to printing **offline.** Contrast with: **OFFLINE PRINTING.** See: **PRINT COMMANDS.**

ONLINE REFERENCE
Use of **online searching** to answer various ready-reference questions or to assist reference librarians in providing reference service.

ONLINE RETRIEVAL
See: **ONLINE SEARCHING.**

ONLINE SEARCHING
Means of retrieving desired information, often bibliographic in nature (although this is rapidly changing), by using a machine, specifically a **computer.**

ONLINE SERVICE
See: **SEARCH SERVICE.**

ONLINE SERVICE COORDINATOR
See: **SEARCH SERVICE COORDINATOR.**

ONLINE SYSTEM
Technically, any computer system which allows immediate interaction and communication between the user and the computer. See: **ONLINE.**

ONLINE THESAURUS
Thesaurus which is available for **online** use. See: **THESAURUS.**

ONLINE TIME
See: **CONNECT TIME.**

ONTAP DATABASES
DIALOG USAGE: Special training files which provide low-cost access to representative portions of certain DIALOG databases to allow for **online** practice. ONTAP stands for Online Training and Practice. Examples of available ONTAP files include: **ONTAP CA SEARCH** (File 204); **ONTAP CHEMNAME** (File 231); **ONTAP DIALINDEX** (File 290); **ONTAP ERIC** (File 201); and **ONTAP PST PROMPT** (File 216).

OPERAND
Data that is operated on. For example, in "CAT AND FOOD," cat and food are operands.

OPERATOR
See: **BOOLEAN OPERATOR**.

OR OPERATOR
Boolean operator which allows any terms connected with OR to be retrieved. Logically expressed as "A is true if and only if either B is true or C is true." For example, a search of "library OR automation" retrieves any items which have either word in any of the **searchable fields**. No degree of **proximity** or **adjacency** is required. See also: **BOOLEAN LOGIC**.

ORBCHEM (Database)
SDC USAGE: See **ORBIT (Database)**.

ORBIT
Technically, the computer **programs** developed by IBM and used by the System Development Corporation, which are employed to allow **online searching** of SDC's databases. ORBIT is an acronym for Online Retrieval of Bibliographic Information Time-shared. Now commonly used as a synonym for the **System Development Corporation**.

ORBIT (Database)
System database to which users of SDC are automatically connected when **logging on**. Can be used to cost-effectively save and store searches and to accomplish various housekeeping functions, e.g., asking for an **online** explanation of a **command**. Two other files, ORBCHEM and ORBPAT, serve similar functions for chemical and patent **search strategy** development, especially when **saving searches**.

ORBPAT (Database)
SDC USAGE: See **ORBIT (Database)**.

ORDER COMMAND
SDC USAGE: **Command** used to order full text copies of documents retrieved from on online search through the SDC **Electronic Maildrop©** Service. See: **DOCUMENT DELIVERY**.

.ORDER COMMAND
DIALOG USAGE: **Command** used to initiate an online request for **document delivery** using DIALOG's **DIALORDER Service**.

ORDER OF EXECUTION
See: **PRIORITY OF EXECUTION**.

ORGANIZATIONAL SOURCE
SDC USAGE: See **CORPORATE SOURCE.**

OUTPUT
1) Results or information generated by the processing of the computer and then made available, usually in a **printout.** Contrast with: **INPUT.** 2) Used synonymously with printout. See: **PRINTOUT.**

OUTPUT COMMANDS
See: **PRINT COMMANDS.**

OUTPUT FORMAT
See: **PRINT FORMAT.**

OUTPUT I/O ERROR MESSAGE
DIALOG USAGE: Indicates momentary **hardware** problem.

OUTPUT OPTIONS
See: **PRINT FORMAT.**

OUTPUT SEQUENCE
See: **PRINT FORMAT.**

OVERFLOW CONDITION
Condition which results because a requested process or function either takes too much time (**time overflow**) or requires too much **storage** space (**storage overflow**).

OVERLAP
Degree of duplication of entries in databases which cover similar topics. It is currently impossible to eliminate duplicate references obtained in different files. It is important to consider the degree of overlap when selecting databases for an **online search**. See also: **MERGE COMMAND.**

P COMMAND
DIALOG USAGE: See **PAGE COMMAND.**

PACIFIC ISLAND ECOSYSTEMS (Database)
Bibliographic database which covers biological, ecological, physical, and socioeconomic information on the Pacific Islands. Available on SDC (PIE file).

PACKET SWITCHING
Technique of dividing messages to be sent through a **communications network** into several short fixed-length packets. These may travel different routes through the network to reach their destination where they are reassembled into complete messages.

PAGE
COMPUTER SCIENCE USAGE: Fixed-length amount of **data** which is considered one entity in **storage**. Data which comprises one screen on a **video terminal. ONLINE SEARCHING USAGE:** General context of one sheet of printed results.

PAGE COMMAND
  DIALOG USAGE: Command used to continue the printing of any display from an **EXPAND command**. The need for a PAGE command is indicated by a **MORE message**.

PAIS INTERNATIONAL (Database)
  Bibliographic database which covers most social science fields, including banking, international relations, political science, public policy, and social welfare. Available on BRS (PAIS file) and DIALOG (File 49).

PAPERCHEM (Database)
  Bibliographic database which indexes the scientific and technical publications related to the pulp and paper industry. Available on DIALOG (File 240) and SDC (PAPERCHEM file).

PARAGRAPH
  BRS USAGE: See **FIELD**.

PARAGRAPH QUALIFICATIONS
  BRS USAGE: See **FIELD QUALIFIER**.

PARENTHESES
  Used to enclose portions of a **search statement** to specify the **priority of execution**. See: **PRIORITY OF EXECUTION** and **NESTING**.

PARITY
  Method of detecting **errors** in the transmission of **data** through a **communications network**. Technically, extra **bits**, known as parity bits, are added to each **character** code before it is transmitted. This is then checked at the receiving end of the line. **Terminals** typically have a switch which distinguishes between even parity and odd parity. Even parity is generally used, but in many cases, it does not matter.

PASSWORD
  Unique code, usually one to eight characters long, which is assigned by a system to identify authorized users. Users must supply this confidential password when they **logon** to the system. See also: **USER NUMBER** and **BUSY PASSWORD**.

PATC (Database)
  BRS USAGE: See **PATCLASS (Database)**.

PATDATA (Database)
  Nonbibliographic database which includes citations and abstracts for all United States patents issued in all scientific and technical categories. Produced by BRS since 1982 to replace PATSEARCH database previously made available on BRS from Pergamon International Information Corporation.

PATCLASS (Database)
  Nonbibliographic database produced by Pergamon International Information Corporation which includes U.S. Classification Classes and Subclasses Codes for all United States Patents. Available until July 1982 on BRS (PATC file). See also: **PATDATA (Database)**.

PATLAW (Database)
　　Nonbibliographic database which reports decisions, made by various federal courts and commissions, regarding copyrights, patents, trademarks, and unfair competition. Available on DIALOG (File 243).

PATRON
　　See: **REQUESTER** and **END USER.**

PATS (Database)
　　BRS USAGE: See **PATDATA (Database).**

PATSEARCH (Database)
　　See: **PATDATA (Database).**

P/E NEWS (Database)
　　Bibliographic database which indexes 12 major petroleum and energy publications. Available on SDC (P/E NEWS file).

PERIODS
　　BRS USAGE: All system **commands** and their abbreviations must be preceded by two periods, e.g., "..PRINT" to enter the print **mode. DIALOG USAGE**: Certain commands must be preceded with one period in order to differentiate them from other commands, e.g., the period in the **.EXECUTE command** is needed to distinguish it from the **EXPAND command.**

PERIPHERAL EQUIPMENT
　　COMPUTER SCIENCE USAGE: Any equipment which is used with a **computer**, but which is not directly a part of it and may not absolutely be necessary for its basic operation. **Terminals** and **printers** are considered peripheral equipment.

PERMANENT SAVES
　　See: **SAVING SEARCHES.**

PERSONAL COMPUTER
　　Microcomputer used by individuals, either at home or at work, to perform a variety of functions, e.g., **word processing** or personal financial accounting. The major **commercial search services** are beginning to make **online searching** available to users of personal computers, e.g., DIALOG's **KNOWLEDGE INDEX database**. Personal computers can also be used as **smart terminals** to facilitate actual online search procedures. Common examples include Radio Shack's TRS 80 and Apple computers. See also: **MICROCOMPUTER.**

PESTDOC (Database)
　　Bibliographic database which covers the areas of pesticides, herbicides, and plant protection, especially as it pertains to agricultural chemical manufacturers. Available on SDC (PESTDOC and PESTDOC-II files).

PHARMACEUTICAL NEWS INDEX (Database)
　　Bibliographic database which provides access to current news about the pharmaceutical industry and related health fields. Available on BRS until 1982 (PNIA file) and DIALOG (File 42).

PHILOSOPHER'S INDEX (Database)
Bibliographic database that indexes and abstracts books and journals which deal with philosophy and related topics. Available on DIALOG (File 57).

PHRASE SEARCHING
See: **ADJACENCY.**

PHYSICAL RECORD
See: **RECORD.**

PIE (Database)
SDC USAGE: See **PACIFIC ISLANDS ECOSYSTEMS (Database).**

PIRA (Database)
Bibliographic database produced by the Research Association for the Paper and Board, Printing and Packaging Industries and which covers all aspects of the paper and printing industries. Available on DIALOG (File 48).

PLEASE TRY AGAIN MESSAGE
TYMNET USAGE: Indicates incorrect or unauthorized user name has been used.

PNIA (Database)
BRS USAGE: See **PHARMACEUTICAL NEWS INDEX (Database).**

POLL (Database)
BRS USAGE: See **POLLUTION ABSTRACTS (Database).**

POLLUTION ABSTRACTS (Database)
Bibliographic database which indexes materials related to various types of pollution, including air, noise, and water pollution. Available on BRS (POLL file) and DIALOG (File 41).

POPLINE (Database)
Bibliographic database which deals with family planning, fertility control, population, and reproduction. Available on MEDLARS (POPLINE file).

POPULATION BIBLIOGRAPHY (Database)
Bibliographic database which indexes a wide variety of materials dealing with all areas of population research, including demography, migration, and fertility studies. Available on DIALOG (File 91).

PORT
Entry or exit point in a **communications network**. Individual channel through which **data** can be received and transmitted by and from a **commercial search service's host computer**. If no channels are available, the user may receive an **"All *ports* busy" message.**

PORTABLE TERMINAL
Terminal which can easily be moved and used from various locations. Generally, such terminals are compact and designed to be carried from location to location. Portable terminals are especially important when **online demonstrations** are to be performed or

when the terminal must be shared with other search operations or sites. Contrast with: **STATIONARY TERMINAL**. See also: **TERMINAL**.

PORTS BUSY
See: **PORT**.

POSITIONAL OPERATORS
System specific operators which determine the degree of **adjacency** or **proximity** retrieved. See: **ADJACENCY** and **PROXIMITY**. See also: **FREE TEXT OPERATORS** (BRS usage), **FULL TEXT OPERATORS** (DIALOG usage), and **PROXIMITY OPERATORS** (SDC usage).

POSTINGS
Total number of items listed under a given term or **access point**. Often synonymous with **hit**, but technically they are equivalent only when a single term is searched. In that case, the number of items retrieved by the search ("hits") equals the total number of items listed under that term ("postings"). See also: **HITS**.

POSTING COUNTS
See: **POSTINGS**.

POSTINGS DICTIONARY
List which gives the number of items assigned or "posted" to each term in a **bibliographic database**. Many print **thesauri** include postings for each **index term** given, but online commands, e.g., **EXPAND** on DIALOG or **NEIGHBOR** on SDC, can also be used to produce lists of terms with postings individually indicated. See also: **POSTINGS**.

POSTINGS FILE
See: **POSTINGS**.

POST-QUALIFICATION OF SEARCH TERMS
BRS USAGE: Ability to **qualify search terms** which have already been retrieved and assigned **set numbers**. Also known as "after the fact" qualification. See: **QUALIFICATION OF SEARCH TERMS**.

POST-SEARCH DEBRIEFING
See: **POST-SEARCH INTERVIEW**.

POST-SEARCH INTERVIEW
Conversation between the **search analyst** and the **requester** after an **online search** has been conducted. This discussion is to explain the **search results**, consider further alternatives, and answer any questions raised either by the search itself or the actual results. See also: **END USER** and **PRESEARCH INTERVIEW**.

POST-SEARCH NEGOTIATIONS
See: **POST-SEARCH INTERVIEW**.

POWER (Database)
Bibliographic and **catalog database** which lists the catalog records of the book collection of the United States Department of Energy's Library. Available on SDC (POWER file).

PRECISION
Degree of exactness. **COMPUTER SCIENCE USAGE**: Computer scientists contrast **accuracy** with precision. Precision indicates the detail used in displaying the results, while accuracy concerns the quality of the results. For example, a computation to two significant decimal points is more precise than a calculation rounded to the nearest whole number, but if it contains an **error**, it is less accurate. **ONLINE SEARCHING USAGE**: Percentage of retrieved items that are relevant to the topic. See: **RECALL**.

PREDICASTS DATABASES
Bibliographic and **numeric databases** which provide business and industrial statistics and information, known as PTS (Predicasts Terminal System) files. See specific **PTS databases**.

PREFIX CODES
DIALOG USAGE: Two-letter code used to identify the particular **fields** in the **additional index**. For example, "AU = " is used for the author field. The two-letter code is known as a **field indicator**.

PREFORMATTED PRINTING OPTIONS
See: **PRINT FORMAT**.

PREM (Database)
BRS USAGE: See **PRE-MED (Database)**.

PRE-MED (Database)
Bibliographic database which provides citations to the most recent months of journals indexed in *Abridged Index Medicus*. Available on BRS (PREM file).

PREP (Database)
BRS USAGE: See **PRE-PSYC (Database)**.

PRE-PSYC (Database)
Bibliographic database which covers the most recent 12 months of major psychological journals. Available on BRS (PREP file).

PRESEARCH INTERVIEW
Conversation between the **search analyst** and the **requester** prior to an **online search** to formulate a **search strategy**. This discussion is very similar to a reference interview and involves such things as determining what information is desired, where to look for it, and how to go about retrieving it. Also known as the Informational Interview to distinguish it from the traditional reference interview. See also: **POST-SEARCH INTERVIEW**.

PRINT
Technically, the presentation of a search in print form, usually using a **print terminal**. However, a distinction is frequently made between "printing" **offline** and "displaying" **online**.

PRINT CHARGES
Fees assessed to have individual citations or references either **displayed online** or **printed offline**. See: **ONLINE PRINT CHARGES** and **OFFLINE PRINT CHARGES**.

PRINT COMMAND

Command that indicates not only what **records**, but also which **fields** for each record, are to be **printed** or **displayed**. Specific commands vary, but in most cases, the **set** to be printed must be identified, the **print format** selected, and the records to be printed indicated. Results can be either printed **online** or **offline**. However, a distinction is frequently made between "printing" offline and "displaying" online. Different print commands are used to differentiate between offline and online prints. See also: **OFFLINE PRINTING** and **ONLINE PRINTING**. BRS USAGE: See **..PRINT COMMAND**. DIALOG USAGE: Command used to print results offline. See also: **TYPE COMMAND** and **PRINT FORMAT**. SDC USAGE: Command used to print results either online or offline. See also **PRINT FORMAT**.

..PRINT COMMAND

BRS USAGE: **Command** used to **display** results online. See also: **PRINT COMMAND, PRINT FORMAT**, and **..PRINTOFF COMMAND**.

PRINT EQUIVALENT

Print version of an **online database**. Most **bibliographic databases** have print equivalents, although there may be significant differences between the two versions. See: **DATABASE**.

PRINT FILE

See: **LINEAR FILE**.

PRINT FORMAT

Designation of the **fields** to be **printed**, either **online** or **offline**. Formats range from only **accession numbers** to complete **records** with **abstracts**. Specific **print commands** vary among the **commercial search services**. For example, DIALOG has relatively standardized print formats, while SDC allows the user to specify exactly which **printable fields** are to be printed.

PRINT FULL COMMAND

SDC USAGE: **Print format** which prints the complete **record** in most databases. This normally contains all **printable fields**, including an **abstract**.

PRINT MODE

BRS USAGE: Operating **mode** in which **search results** can be **displayed online** or **printed offline**.

PRINT OFFLINE COMMAND

SDC USAGE: **Print format** used to have items **printed offline** and mailed to the user. Various options are available, but the most commonly used is "PRINT FULL OFFLINE INDENTED STORAD." This **command** is abbreviated "PRTOFF" and is used to have offline prints produced in the **indented (print option)** and to be mailed directly to the address stored earlier **(STORAD)**.

PRINT SELECT COMMAND

SDC USAGE: **Command** used to transform terms from a specific **field**, usually the **Index Term** (IT) field, into individually numbered **search statements**.

PRINT TERMINAL

Terminal which functions like an electric typewriter and produces a print record of all searches. Contrast with: **VIDEO TERMINAL**. Two types of **printers** are generally available: **thermal printers** and **impact printers**.

PRINT TRIAL COMMAND

SDC USAGE: Online print format that prints only titles, **index terms,** and other subject-related **fields,** except for abstracts. Can be used to determine quickly the relevance of retrieved items and to identify additional subject terms which can be used.

PRINTABLE FIELDS

The **fields** or parts of a **record** that can be **displayed** or **printed**. See: **PRINT FORMAT**.

PRINTED INDEX

Hardcopy version of a periodical index. Typically contrasted with a **bibliographic database**. The **database** may be the **online** equivalent of the printed index. For example, the printed ERIC index is directly equivalent to the online **ERIC database**. However, in many cases there are significant differences between the print and online versions of the same index. See: **DATABASE**.

PRINTER

Device used as either part of a **print terminal** or as a piece of **peripheral equipment** attached to a **video terminal** to produce hardcopy output from an **online search**. Two types of **printers** are generally available: **thermal printers** and **impact printers**. Printers used in online searching are usually **line printers,** which print out the results one line at a time. See also: **IMPACT PRINTERS** and **THERMAL PRINTERS**.

.PRINTOFF COMMAND

BRS USAGE: Command used to **print** results **offline**. See also: **..PRINT COMMAND, PRINT COMMAND,** and **PRINT FORMAT**.

PRINTOUT

Printed results or **output** of a search. Often used synonymously with output. See: **OUTPUT**.

PRIORITY OF EXECUTION

Order in which a system operates on search elements linked by **Boolean operators**. For example, DIALOG first processes the **NOT operator,** then the **AND operator,** and finally the **OR operator**. This is known as implicit **nesting. Parentheses** can be used to guarantee the order of execution. Items enclosed in parentheses are executed before those that are not. This use of parentheses is known as explicit nesting. See also: **BOOLEAN OPERATOR** and **NESTING**.

PROCESSING CUE

Signal to a user that the **host computer** has received and is processing the previous **command**. On most **terminals,** the print head quickly moves over 10 spaces and then returns to its original position without printing. This movement is referred to as a "blip," "flicker," "stutter," or "twitch."

PROFILE
See: **SEARCH PROFILE**.

PROGRAM MESSAGES
SDC USAGE: System messages which either prompt the user to do something, ask the user questions, or provide information to the user.

PROGRAMMER
Person who writes **programs**. See: **PROGRAMS**.

PROGRAMMING
See: **PROGRAMS**.

PROGRAMS
COMPUTER SCIENCE USAGE: Coded operating instructions which direct the activity of the **computer**. The process of writing these instructions is known as "programming" and is commonly done by a **"programmer."** Often considered synonymous with **software**. See: **SOFTWARE. ONLINE SEARCHING USAGE:** No knowledge of programming is required for most **online searching** applications.

PROPERTIES DATABASE
See: **DICTIONARY DATABASE**.

PROMPT
Symbol which indicates that the **host computer** is ready to accept input from the user. Prompt may be a piece of punctuation, e.g., DIALOG uses a **question mark**, or a brief statement, e.g., SDC prompts with "USER:."

PROXIMITY
Requirement that two or more terms have a specified hierarchical relationship, but not necessarily be **adjacent** to each other. Contrast with: **ADJACENCY**. For example, in DIALOG "sex(F)discrimination" retrieves not only the phrase "sex discrimination," but also any citation in which both words appear in the same **field**, e.g., the title "Discrimination in Sex" will be retrieved. See: **POSITIONAL OPERATORS**.

PROXIMITY OPERATORS
SDC USAGE: Special operators which allow a user to specify various hierarchical relationships between **search terms**. See also: **ADJACENCY, POSITIONAL OPERATORS**, and **PROXIMITY**. Proximity cannot be used in all SDC databases. The **STRINGSEARCH command** and the **SENSEARCH command** must be used in some databases. Proximity operators available on SDC include:

(W) or ADJ	Requires terms to be directly adjacent in specified order.
(nW) or (n)	Requires first term to be within n words of the second.
(L) or LINK	Requires terms to be in the same subfield or subrecord.
(S) or W/S	Requires terms to be in the same sentence.
(F) or W/F	Requires terms to be in the same **field**.
(C) or (R)	Requires terms to simply be in the same **record**.

PRTOFF COMMAND
SDC USAGE: Stands for "Print Full Offline Indented Storad." See: **PRINT OFFLINE COMMAND**.

PRT SEL COMMAND
SDC USAGE: See **PRINT SELECT COMMAND**.

PSYC (Database)
BRS USAGE: See **PSYCINFO (Database)**.

PSYCHOLOGICAL ABSTRACTS (Database)
See: **PSYCINFO (Database)**.

PSYCINFO (Database)
Bibliographic database which covers the literature of psychology and related disciplines. Available on BRS (PSYC file), DIALOG (File 11), and SDC (PSYCINFO file).

PTS F & S INDEXES (Database)
Bibliographic database which provides information on domestic and foreign companies, products, and industries. Available on BRS (PTSI file) and DIALOG (Files 18 and 98).

PTS INTERNATIONAL FORECASTS (Database)
Numeric database which abstracts published forecasts prepared for all countries of the world, except the United States. Available on DIALOG (File 83).

PTS INTERNATIONAL TIME SERIES (Database)
Numeric database which includes about 2,500 forecast time series for 50 major countries, except the United States. Available on DIALOG (File 84).

PTS PREDALERT (Database)
Bibliographic database which is the current weekly updated file for both **PTS PROMPT** and **PTS F & S INDEXES** databases. Available on DIALOG (File 17).

PTS DATABASES
Predicasts Terminal System. See: **PREDICASTS DATABASES**.

PTS/F & S INDEX WEEKLY UPDATE FILE (Database)
Bibliographic database which is the weekly updated version of the **PTS F & S INDEX database**. Available on BRS (PTSW file).

PTS/FORECASTS (Database)
Numeric database which provides statistical forecasts for products, industries, population, and national income, as reported in trade journals and reports. Available on BRS (PTSF file).

PTS/HISTORICAL TIME SERIES (Database)
Numeric database which provides statistical time series for products, industries, population, and national income, as reported in various trade journals and reports. Available on BRS (PTSH file).

PTS PROMPT (Database)
Bibliographic database which abstracts various aspects of business information, e.g., acquisitions, market data, and production, as reported in major newspapers, magazines, government reports, and other related publications. Available on BRS (PTSP file) and DIALOG (File 16).

PTR/PROMPT WEEKLY UPDATE FILE (Database)
Bibliographic database which is the weekly updated version of the **PTS PROMPT** database. Available on BRS (PTSD file).

PTS U.S. TIME SERIES (Database)
Numeric database which contains time series on the United States, including both composite statistics and annual data reports for over 37,000 series. Available on DIALOG (File 82).

PTS U.S. FORECASTS (Database)
Numeric database which presents abstracts of forecasts for the United States, as reported in trade journals, newspapers, government studies, and other related types of publications. Available on DIALOG (File 81).

PTSD (Database)
BRS USAGE: See **PTS/PROMPT WEEKLY UPDATE FILE (Database)**.

PTSF (Database)
BRS USAGE: **PTS/FORECASTS (Database)**.

PTSH (Database)
BRS USAGE: See **PTS/HISTORICAL TIME SERIES (Database)**.

PTSI (Database)
BRS USAGE: See **PTS F & S INDEXES (Database)**.

PTSP (Database)
BRS USAGE: See **PTS PROMPT (Database)**.

PTSW (Database)
BRS USAGE: See **PTS/F & S INDEXES WEEKLY UPDATE FILE (Database)**.

PUBLIC AFFAIRS INFORMATION SERVICE (Database)
See: **PAIS INTERNATIONAL (Database)**.

PURGE COMMAND
SDC USAGE: **Command** used to delete searches saved by the **STORESEARCH feature**. See also: **SAVING SEARCHES**.

..PURGE COMMAND
BRS USAGE: **Command** which can be used to eliminate or delete **search statements** which are no longer needed for the search. This command can also be used to cancel **offline prints** and any **saved searches**.

Q NUMBERS
    See: **QUERIES**.

QUALIFICATION OF SEARCH TERMS
    Restriction of a **search term** to one or more specific **fields**. This is normally accomplished by using a **field qualifier**, but each **commercial search service** uses a slightly different technque. See: **FIELD QUALIFIER**. In some cases, post-qualification of search terms is possible.

QUALIFIER
    Field qualifier used in the qualification of **search terms**. See: **QUALIFICATION OF SEARCH TERMS**.

QUERIES
    BRS USAGE: Number assigned to certain **commands** or "queries." The **PRINTOFF, SEARCHOFF,** and **SDI** commands result in the following acknowledgment and the assignment of an identification number: "Your offline *query* has been saved under the name *Q*0011." Each individual command is labeled a "Query" and assigned a "Q" number. This Q number can be subsequently used to eliminate the query.

QUERY FORMULATION
    See: **SEARCH STRATEGY**.

QUESTEL
    Major French **commercial search service**.

QUESTION MARK
    BRS USAGE: Key used in **line deletion** to erase an entire line of input before it is transmitted to the computer. **DIALOG USAGE:** 1) System **prompts**. 2) Used to indicate the point of **truncation**.

QUESTION NUMBER
    See: **SET NUMBER**.

QUICK BROWSE CAPABILITY
    BRS USAGE: Special BRS technique which allows users to scan citations quickly as they are **displayed online,** without requiring the complete citation to be displayed.

R OPERATOR
    SDC USAGE: See **PROXIMITY OPERATORS**.

R REFERENCE NUMBER
    DIALOG USAGE: Number assigned to each subject-related term listed as a result of an **EXPAND command** of the appropriate **E Reference Number** of the term for which subject terms are desired.

RANDOM ACCESS
    COMPUTER SEARCHING USAGE: Method of directly retrieving any **record** in a **file** without the necessity of searching all of the other records. Consequently, the amount of time needed to retrieve an item is totally independent of its location within the file. Random access makes **online searching** feasible because without this capability each record

in a database would have to be searched sequentially to retrieve any item. Also known as direct access.

RANGE SEARCHING
DIALOG USAGE: Allows searching over a range of **data**, especially sequential items such as publication years or share of market. For example, "PY = 1979:PY = 1983" will retrieve all items published in the years 1979, 1980, 1981, 1982, and 1983. Since a colon must be used, this is also commonly referred to as colon searching.

RANGING
DIALOG USAGE: See **RANGE SEARCHING**. **SDC USAGE**: See **DATA RANGING**.

RAPRA ABSTRACTS (Database)
Bibliographic database which covers all aspects of the rubber and plastics industries. Available on DIALOG (File 95).

READOUT
See: **PRINTOUT**.

REAL TIME
COMPUTER SCIENCE USAGE: Actual time required for a **computer** to complete a process or **program**. **ONLINE SEARCHING USAGE**: Online search **systems** are real time operations because the response of the computer is fast enough to allow immediate interaction between the user and the computer. See also: **INTERACTIVE SYSTEM**.

RECALL
Items retrieved by an **online search**. Generally considered to be the percentage of relevant items retrieved by a search. See also: **ACCURACY, PRECISION**, and **SEARCH RESULTS**.

RECALL COMMAND
SDC USAGE: **Command** used to execute a search that has previously been saved. See: **SAVING SEARCHES**.

RECON
Online system used for **information retrieval**. Originally designed by the Lockheed Corporation for the United States National Aeronautics and Space Administration (NASA), RECON is now used by various agencies, e.g., NASA/RECON, DOE/RECON (Department of Energy), and ESA/RECON (European Space Agency). RECON stands for Remote Console.

RECONNECT
To reestablish a direct connection between a **terminal** and the **host computer** after being momentarily disconnected. In most cases, the search can be continued from the point at which it was interrupted. This reconnect capability is useful when a search has been interrupted by **communications** or system problems. Also, it is generally possible to intentionally discontinue a search temporarily by using an established **command**, e.g., **LOGOFF HOLD** in DIALOG, with the intent of shortly reconnecting and completing the search. Also known as restart.

RECORD

Group of related **information** contained in a **database** which is treated as a unit by the **computer**. In general, a record is all of the information stored for one item. For example, in a **bibliographic database**, the author, title, journal or publishing information, abstract, and all other **fields** directly related to the item constitute one record. In this case, it is also known as a bibliographic record. If the record can be described in terms of physical characteristics, e.g., the form in which it is stored or retrieved, it is referred to as a physical record.

REMOTE ACCESS

To have **access** or be able to communicate with a **computer** that is physically distant from the **terminal**. Typically necessitates using a **dialup terminal**. Contrast with: **HARDWIRED TERMINAL**. Searches done on the databases from the major **commercial search services** are done on a remote access basis.

REFERENCE

Generally considered synonymous with **citation**. See: **CITATION**.

REFERENCE DATABASE

Any type of database, whether **bibliographic** or **nonbibliographic**, which is frequently consulted as a source to answer a specific question. While virtually any file could be considered a reference database, general use files, such as **MAGAZINE INDEX** and **ENCYCLOPEDIA OF ASSOCIATIONS**, are more commonly referred to as "reference databases."

REFERRAL DATABASE

Virtually synonymous with **bibliographic database** in that it does not directly provide an answer, but refers users to other sources. However, many types of **nonbibliographic databases** are also commonly considered referral databases because they similarly refer users to additional sources of information. An example of a referral database is the **NATIONAL INFORMATION SOURCES ON THE HANDICAPPED database**.

REGISTRY NUMBER

See: **CHEMICAL DICTIONARY DATABASES**.

REGISTRY OF TOXIC EFFECTS OF CHEMICAL SUBSTANCES (Database)

Nonbibliographic database which directly provides basic toxicity information concerning individual chemical substances. Also known as RTECS. Available on MEDLARS (RTECS file).

RELATED TERMS

Terms indicated as being subject-related to specific terms identified in a **thesaurus**. The relationship may be hierarchical, e.g., narrower or boarder terms. See also: **HIERARCHICAL VOCABULARY**.

RELEVANCE

Appropriateness of the topic or usefulness of the **data** to the **end user**. See also: **ACCURACY, PRECISION**, and **RECALL**.

RELI (Database)

BRS USAGE: See **ALTA RELIGION (Database)**.

RELOAD

To **load** the previously available **database** back into the **computer** and make it accessible **online** again. A **commercial search service** "reloads" a file every time it is **updated** or when changes have been made in the search features available.

REMARC (Database)

Catalog database which represents the items cataloged by the Library of Congress from 1897 to January 1978. Available on DIALOG (Files 421, 422, 423, 424, 425).

REMOTE ACCESS

Ability to communicate with a **computer** from a **terminal** not directly connected to it. **Online searching** is dependent on the use of some sort of **communications,** most often a **communications network,** to establish this connection between a **host computer** and a terminal physically separate from it.

REMOTE MODE

Setting on a **terminal** which allows it to both transmit to and receive **data** from a **host computer.** Contrast with: **LOCAL MODE.** See also: **MODE.**

RENAME COMMAND

SDC USAGE: Command which allows the user to change any system keyword, such as a command name, to any name or symbol that is not already an **ORBIT** keyword. The original name will no longer work. See also: **SYNONYM COMMAND.**

REQUESTER

Person seeking information who asks for an **online search.** Also known as the **end user.** See also: **END USER.**

REQUESTS

See: **SEARCH REQUEST.**

RERUN

To repeat an **online search.** May be done to correct an error, modify the **search strategy,** or to **update** the results. See also: **RUN.**

RESOURCES IN VOCATIONAL EDUCATION (Database)

Directory database which reports on current and completed research projects in the field of vocational education. Available on BRS (RIVE file).

RESPONSE

Reply to an **online command** or **search statement** by the **host computer.**

RESPONSE TIME

Commonly used term for **access time.** Time taken for a system to reply to a **command** or **search statement** transmitted to the system by the user.

RESTART

See: **RECONNECT. SDC USAGE:** To totally erase a search and start the online session over.

RESTART COMMAND
    SDC USAGE: Command used to initiate a new search session without **logging off** and then **logging on** again. See: **RESTART**.

RESTRICTING SEARCHES
    See: **LIMITING SEARCHES**.

RESULT STATEMENT
    See: **SEARCH NUMBER** and **SEARCH STATEMENT**.

RESULTS
    See: **SEARCH RESULTS**.

RETRIEVAL
    See: **INFORMATION RETRIEVAL**.

RETRIEVAL SERVICE
    See: **SEARCH SERVICE** and **INFORMATION RETREIVAL CENTER**.

RETRIEVED RECORD
    Item retrieved by an **online search**. See also: **RECALL, RECORD**, and **SEARCH RESULTS**.

RETROSPECTIVE SEARCH
    Search of a database for a given period of time to retrieve items on a particular topic. If the same **search strategy** is subsequently executed to **update** this original search, it is known as a **current awareness search**. A regularly performed current awareness search is referred to as **selective dissemination of information**. See: **CURRENT AWARENESS SEARCH**. See also: **SELECTIVE DISSEMINATION OF INFORMATION**.

RETURN COMMAND
    SDC USAGE: Command used with the **TFILE command** to return to the original database. See: **TFILE COMMAND**.

RETURN KEY
    See: **CARRIAGE RETURN**.

RIGHT TRUNCATION
    Truncation used to retrieve all terms beginning with a specific **word stem**. For example, a search of the truncated word "librar" will retrieve all words beginning with those six letters, e.g., library, librarian, and librarianship.

RILM ABSTRACTS (Database)
    Bibliographic database which provides international coverage of all aspects of music and musicology. Available on DIALOG (File 97).

RINGDOC (Database)
    Bibliographic database which covers all areas of pharmaceutical information. Available on SDC (RINGDOC and RING6475 files).

RIVE (Database)
BRS USAGE: See **RESOURCES IN VOCATIONAL EDUCATION (Database)**.

RNM COMMAND
SDC USAGE: See **RENAME COMMAND**.

ROOT
See: **WORD STEM**.

ROOT COMMAND
BRS USAGE: **Command** which displays a list of all entries in the **inverted file** that begin with a particular **word stem**. Similar to DIALOG's **EXPAND command** and SDC's **NEIGHBOR command**.

ROYALTY FEE
Fee accessed by certain **database producers** when their files are used online through the major **commercial search services**. These charges are in addition to the regular connect hour rates.

RST COMMAND
SDC USAGE: See **RESTART COMMAND**.

RTECS (Database)
MEDLARS USAGE: See **REGISTRY OF TOXIC EFFECTS OF CHEMICAL SUBSTANCES (Database)**.

RUN
COMPUTER SCIENCE USAGE: Execution of one **program** by a **computer**. ONLINE SEARCHING USAGE: To perform an **online search**.

S COMMAND
DIALOG USAGE: See **SELECT COMMAND**.

SAE (Database)
SDC USAGE: See **SOCIETY OF AUTOMOTIVE ENGINEERS (Database)**.

SAFETY (Database)
Bibliographic database which covers the broad area of safety, with particular emphasis on identifying, evaluating, eliminating, or controlling hazards. Available on SDC (SAFETY file).

SAME OPERATOR
BRS USAGE: See **FREE TEXT OPERATORS**.

..SAVE COMMAND
BRS USAGE: **Command** which permanently saves a **search strategy** until it is released with the **..PURGE command**. See also: **SAVING SEARCHES**.

SAVE COMMAND
SDC USAGE: **Command** used in **saving searches** after the **search strategy** has been executed in a database. The saved strategy is retained for only one day. Contrast with: **STORE COMMAND**. See also: **SAVING SEARCHES**.

SAVESEARCH FEATURE

BRS USAGE: Technique used in **saving searches**. Searches can be retained either temporarily (for one day) or permanently (until specifically released by the **..PURGE command**). See also: **SAVING SEARCHES**.

SAVEsearch FEATURE

SDC USAGE: Technique used in **saving searches**. This feature only saves a search for one day. Contrast with: **STOREsearch FEATURE**.

SAVING SEARCHES

Technique used to retain and store **online search strategies** so that they can be reused in a later search without reentering the **search statements**. See: **SAVEsearch FEATURE** (SDC usage), **SAVESEARCH FEATURE** (BRS usage), and **SEARCH*SAVE FEATURE** (DIALOG usage).

SCAN

COMPUTER SEARCHING USAGE: To examine each part in every item in a file in a logical sequence.

SCHOOL PRACTICES INFORMATION FILE (Database)

Directory database which provides information on educational practices, programs, and materials currently being used in various educational settings. Available on BRS (SPIF file).

SCISEARCH (Database)

Bibliographic database which corresponds to the printed *Science Citation Index*. Available on BRS until 1982 (ISCI file) and DIALOG (Files 34, 94, 186, and 187).

SCREEN

Surface of a **cathode ray tube** on which a visual display is presented.

SDC

See: **SYSTEM DEVELOPMENT CORPORATION**.

SDI

See: **SELECTIVE DISSEMINATION OF INFORMATION**.

SDILINE

Selective dissemination of information service available for the **MEDLINE database**. SDILINE stands for S̲elective D̲issemination of I̲nformation O̲nline. Available on MEDLARS (SDILINE file).

SDIsearch FEATURE

SDC USAGE: Technique in which **saved searches** are automatically executed whenever the given database is **updated**. See: **SELECTIVE DISSEMINATION OF INFORMATION** and **SAVING SEARCHES**.

SEARCH

Process of finding information or records containing the desired information. **ONLINE SEARCHING USAGE:** The online examination of data to retrieve records relevant to the search request. See: **ONLINE SEARCHING**.

SEARCH AIDS

Aids, generally print publications, which assist the user in conducting an **online search**. Search aids include **user manuals, thesauri, word frequency lists**, and other types of **documentation**. They are produced by **commercial search services, database producers**, and independent organizations and publishers.

SEARCH ANALYST

Individual **trained** in **online searching** who typically serves as an **intermediary** between the **requester** and the **information** contained in the database. The search analyst conducts the **presearch interview**, prepares the **search strategy**, and executes the search.

..SEARCH COMMAND

BRS USAGE: Command used to return the user to the **SEARCH MODE**.

SEARCH COMMANDS

See: **COMMAND** and **COMMAND LANGUAGE**.

SEARCH CONSULTANTS

See: **SEARCH ANALYSTS**.

SEARCH EVALUATION

Judging the quality of **search results** during and after an **online search**.

SEARCH FORM

See: **SEARCH REQUEST FORM**.

SEARCH FORMULATION

See: **SEARCH STRATEGY**.

SEARCH HISTORY

Listing of all **search statements** and **postings** retrieved up to that point in an **online search**. Particularly useful when using a **video terminal** or when the search involves a large number of search statements. All of the **commercial search services** have such capabilities, but the actual commands vary.

SEARCH KEY

See: **ACCESS POINT**.

SEARCH LABEL

BRS USAGE: Four-letter code assigned to each BRS database. This search label must be entered by the user to gain access to the database. Generally, the four letters represent an abbreviation for the database's actual name, e.g., "DRUG" stands for the **DRUGINFO database**.

SEARCH LOG

Record of what searches have been conducted. Typically includes names of the **search analyst, requester, commercial search service** and **databases** used, amount of time spent **online**, topic of the search, and number of items retrieved, whether **displayed** online or **printed offline**. Generally kept manually, although using a **microcomputer** as a **terminal** can result in a type of computer-generated search log.

SEARCH LOGIC
see: **BOOLEAN LOGIC.**

SEARCH MODE
BRS USAGE: Operating **mode** in which terms can be entered by the user, searched by the system, and a resulting **set** produced.

SEARCH OPTIONS
Various ways a **search strategy** can be conducted or modified. For example, the **searchable fields** available and methods of **limiting searches** are considered search options.

SEARCH PROFILE
Search strategy which is in a form acceptable to both the **commercial search service** and the **database** on which it is to be executed. Sometimes used synonymously with **search request,** but actually a search request is translated into a completed search profile through the **presearch interview.**

SEARCH PROTOCOL
See: **SEARCH STRATEGY.**

SEARCH QUERY DEVELOPMENT
See: **SEARCH PROFILE** and **SEARCH STRATEGY.**

SEARCH REQUEST
Communication of the search topic to the **search analyst** who will perform the search. Normally done through a **presearch interview** and may involve the use of a **search request form.**

SEARCH REQUEST FORM
Printed form designed to facilitate the preparation of a **search strategy** by requiring the **requester** to describe the search topic and answer certain questions relevant to the type of search desired. Normally completed prior to the **presearch interview.**

SEARCH RESULTS
Items and information retrieved from an **online search.** Often used synonymously with **recall.** See also: **RETRIEVED RECORD.**

SEARCH SAVING
See: **SAVING SEARCHES.**

SEARCH SERVICE
Two common usages: 1) Synonymous term for **commercial search services,** the organizations which offer access to one or more databases by providing all necessary computer operations and support services; and 2) **Online search** operation which uses the databases available from the commercial search services. See: **COMMERCIAL SEARCH SERVICES.**

SEARCH SERVICE COORDINATOR
Person designated to be in charge of the local **search service.**

SEARCH STATEMENT

Search terms used to retrieve a **set** of items on a desired topic. While a search statement can consist of only one term, it typically includes various search items, **Boolean operators**, and **set numbers**. Each search statement is generally assigned a set number.

SEARCH STATEMENT NUMBER

See: **SET NUMBER.**

SEARCH STRATEGY

Set of prepared **search statements** which represent a plan for accessing a database and retrieving desired information. A completed search strategy is also known as a **search profile.**

SEARCH STRATEGY FORMULATION

See: **SEARCH PROFILE** and **SEARCH STRATEGY.**

SEARCH SYSTEM

Technically, the **computer program** used by a **commercial search service** to provide access to their **databases**. For example, SDC's search system is known as **ORBIT**, while BRS uses the **STAIRS** search system.

SEARCH TERMS

Words or phrases searched to retrieve relevant documents or items. May be only **key words**, e.g., subject-related words from the title or abstract, or **index terms**, e.g., assigned **identifiers** or **descriptors.**

SEARCH TIME

See: **CONNECT TIME.**

SEARCHABLE FIELDS

Any **field** that can be directly searched by the computer. synonymous with **access points.**

SEARCHER

See: **SEARCH ANALYST.**

..SEARCHOFF COMMAND

BRS USAGE: Command used in performing **offline searching.**

SEARCH*SAVE FEATURE

DIALOG USAGE: Techniques used in **saving searches.** Three types of SEARCH*SAVE options are available: standard (permanent until released), temporary (held for one day), and SDI (run automatically whenever the given database is **updated**). See: **SAVING SEARCHES** and **SELECTIVE DISSEMINATION OF INFORMATION.**

SECURITY CODE

SDC USAGE: Required security code of up to 10 characters which must initially be asigned by a user and then is used whenever access to the system is desired. Designed to prevent unauthorized charges to a user's account.

SECURITY PASSWORD
   BRS USAGE: Second **password** assigned by a user to guard against unauthorized use.

SEL COMMAND
   SDC USAGE: See **SELECT COMMAND**.

SELECT COMMAND
   DIALOG USAGE: Basic **command** used to gather **index terms** or groups of terms in numbered sets. When **Boolean operators** are used in combining various terms into one **search statement**, this use of the SELECT command is known as SUPERSELECT. A variation of the SUPERSELECT command is the SELECT STEPS command, which causes separate **set numbers** to be assigned to each step in the search. SELECT is commonly abbreviated "S," and SELECT STEPS can be entered as either "S STEPS" or "SS." See also: **COMBINE COMMAND. SDC USAGE:** Used to retrieve items by set number from the list produced by **NEIGHBOR** and **PRINT SELECT commands**.

SELECT STEPS COMMAND
   DIALOG USAGE: See **SELECT COMMAND**.

SELECTIVE DISSEMINATION OF INFORMATION
   Regular use of **current awareness searches** to provide **end users** or requesters with the most current references to items of potential interest. A **search strategy** originally developed and used to perform an initial **retrospective search** is typically stored and automatically executed by a **commercial search service** each time a specific file is **updated**. Often used synonymously with current awareness. The commercial search service may charge a minimal fee for storing the original search strategy. Normally abbreviated SDI.

SEND
   See: **ENTER**.

SENSEARCH COMMAND
   SDC USAGE: Technique similar to the **STRINGSEARCH command** which searches any sentence for a specified **string** of characters or words. See: **STRINGSEARCH**.

SEQUENTIAL FILE
   See: **LINEAR FILE**.

SERLINE (Database)
   Catalog database which includes all serials currently being received or on order by the National Library of Medicine. SERLINE stands for Serials Online. Available on MEDLARS (SERLINE file).

SERVICE VENDOR
   See: **COMMERCIAL SEARCH SERVICE**.

SET
   Collection of items retrieved as the result of an **online search**. The number typically assigned to each set is known as the **set number**.

SET DETAIL COMMAND
BRS USAGE: Command used to have individual **set numbers** assigned for each term searched.

SET 99
DIALOG USAGE: See **KEEP COMMAND.**

SET NUMBER
Numerical label assigned to each **search statement** in an **online search**. Also known as a search statement number.

SET NUMBER SYNTAX ERROR MESSAGE
DIALOG USAGE: Indicates that an incorrect **set number** has been used in a **search statement.**

SIGNAL LIGHT
See: **CARRIER LIGHT.**

SIGNOFF
See: **LOGOFF.**

SIGNON
See: **LOGON.**

SINGLE CHARACTER TRUNCATION
Truncation which allows only one additional character. Depending on the **commercial search service,** single character truncation can be used with **internal, left,** and **right truncation.** See: **TRUNCATION.**

SMART TERMINAL
Terminal which contains a **microprocessor** and can be used not only to transmit and receive data, but also to process and manipulate it. Contrast with: **DUMB TERMINAL.** See also: **PERSONAL COMPUTER** and **TERMINAL.**

SMIE (Database)
BRS USAGE: See **SSIE CURRENT RESEARCH (Database).**

SOCIAL SCISEARCH (Database)
Bibliographic database which corresponds to the printed *Social Science Citation Index.* Available on DIALOG (File 7).

SOCIETY OF AUTOMOTIVE ENGINEERS (Database)
Bibliographic database which covers technical papers dealing with automotive and other self-propelled vehicles. Available on SDC (SAE file).

SOCIOLOGICAL ABSTRACTS (Database)
Bibliographic database which covers the literature of sociology and related social and behavioral areas. Available on DIALOG (File 37).

SOFTWARE

All **programs** needed to cause a **computer** to perform certain operations. Contrast with: **HARDWARE**. See also: **PROGRAMS**.

SORT

To arrange output into a chosen sequence for either **online** or **offline printing**. For example, a set of retrieved items can be sorted in order by geographical areas, amount of sales, or product classifications. Not all databases can be sorted. In some cases, it is also possible to sort results and arrange them alphabetically by author or journal name.

SORT (PRINT OPTION)

SDC USAGE: Print option which allows **offline printouts** to be arranged alphabetically, e.g., by author or journal, or sequentially, e.g., by publication date. See: **SORT**.

.SORT COMMAND

DIALOG USAGE: Command used to **sort** or arrange retrieved items into a specified order for **online display**. See: **SORT**.

SOURCE, THE

Information and entertainment service available to owners of **microcomputers**.

SOURCE DATABASE

Synonymous with **nonbibliographic database**. See: **NONBIBLIOGRAPHIC DATABASE**.

SOURCE DOCUMENTS

Primary or original documents. From these documents information is extracted or indexed and put into **machine readable** form to allow it to be retrieved through **online searching**. See: **DOCUMENT** and **RECORD**.

SPECIAL LIBRARY ASSOCIATION

International organization of special librarians and information managers. Publishes *Special Libraries*.

SPECIFIED CHARACTER TRUNCATION

Truncation which specifies the maximum number of additional characters which can be retrieved. Depending on the **commercial search service**, specified letter truncation can be used as **internal, left,** and **right truncation**. See also: **SINGLE CHARACTER TRUNCATION** and **TRUNCATION**.

SPEED OF TRANSMISSION

See: **TRANSMISSION SPEED**.

SPIF (Database)

BRS USAGE: See **SCHOOL PRACTICES INFORMATION FILE (Database)**.

SPIN (Database)

Bibliographic database which indexes and abstracts the contents of major physics journals. Available on DIALOG (File 62).

SPORT (Database)
Bibliographic database which provides coverage of most sports and related areas of recreation and physical education. Available on SDC (SPORT file).

SSCI (Database)
BRS USAGE: See **SOCIAL SCISEARCH (Database)**.

SSIE CURRENT RESEARCH (Database)
Directory database which contains reports and summaries of current scientific research projects. Produced by the Smithsonian Science Information Exchange (SSI). Available on BRS (SMIE file), DIALOG (File 65), and SDC (SSIE file).

STACKING COMMANDS
Entering of several. **commands** into a system in a single line of typing. Commands typically have to be separated by a piece of punctuation, e.g., on SDC and DIALOG stacked commands are separated by semicolons, but BRS uses a slash for the same purpose. Not all commands can be stacked.

STAIRS
Computer programs developed by IBM which were used as the basis for BRS's **software** system. STAIRS stands for Storage and Information Retrieval System.

STANDARD & POOR'S NEWS (Database)
Bibliographic database which provides both news and financial information about more than 9,000 publicly-owned American companies. Available on DIALOG (File 132).

STANDARDS & SPECIFICATIONS (Database)
Directory database which includes all government and industry standards and specifications issued for particular products or industries. Available on DIALOG (File 113).

STATE PUBLICATIONS INDEX (Database)
Bibliographic database covering current state documents issued by the 50 states, Puerto Rico, and the Virgin Islands. Available on BRS (IHSP file).

STATEMENT
See: **SEARCH STATEMENT**.

STATEMENT NUMBER
See: **SET NUMBER**.

STATIONARY TERMINAL
Terminal which is not intended to be moved from location to location. A relatively permanent site for the **terminal** is selected and the terminal is not generally used for **online demonstrations** away from that location. Contrast with: **PORTABLE TERMINAL**. See also: **TERMINAL**.

STDS (Database)
BRS USAGE: See **INDUSTRY AND INTERNATIONAL STANDARDS (Database)**.

STEM
See: **WORD STEM**.

STOP COMMAND
SDC USAGE: **Command** used to **logoff** and terminate an **online** search.

STOP LIST
See: **STOP WORDS**.

STOP WORDS
Trivial words, such as "the," "an," or "by," that are not normally included as searchable terms. Stop lists are provided by each **commercial search service**.

STORAD COMMAND
SDC USAGE: **Command** which allows a user to permanently store an address to which all **printouts** will automatically be mailed.

STORAGE
Generally considered synonymous with **memory. COMPUTER SCIENCE USAGE:** Any device or medium that can accept **data**, store it, and display it when requested. Distinction is occasionally made between internal storage, known as "memory," and external storage devices, referred to as "storage." See: **MEMORY**.

STORAGE OVERFLOW
Condition which occurs because a search or **search statement** exceeds the temporary allocated **storage** space. See also: **OVERFLOW CONDITIONS**.

STORE COMMAND
SDC USAGE: **Command** used in **saving searches** after the **search strategy** has been entered in a database. Saved strategy is retained until specifically **purged** by the user. Contrast with: **SAVE COMMAND, SAVING SEARCHES,** and **STOREsearch FEATURE**.

STOREsearch FEATURE
SDC USAGE: Techniques used in **saving searches**. This feature stores any saved searches until they are specifically **purged** by the user. Contrast with: **SAVEsearch FEATURE**. See also: **SAVE COMMAND, SAVING SEARCHES,** and **STORE COMMAND**.

STORING SEARCHES
See: **SAVING SEARCHES**.

STRING
Set of consecutive **characters** or words to be **STRING SEARCHED**. See: **STRING SEARCHING**.

STRING SEARCHING
Technique for retrieving a specific **string** of **characters**, even if it is totally embedded in a larger word. For example, string searching "qualif" might retrieve both "*prequalify*" and "qualif*ications*." **SDC USAGE:** Used in those databases which do not recognize **proximity operators** to specify both **adjacency** and **proximity**. The **STRINGSEARCH command** can

also be used to search fields not directly searchable, to search for **stop words**, and to search for the location of terms within a specific part of a **field**. See also: **STRINGSEARCH COMMAND**.

STRINGSEARCH COMMAND
SDC USAGE: **Command** used to perform a **STRING SEARCH**.

STUTTER
See: **PROCESING CUE**.

SUBFILE
Subdivision of a **database**. See also: **FILE SEGMENT**.

SUBHEADINGS COMMAND
SDC USAGE: **Command** used to indicate certain **fields** to be searched for all **search terms** subsequently input.

SUBJECT RELATED TERMS
See: **RELATED TERMS**.

SUBJECT TERMS
See: **CONTROLLED VOCABULARY** and **DESCRIPTORS**.

SUBS COMMAND
SDC USAGE: See **SUBHEADINGS COMMAND**.

SUFFIX CODES
DIALOG USAGE: Two-letter code used to identify the particular **fields** in the **basic index**. For example, "/DE" is used for the **descriptor** field. The two-letter code is known as a **field indicator**.

SUPERINDEX
Directory database which is composed of the index entries from almost 600 scientific, technical, and medical reference books. Can be used to identify specific page references for items cited in any of the books' indexes. Available on DIALOG (File 121).

SUPERSELECT COMMAND
DIALOG USAGE: See **SELECT COMMAND**.

SUPPLEMENTARY TERM FIELD
SDC USAGE: **Field** which contains additional **controlled vocabulary** words beyond the assigned **index terms** which further describe the item.

SURFACE COATING ABSTRACTS (Database)
Bibliographic database which covers the research literature related to paint and surface coatings. Available on DIALOG (File 115).

SWRA (Database)
SDC USAGE: See **WATER RESOURCES ABSTRACTS (Database)**.

SYMBOL, LOGIC
See: **LOGICAL OPERATORS.**

SYN COMMAND
SDC USAGE: See **SYNONYM COMMAND.**

SYNCHRONOUS TRANSMISSION
COMPUTER SCIENCE USAGE: **Data communications** term which refers to the transmission of **data** in a continuous flow with an equal amount of time between each **character.** Contrast with: **ASYNCHRONOUS TRANSMISSION.**

SYNONYM COMMAND
SDC USAGE: **Command** which permits a user to create synonymous names for **ORBIT** keywords, such as commands or **Boolean operators.** Either the original or newly created name can then be used. See also: **RENAME COMMAND.**

SYNTAX ERROR MESSAGE
BRS USAGE: Indicates that a **mistake** has been made in the use of **Boolean logic** or **free text operators.**

SYSTEM
COMPUTER SCIENCE USAGE: Combination of equipment, personnel, and procedures needed to accomplish a specific objective. **ONLINE SEARCHING USAGE:** Frequently used synonymously with **commercial search service,** as in, "I use the DIALOG system."

SYSTEM DEVELOPMENT CORPORATION
Major **commercial search service.** Commonly referred to as "SDC." Also known as **ORBIT.** Major SDC databases ("SDC file") and **system specific commands** ("SDC USAGE") are identified and described in this dictionary.

SYSTEM DOCUMENTATION
See: **DOCUMENTATION.**

SYSTEM FAILURE
See: **DOWN TIME.**

SYSTEM MESSAGE
Short message provided to the user to identify problems or difficulties encountered. System messages may originate either from the **commercial search services** or the **communications networks.** Commonly received system messages are identified and described in this dictionary.

SYSTEM RESPONSE
See: **RESPONSE.**

SYSTEM SPECIFIC
Commands or features that are directly related to a specific **commercial search service.** The techniques may be similar, but the actual commands vary. For example, each system has a command to retrieve a list of alphabetically related terms, but the commands are

different, e.g., **EXPAND** (DIALOG usage), **NEIGHBOR** (SDC usage), and **ROOT** (BRS usage).

T COMMAND
 DIALOG USAGE: See **TYPE COMMAND**.

T NUMBER
 BRS USAGE: Unique number assigned to each user organization by BRS. This number can be used to send and receive **electronic mail** through the message switching system available in BRS's **MSGS database**. A directory of T numbers is made available to BRS users.

TAG
 See: **FIELD TAG**.

TAILORED PRINT COMMAND
 SDC USAGE: Allows the user to specify exactly which **fields** are to be **printed**. See also: **PRINT FORMAT**.

TAPE, MAGNETIC
 See: **MAGNETIC TAPE**.

TELECOMMUNICATIONS
 See: **COMMUNICATIONS**.

TELECOMMUNICATIONS NETWORK
 See: **COMMUNICATIONS NETWORK**.

TELEGEN (Database)
 Bibliographic database which provides international coverage of the field of biotechnology. Available on SDC (TELEGEN file).

TELENET
 Major **communications network** used to access the major **commercial search services**.

TERM (Database)
 BRS USAGE: Integrated vocabulary aid being developed by BRS to aid in selecting and searching databases in the social sciences.

TERMINAL
 Device used to **transmit data** to and from a **computer**, generally through a **communications network**. There are basically two types: 1) **print terminal**, which functions much like an electric typewriter and produces a print record of all searches, and 2) **video terminal**, which uses a **cathode ray tube** to display results. Regardless of the type of terminal used, a **printer** is generally considered essential. A choice must typically be made between a **portable terminal** and a **stationary terminal**. Differences in **transmission speeds** are also an important consideration when selecting a terminal. A **dumb terminal** is generally used in **online searching**, but **microcomputers**, such as the increasingly popular **personal computers**, can be used as **smart terminals** to not only transmit and receive **data**, but also to further process and manipulate it.

TERMINAL IDENTIFIER
Alphanumeric code, usually one or two letters and/or numbers, which allows the **communication network** and the **host computer** to adjust their responses to meet the capabilities of the specific **terminal** being used. One of the initial responses required when **logging on** to any communications network is to identify what model of terminal is being used.

TERMINAL PRINTOUT
See: **PRINTOUT**.

TERMS
See: **SEARCH TERMS**.

TEXT EDITED
BRS USAGE: Refers to the removal of certain punctuation marks and special characters to facilitate searching. For example, on a text edited BRS database the word "on-line" would be searched without the hyphen. This feature is **database specific**, and not all BRS databases have been text edited.

TEXT EDITING
Reformatting a **print record**. Generally used to describe **word processing**. See: **WORD PROCESSING**.

TEXT SEARCHING
SDC USAGE: See **FULL TEXT SEARCHING**.

TFILE COMMAND
SDC USAGE: Allows a user to access a "temporary **file**" in the middle of another search without losing **search statements** in the original database. The TFILE command is typically used to search **dictionary databases**, e.g., **CHEMDEX** or **BIOCODES,** in order to retrieve codes or other synonyms to aid in the original search. The **RETURN command** is used to return to the initial file.

THERMAL PRINTER
Printer which imprints by using a heat process which forms a matrix of small dots on special heat-sensitive paper. Usually extremely quiet and lightweight. Contrast with: **IMPACT PRINTER**. May also be known as a dot matrix printer.

THESAURUS
List of standardized **index terms**, which are generally known as **descriptors**. Cross-references and brief definitions are typically given. Used to select appropriate **search terms** when using a **controlled vocabulary** approach. The thesaurus may be available **online**, on microform, or in printed form.

TIME COMMAND
SDC USAGE: Simply gives actual time in Pacific Time Zone. See also: **TIME INTERVAL COMMAND** and **TIME RESET COMMAND**.

..TIME COMMAND
BRS USAGE: Allows the user to ask for the elapsed time at any point during an **online** search.

TIME INTERVAL COMMAND
SDC USAGE: Presents the total elapsed time since **logon**. See also: **TIME COMMAND** and **TIME RESET COMMAND**.

TIME OVERFLOW
Condition which results when requested processes or functions take too much processing time. See: **OVERFLOW CONDITIONS** and **TIME-SLICING**.

TIME RESET COMMAND
SDC USAGE: Presents total elapsed time since **logon** and resets the time from zero. See also: **TIME COMMAND** and **TIME INTERVAL COMMAND**.

TIME SHARING
Simultaneous utilization of a **computer** by a number of users. **Online searching** is dependent upon time sharing computers.

TIME-SLICING
Computer processing technique which allows the system to interrupt any requested function that takes more than an established amount of time ("time-slice"). A message is sent to the user to explain that additional time will be required and to give the user the option of discontinuing the search. See also: **OVERFLOW CONDITIONS** and **TIME OVERFLOW**.

TITLE ENRICHMENT
Technique used in **citation indexing** in which a vague title, e.g., "Where Are We Going?," is assigned additional words to facilitate retrieval, e.g., "Where Are We Going (Summer Travel Planning)."

TOXIC SUBSTANCES CONTROL ACT (Database)
Dictionary database which lists chemicals in commercial use in the United States and provides molecular formula, registry number, and chemical name. Available on DIALOG (File 52, TSCA Initial Inventory and updates only) and SDC (TSCA file, TSCA Initial Inventory and updates, plus plant and production data).

TOXICOLOGY DATA BANK (Database)
Nonbibliographic database which summarizes and directly provides chemical, pharmacological, and toxicological data. Available on MEDLARS (TBD file).

TOXLINE (Database)
Bibliographic database which covers all aspects of toxicological information. TOXLINE stands for Toxicology Online. Available on MEDLARS (TOXLINE, TOXBACK74, and TOXBACK65 files).

TRADE OPPORTUNITIES (Database)
Directory database which provides information on export opportunities for American businesses as supplied by the Foreign Service to the United States Department of Commerce. Available on DIALOG (File 106, 1976—last quarter, and File 107, current weekly **updates**).

TRADE AND INDUSTRY INDEX (Database)
Bibliographic database which covers the business, industry, and trade literature as reported in major trade journals, newspapers, and other business publications. Available on DIALOG (File 148).

TRAINER
Online training program developed at the University of Pittsburgh. TRAINER is a computer-based tutorial system which introduces users to basic search commands and techniques. See also: **EMULATOR**.

TRAINING OF SEARCH ANALYSTS
Instruction of **search analysts** in the actual mechanics of **online searching**. Contrast with the **education** of all library staff members about the potential applications of online searching.

TRANSMISSION SPEED
Speed of transmitting **data**. Expressed as either characters-per-second or as **baud** rate. **Terminals** used for **online searching** usually communicate at 10, 15, 30, or 120 characters-per-second (cps). The 120 cps is known as **high speed,** while the slower speed terminals are referred to as **low speed.** Currently, most online searching is done at 30 cps, although 120 cps terminals are becoming more widely used. See: **HIGH SPEED, LOW SPEED,** and **TERMINAL**.

TRANSMIT
To send **data** from a **terminal** to the **computer,** or vice versa.

TRANSPORTATION RESEARCH INFORMATION SERVICE (Database)
Bibliographic database which covers all areas of transportation, including air, highway, rail, shipping, and mass transit. Available on DIALOG (File 63).

TREE
COMPUTER SEARCHING USAGE: Outline or representation of the hierarchy of a program. **ONLINE SEARCHING USAGE**: Hierarchical relationship between **controlled vocabulary** terms. **MEDLINE database** uses tree structures to identify relationships between subject terms. See also: **HIERARCHICAL VOCABULARY**.

TRIAL (PRINT OPTION)
SDC USAGE: See **PRINT TRIAL COMMAND**.

TRIS (Database)
See: **TRANSPORTATION RESEARCH INFORMATION SERVICE (Databasae)**.

TROPAG (Database)
Bibliographic database which offers international coverage of tropical and subtropical agriculture. Available on SDC (TROPAG file).

TRUNCATION
Technique used to retrieve all terms which include a specific **word stem**. This normally means retrieving all items beginning with this word stem or root (**"right truncation"**), but it is also possible to allow for various prefixes when searching (**"left truncation"**), to specify the number of additional characters to be retrieved (**"specific character truncation"**), and to retrieve characters embedded within a term (**"internal truncation"**).

TSCA (Database)
SDC USAGE: See **TOXIC SUBSTANCES CONTROL ACT (Database)**.

TSCA INITIAL INVENTORY (Database)
DIALOG USAGE: See **TOXIC SUBSTANCES CONTROL ACT (Database)**.

TULSA (Database)
Bibliographic database prepared by the University of Tulsa which provides international coverage of patents and literature related to oil and gas exploration, drilling, development, and production. Available on SDC (TULSA file).

TURNKEY SYSTEM
COMPUTER SCIENCE USAGE: System which is totally designed, **programmed**, and installed by an outside company and can be used with minimal preparation by the user. **ONLINE SEARCHING USAGE:** To a limited extent, **online searching** can be considered a turnkey system because the **commercial search services** have standardized and prepared their systems so they are relatively easy to use and so they require minimal user preparation, except for some **training of search analysts** and **terminal** selection.

TUTORIAL FEATURES
See: **HELP COMMAND**.

"TWITCH"
See: **PROCESSING CUE**.

TYMNET
Major **communications network** used to access the various **commercial search services**. Division of Tymshare Corporation.

TYPE COMMAND
DIALOG USAGE: Command used to display records **online** from previously established **sets**. See also: **PRINT FORMATS**.

ULRI (Database)
BRS USAGE: See **ULRICH'S INTERNATIONAL PERIODICAL DIRECTORY (Database)**.

ULTICH'S INTERNATIONAL PERIODICAL DIRECTORY (Database)
Directory database which corresponds to the print publication by the same name, plus other related R. R. Bowker publications, e.g., *Ulrich's Quarterly*. Available on BRS (ULRI file) and DIALOG (File 480).

UNAUTHORIZED FILE
File is not valid for user's **password**. Certain files have restricted **access**. For example, in DIALOG certain databases are not searchable as part of the **Classroom Instruction Program**. If a student attempts to enter the **CHEMICAL INDUSTRY NOTES database**, he will be told the file is "unauthorized."

UNAUTHORIZED FILE MESSAGE
DIALOG USAGE: Indicates that the use of the requested database has been restricted by the **database producer**. The most common restriction is geogaphical, e.g., some databases cannot be accessed by certain foreign users.

UNAVAILABLE FILE MESSAGE

DIALOG USAGE: Indicates that the requested file is either nonexistent or not yet available for searching.

UNCONTROLLED VOCABULARY

No assigned **descriptors** or **index terms**. A database with an uncontrolled vocabulary is known as a **natural language database** and can be searched only by using **free text searching** techniques. See: **FREE TEXT SEARCHING**.

UNINET

Major **communications network** used to access the major **commercial search services**.

UNIT RECORD

See: **RECORD**.

UNITED STATES POLITICAL SCIENCE DOCUMENTS (Database)

Bibliographic database which indexes and abstracts, from a broad range of scholarly journals, articles dealing with all aspects of political science. Commonly abbreviated USPSD. Available on DIALOG (File 93).

UNIVERSAL SERIALS AND BOOK EXCHANGE BIBLIOGRAPHY (Database)

Directory database which contains citations to over ten thousand serial titles always available at the Universal Serials and Book Exchange, a nonprofit organization which facilitates the exchange of publications among member institutions. Available on BRS (USBE file).

UPDATE

Most recent addition to a database. Databases are typically updated on a regular basis as part of normal **file maintenance**. Searches can often be restricted to items included only in the latest update. This can serve as a means of conducting a **current awareness search**.

UPDATES COMMAND

SDC USAGE: Provides the current coverage dates and **update** information for all **ORBIT** databases.

U.S. EXPORTS (Database)

Numeric database which provides detailed export statistics for all commodities exports from the United States to foreign countries. Available on DIALOG (File 126).

U.S. GOVERNMENT CONTRACT AWARDS (Database)

Directory database which lists current contracts awarded to both private and public companies or agencies by the federal government. Available on SDC (USGCA file).

U.S. PATENTS OFFICE (Database)

Nonbibliographic database which covers all United States patents, continuations, divisionals, and defensive documents awarded since 1971. Available on SDC (USPA, USP77, USP70 files).

U.S. PUBLIC SCHOOL DIRECTORY (Database)

Directory database which provides information, including address and size, for all American public schools. Available on DIALOG (File 120).

..USAGE COMMAND
BRS USAGE: Allows the user to check the level of activity on the system. System will indicate one of three levels: High, Above Normal, or Normal.

USBE (Database)
BRS USAGE: See **UNIVERSAL SERIALS AND BOOK EXCHANGE (Database)**.

USCLASS (Database)
Dictionary database which lists all United States Classifications, Cross-Reference Classifications, and Unofficial Classifications for all patents ever issued in the United States. Available on SDC (USCLASS file).

USER
See: **END USER** and **REQUESTER**.

USER-COMPUTER INTERFACE
See: **INTERFACE**.

USER FEES
Charges assessed by local **search services** to pay for the costs of performing a specific **online search**. If user fees are charged, they are typically composed of **direct costs** and possibly some of the **indirect costs** involved in conducting the search. See also: **DIRECT COSTS** and **INDIRECT COSTS**.

USER FRIENDLY
System which minimizes the problems and fears involved in the **interface** between inexperienced or untrained users and computer systems.

USER IDENTIFICATION
See: **USER NUMBER**.

USER INTERFACE
See: **INTERFACE**.

USER MANUALS
Principal **search aids** prepared by the **commercial search services** and **database producers** to instruct users and to provide detailed descriptions of **search strategies** relevant to a particular system or database. The user manuals provided by the commercial search services are essential to efficient searching of the databases available. These manuals are frequently loose-leaf so they can be regularly updated and are available in both detailed and summarized versions.

USER NUMBER
Unique number assigned to each user of a system. Does not function as a **password**, but identifies a user for billing and other administrative purposes. Also known as customer number. See: **PASSWORD**.

USER PROFILE
See: PROFILE.

USERS GROUPS
Local groups of **online search analysts** who arrange meetings, sponsor presentations on specific databases or subjects, and exchange information concerning all aspects of searching.

USGCA (Database)
SDC USAGE: See **U.S. GOVERNMENT CONTRACT AWARDS (Database)**.

USPA (Database)
SDC USAGE: See **U.S. PATENT OFFICE (Database)**.

USPSD (Database)
See: **UNITED STATES POLITICAL SCIENCE DOCUMENTS (Database)**.

VARIABLE CHARACTER TRUNCATION
See: INTERNAL TRUNCATION.

VARIABLE FIELD
Field whose length can vary depending on the amount of **data** that needs to be included. For example, the title field typically is a variable field to allow for titles of different lengths. See also: **FIXED FIELD**.

VDT
See: **VIDEO DISPLAY TERMINAL**.

VDU
See: **VIDEO DISPLAY UNIT**.

VENDORS
Synonymous term for **commercial search services**. Since the major commercial search services are private companies, they have commonly been referred to as vendors or database vendors. See: **COMMERCIAL SEARCH SERVICE**.

VENN DIAGRAM
Graphic presentation, generally interconnected circles, used to demonstrate the relationship between **sets**. Generally used to explain **Boolean logic**.

VERSION COMMAND
SDC USAGE: Allows French-speaking users to request "VERSION FRENCH" to get all **ORBIT** messages in French.

VETDOC (Database)
Bibliographic database which provides international coverage of drug applications in veterinary medicine, especially designed for veterinary pharmaceutical manufacturers. Available on SDC (VETDOC file).

VIDEO DISPLAY TERMINAL
See: **VIDEO TERMINAL**.

VIDEO DISPLAY UNIT

Device which presents a visual representation of an **online search**. This generally involves the use of a **cathode ray tube**. Abbreviated VDU and also known as visual display unit. **Terminals** using such a video display unit are called **video terminals**. See also: **VIDEO TERMINAL**.

VIDEO TERMINAL

Terminal which displays the search on a **cathode ray tube**. For **online searching**, a **printer** is usually attached to the video terminal to produce a print record of the search. Contrast with: **PRINT TERMINAL**. Also known as a CRT terminal or as either a video display terminal or a visual display terminal, both abbreviated VDT.

VISUAL DISPLAY TERMINAL

See: **VIDEO TERMINAL**.

VOCABULARY

See: **SEARCH TERMS** and **CONTROLLED VOCABULARY**.

VOCABULARY AIDS

See: **THESAURUS**.

VOTES (Database)

Nonbibliographic database which records all roll-call votes by members of the United States Congress. Available on SDC (VOTES file).

W OPERATOR

DIALOG USAGE: See **FULL TEXT OPERATORS**. **SDC USAGE**: See **PROXIMITY OPERATORS**.

W/F OPERATOR

SDC USAGE: See **PROXIMITY OPERATORS**.

W/R OPERATOR

SDC USAGE: See **PROXIMITY OPERATORS**.

W/S OPERATOR

SDC USAGE: See **PROXIMITY OPERATORS**.

WARM RESTART

See: **RECONNECT**.

WATER RESOURCES ABSTRACTS (Database)

Bibliographic database which covers all areas of water research, including water planning, hydrology, and water quality. Available on DIALOG (File 117).

WATERLIT (Database)

Bibliographic database produced by the South African Water Information Centre, which covers international aspects of water resources. Available on SDC (WATERLIT file).

WEIGHTED INDEX TERM
See: **INDEX TERM**.

WELDASEARCH (Database)
Bibliographic database which provides international coverage of the processes involved in joining metals and plastics. Available on DIALOG (File 99).

WESTLAW (Database)
Major legal **full text** database which offers searching of legal texts and decisions. Produced and made available by West Publishing Company.

WITH OPERATOR
BRS USAGE: See **FREE TEXT OPERATORS**.

WORD
Set of **characters**, generally considered as a whole, which is often identified by the computer by the spaces and, in some cases, punctuation marks which precede and follow it. For example, on DIALOG "on-line" is considered two words ("on" and "line"). A word may or may not have an actual literal meaning. For example, the computer would consider "XYZ" a "word."

WORD FREQUENCY LIST
List which indicates the **postings** for the terms contained in a specific database. See: **POSTINGS**.

WORD PROCESSING
Use of a computer to manipulate or **text edit** a document.

WORD PROXIMITY SEARCHING
See: **PROXIMITY**.

WORD SEQUENCE SEARCHING
See: **ADJACENCY**.

WORD STEM
Initial portion of a word that, through the use of **truncation**, can be used to retrieve other words beginning with that stem or root. For example, "librar" is the stem for all words beginning with those same six letters, e.g., library, librarians, or librarianship. See also: **TRUNCATION**.

WORD-BY-WORD FILING
Alphabetical filing procedure in which words are arranged word by word. **Words** are typically defined by spaces or punctuation. For example, in word-by-word filing, the following words would be filed in this order: New Data, New Technology, Newberry, and Newsweek. See: **LETTER-BY-LETTER FILING**. See also: **WORD**.

WORLD AFFAIRS REPORT (Database)
Bibliographic database which abstracts worldwide news items as reported from Soviet sources. Available on DIALOG (File 167).

WORLD ALUMINUM ABSTRACTS (Database)

Bibliographic database which covers the technical literature on all aspects of aluminum. Available on DIALOG (File 33).

WORLD PATENTS INDEX (Database)

Nonbibliographic database which lists information pertaining to patent specifications issued by patent offices located in 24 major industrial countries. Available on SDC (WPI/WPIL file).

WORLD TEXTILES (Database)

Bibliographic database which provides international coverage of the scientific and technological literature on textiles and the textile industry. Available on DIALOG (File 67).

WPI/WPIL (Database)

SDC USAGE: See **WORLD PATENTS INDEX (Database).**

X OPERATOR

DIALOG USAGE: See **FULL TEXT OPERATOR.**

XOR OPERATOR

Boolean operator which requires either one or the other term to be in the **record,** but not both. See also: **BOOLEAN OPERATOR.**

Bibliography

Journal Articles

Part I
GENERAL OVERVIEW OF ONLINE SEARCHING

ACADEMIC LIBRARIES AND ONLINE SEARCHING

Large academic libraries typically offer a wide range of online search services. Traditionally, these have involved providing annotated bibliographies on specialized topics, but more and more academic libraries are using online searching as an aid in answering reference questions. Differences between large and small libraries and undergraduate and graduate students' use of online searching are discussed in the articles annotated in this section.

Related sections in this bibliography include:

Impact of Online Searching (Entries 208-221)
Reference Uses of Online Searching (Entries 279-285)
Setting Up and Managing an Online Search Service (Entries 345-367)

1. Akeroyd, J. and J. Foster. **"Online Information Services in U.K. Academic Libraries."** *Online Review* 3 (June 1979): 195-204.
    Summarizes the results of a survey of all university and polytechnic libraries in the United Kingdom, conducted in April 1978 to determine the extent to which online search services were available. The use of online information retrieval is "relatively widespread," and 70% of the respondents indicated that they were online users. Benefits cited include cost-effectiveness and increased retrieval. The issue of user fees was also discussed.

2. Hitchingham, Eileen. **"Medline Use in a University without a School of Medicine."** *Special Libraries* 67 (April 1976): 188-99.
    Analyzes the potential use of MEDLINE in a university which does not have a school of medicine. Graduate students in biology, engineering, physics, education, and psychology were given an opportunity to have searches conducted on MEDLINE. Evaluation forms were completed and analyzed. Students were generally satisfied with the results and indicated they would pay for MEDLINE searches in the future. Searches had a minimal effect on interlibrary loan.

3. Holl, Deborah H. **"Cooperative Online Services for Small Academic Libraries."** *Catholic Library World* 5 (April 1980): 392-94.
    Presents the history and development of the Tri-State College Library Cooperative (TCLC) Library Search Center involving 28 smaller college libraries in Pennsylvania, New Jersey, and Delaware. Preliminary preparations and financial considerations are detailed.

The need for good record keeping and evaluation is stressed. After one year of service, the Search Center was authorized to expand service in 1980.

4. Kidd, J. S. **"On-Line Bibliographic Services: Selected British Experiences."** *College and Research Libraries* 38 (July 1977): 285-90.

Describes the introduction of online searching at six British colleges and universities. All institutions specialized in engineering, and differences in operational procedures are noted. Users were very receptive to the service. The importance of the location and publicity of the search center is stressed. Concludes that online searching "while eminently attractive is not likely to be an unalloyed blessing."

5. Kobelski, Pamela and Jean Trumbore. **"Student Use of Online Bibliographic Services."** *Journal of Academic Librarianship* 4 (March 1978): 14-18.

Describes student use of online services at discounted rates. Searches for students at the University of Delaware were partially subsidized by the library for the academic year 1976-1977. Evaluations were conducted, and satisfied and dissatisfied requesters were compared. Emphasizes the effects student searching has on reference services in general.

6. Lamb, Connie. **"Searching in Academia—Nearly 50 Libraries Tell What They're Doing."** *Online* 5 (April 1981): 78-81.

Summarizes the responses to a questionnaire distributed to 47 academic libraries in 1980 to determine the extent of online searching. Primarily descriptive comments were solicited in the following areas: 1) names and titles; 2) number of searches and search analysts; 3) finances; 4) patrons served; 5) systems accessed; 6) equipment; 7) organization; 8) procedures; and 9) promotion. Comments are generally reported and discussed. Responses to the questionnaire indicated online searching is very important in academic libraries, but the variations in answers to specific questions indicate the lack of overall standardization.

7. Lee, Joann H. and Arthur H. Miller, Jr. **"Introducing Online Data Base Searching in the Small Academic Library: A Model for Service without Charge to Undergraduates."** *Journal of Academic Librarianship* 7 (March 1981): 14-22.

Recounts the experiences of Lake Forest College in introducing online services over a two-year period in 1977 and 1978. Objectives of the program, initially funded by a research grant, are detailed and the following aspects described: 1) planning and implementation; 2) equipment selection; 3) selecting commercial search services; 4) personnel; 5) education of the staff; 6) paperwork; and 7) search fees. The experiment was successful and a need for an expansion of the service was evident.

8. McKee, Anna Marie and Cyril C. H. Feng. **"Using Computerized Literature Searches to Produce Faculty Publications Lists."** *Bulletin of the Medical Library Association* 67 (July 1979): 333-35.

Considers the practicality of using online searches of MEDLINE and SCISEARCH to produce and update faculty publications lists. SCISEARCH is judged to be clearly superior to MEDLINE for this purpose, and the advantages of SCISEARCH are enumerated. However, use of online searching greatly increased the quantity of items included in the annual faculty publications lists.

9. Maina, William E. **"Undergraduate Use of Online Bibliographic Retrieval Services: Experiences at the University of California, San Diego."** *Online* 1 (April 1977): 45-50.

Recounts the introduction of online searches, specifically to undergraduate students, at the University of California, San Diego, in early 1976. Searches were provided free, and the search requests were found to be "surprisingly sophisticated." Posters, word of mouth, and classroom discussions were found to be much more efficient publicity than notices to professors. Most students were satisfied with the results of their search, but only a small minority indicated they would pay for such searches.

10.   Matzek, Dick and Scott Smith. **"Online Searching in the Small College Library — The Economics and the Results."** *Online* 6 (March 1982): 21-29.
Argues that online searching is not a luxury even in a small college library, but must be considered simply a "logical, cost-effective extension of traditional reference service." Describes the introduction of online searching at Nazareth College of Rochester in 1980 and its continuation and evaluation in 1981. Policies and cost figures are presented and evaluation techniques described. Benefits of providing online searching are enumerated. Concludes that there really is "no need to have overwhelming concern about online search costs."

11.   Sandy, Gerald C. and James D. Evans. **"On-Line Information Systems in Non-Research Academic Libraries: A Missed Opportunity?"** *Educational Technology* 21 (January 1981): 38-40.
Reports the results of a survey sent to the directors of 53 college libraries in Alabama, Florida, Georgia, and South Carolina to determine the availability of online search services for faculty and students at smaller academic institutions. Responses indicate that online services are not readily available and are not generally being considered for implementation. Directors are typically unaware of the uses of such services and have only infrequently been exposed to online searching. Acknowledges possible geographic limitations of results.

COMMERCIAL SEARCH SERVICES

Three major commercial search services (BRS, DIALOG, and SDC) are readily available and are extensively covered in this bibliography. Descriptions of individual services and comparisons and evaluations of the major services are included here. Differences in search techniques and databases available, as well as cost comparisons, must be taken into account when selecting a commercial search service.
Related sections in this bibliography include:

Databases and Database Producers (Entries 49-67)
Design and Theory of Online Searching (Entries 68-87)

12.   Bement, James. **"The New Prices — Some Comparisons."** *Online* 1 (April 1977): 9-22.
Attempts to compare actual search costs for conducting searches on DIALOG, SDC, and BRS in February 1977. Searches were run on both ABI/INFORM and ERIC and their costs compared. Actual search strategies are presented. Pricing schedules and performance evaluations are given in tables. Notes the benefits of monthly minimum contracts with DIALOG and recommends BRS as a potential third search service for heavy online users. Urges that more comparisons of commercial search services be conducted.

13. **"BRS Picture Story."** *Online* 3 (April 1979): 58-61.

Describes BRS generally and notes its "revolutionary new pricing schedule." Various staff members are identified and individually pictured.

14. Cuadra, Carlos A. **"SDC Experiences with Large Databases."** *Journal of Chemical Information and Computer Sciences* 15 (February 1975): 48-51.

Describes the growth of online search services, with particular emphasis given to the development of SDC. Technical considerations, such as computer storage and structuring of the database, are presented. Stresses the importance of making information specialists and researchers aware of these services. Only if a sizable number of people make use of the services will the large costs of developing the systems and adding new databases be feasible.

15. Conger, Lucinda D. **"Multiple System Searching: A Searcher's Guide to Making Use of Real Differences between Systems."** *Online* 4 (April 1980): 10-21.

Provides a detailed examination of the similarities and differences between nine major online systems. Systems are compared in terms of their size, accessibility, search procedures, access points, online dictionaries, field specifications, adjacency and truncation features, logic, and display formats. No overall conclusions are drawn, but a list of "Do's and Don'ts" summarizes points to be considered in comparing commercial search services.

16. Folke, Carolyn. **"Optimizing Search Costs: A Comparative Study of Three Systems to Find the Best One ... or Two ... or Three.... "** *Online* 5 (April 1981): 38-43.

Considers the cost-effectiveness of using a subsidized state-supported service, a single commercial search service, two or more commercial search services, or some combination of these. Results of a small study undertaken by the Wisconsin Dissemination Project in June 1980 are summarized. Search parameters and cost factors were evaluated and advantages of each option noted. Actual costs are compared and the importance of certain search techniques emphasized. Study resulted in continuation of using three different search services.

17. Hoover, Ryan E. **"A Comparison of Three Commercial Online Vendors."** *Online* 3 (January 1979): 12-21.

Attempts to impartially and accurately compare three major commercial search services (BRS, DIALOG, and SDC) by conducting identical searches on four different databases (CA CONDENSATES, ERIC, MANAGEMENT CONTENTS, and POLLUTION ABSTRACTS). Results are reproduced and compared in various tables. No overall qualitative judgment was made, but numerous "subjective opinions" are discussed.

18. Krichmar, Albert. **"Command Language Ease of Use: A Comparison of DIALOG and ORBIT."** *Online Review* 5 (June 1981): 227-40.

Investigates the ease of use of the command languages employed by DIALOG and SDC in 1979. Responses to questionnaires sent to 171 online searchers in Southern California are analyzed. Perceived ease of use of the command language is a significant factor in the selection of a commercial search service. Specific search features are compared, but most respondents preferred DIALOG. The actual questionnaire and responses are appended.

19. Langlois, M. C. **"On-Line Information Systems. Comparison of COMPENDEX, INSPEC and NTIS Search Files via LMS/DIALOG, SDC/ORBIT and SDS/RECON."** *Online Review* 1 (September 1977): 231-37.

Compares three databases (COMPENDEX, NTIS, and INSPEC) as they were searched in 1976 on three search services (DIALOG, SDC, and RECON). Procedures and problems encountered in searching by title, controlled index terms, free index terms, and standardized codes are presented for each. Most detailed analysis involves the COMPENDEX database.

20. Marshall, Doris B. **"User Criteria for Selection of Commercial On-Line Computer-Based Bibliographic Services."** *Special Libraries* 66 (November 1975): 501-508.

Considers the various factors which must be evaluated when choosing which commercial search service to use. Stresses that the needs of the user, hardware selection, data transmission, the search services themselves, databases available, search features, and evaluation techniques must be investigated prior to making any final decisions. A "Quick Checklist" of items to consider is included.

21. **"Online Goes West."** *Online* 2 (January 1978): 60-61.

Presents a pictorial view of various online facilities located on the West Coast. Pictures are included from SDC, Info-Mart, and Information Unlimited. No descriptions are provided.

22. **"Online Visits BRS Headquarters Open House."** *Online* 6 (January 1982): 77-79.

Presents a pictorial tour of the new headquarters of BRS. Visitors at an open house held in November 1981 are pictured, as are various BRS staff members.

23. **"Online Visits Lockheed."** *Online* 2 (October 1978): 61-64.

Presents pictures of major staff and administrators at DIALOG. Pictures and job titles are given, but no additional information is provided.

24. Pickup, J. A. **"Commercially Funded Services – An Appraisal from the Viewpoint of the Smaller User."** *Aslib Proceedings* 30 (January 1978): 25-33.

Notes the potential market for online services to small or specialized users. Concludes that this market is "relatively untapped" and suggests ways commercial search services can successfully attract these small users. Commercial search services are urged to be flexible in dealing with user needs and a "partnership" between users and suppliers should be established. Finally, users must develop awareness of the online services available within their own institutions.

25. Pope, Nolan F. **"Database Users: Their Opinions and Needs."** *Special Libraries* 71 (May 1980): 265-69.

Reports the results of a survey conducted by the Information Technology Division of the Special Library Association to determine the opinions of searchers concerning current system capabilities and to solicit their suggestions for improvement. Responses indicate the searchers strongly believe systems should be easy to use, inexpensive, well indexed, and straightforward. Major suggestion was for standardized search commands among the various search services. The actual questionnaire is included in an appendix.

26. Rettig, James. **"A Comparative Review of BRS, DIALOG and ORBIT."** *Reference Services Review* 9 (January-March 1981): 39-51.

Compares the three major commercial search services (DIALOG, BRS, and SDC) in four general areas: 1) databases available; 2) price structure; 3) ease of use; and 4) special features and support services. BRS has the lowest rates and the basic databases needed by an academic library. SDC is more costly, but has several unique databases. DIALOG has the most files, including many exclusives, and is comparably priced. Judges DIALOG to be the system of first choice. Notes that these comparisons may be "obsolete within six months."

27. Rouse, Sandra H. and Lawrence W. Lannom. **"Some Differences between Three On-Line Systems: Impact on Search Results."** *Online Review* 1 (June 1977): 117-32.

Compares the three major commercial search services and attempts to develop some objective criteria to be used in choosing which service to use. Specific system differences in data fields, overall file structure, and search features are presented. Identical searches were performed on CA CONDENSATES, ERIC, ABI/INFORM, and NTIS on the three services and the results compared. Differences in items retrieved were noted and explained. Important search features, such as truncation and word proximity, which must be considered when selecting a service to use, are identified.

28. **"SDC Picture Story."** *Online* 2 (July 1978): 68-71.

Presents a pictorial look at the staff of SDC. Persons pictured range from programmer specialists to members of the billing department.

29. Summit, Roger K. **"Lockheed Experience in Processing Large Databases for Information Retrieval Service."** *Journal of Chemical Information and Computer Sciences* 15 (February 1975): 40-42.

Summarizes the role of Lockheed Information Service as a major commercial search service. Brief historical background is provided and the general file organization is described. Notes the direct relationships between search services, database producers, and the end users. Fear of increased government competition is expressed.

30. Weiss, Irvin. **"Evaluation of ORBIT and DIALOG Using Six Data Bases."** *Special Libraries* 67 (December 1976): 574-81.

Compares six databases that were available on both SDC and DIALOG in 1976. The databases are: CHEMCON, ERIC, CAIN, ABI/INFORM, NTIS, and COMPENDEX. Tables provide the following information for each database: hours accessible, dates of coverage, updates, size, and cost. Differences in online commands between SDC and DIALOG are also presented. Advantages and disadvantages of the two commercial search services are briefly summarized.

31. Weiss, Susan. **"Online Bibliographic Services. A Comparison."** *Special Libraries* 72 (October 1981): 379-89.

Compares four major online search services: SDC, DIALOG, BRS, and DROLS (produced by the Defense Technical Information Center). Charts are used for a comparison of online commands, cost, and available databases. Individual tables are given which summarize basic commands for each system, and one table compares cost and database availability. Basic evaluative comparisons are made, but no major conclusions are drawn.

32. Williams, Martha E. **"Criteria for Evaluation and Selection of Data Bases and Data Base Services."** *Special Libraries* 66 (December 1975): 561-69.

Presents criteria to be used to evaluate both databases available and the various services which make them accessible. Factors considered include search features, logical capabilities, document delivery, output formats, and cost. Notes that organizations which use such databases should also periodically evaluate their own needs and services.

CONFERENCE PROCEEDINGS AND MEETINGS

The proceedings of conferences, workshops, and annual conventions that relate to online searching are often reported in the major online journals.

33. **"ASDIC."** *Online* 2 (January 1978): 71.
Reports on the annual meetings of ASDIC (Association of Information and Dissemination Centers) held in San Francisco in October 1977. The purpose of the association and views expressed by various speakers at the conference are summarized.

34. **"Conference Report. Second International Online Information Meeting."** *Online Review* 3 (March 1979): 27-33.
Summarizes the presentations and activities at the Second International Online Information Meeting held in London in December 1978. Major sessions are reviewed and the exhibits and product review seminars briefly discussed. (See also #45.)

35. **"First International On-Line Information Meeting. Abstracts of Papers."** *Online Review* 1 (December 1977): 271-77.
Lists abstracts of the papers to be presented at the First International Online Information Meeting. (See also #48.)

36. **"The Fourth International Online Information Meeting."** *Online Review* 4 (September 1980): 325-30.
Lists the provisional conference program for the Fourth International Online Information Meeting to be held in London in December 1980. Topics and speakers are identified, but no additional information is provided. Exhibitors are also listed. (See also #41.)

37. Hawkins, Donald T. **"ASIS."** *Online* 2 (January 1978): 72-73.
Reports on the Fortieth ASIS annual meeting held in Chicago in September 1977. Technical sessions, panel discussions, and special interest group meetings are briefly noted. Describes the National Online Users Forum and a tutorial on "Telecommunications and Terminals for Online System Use."

38. **"IIA Picture Story."** *Online* 2 (July 1978): 72-73.
Provides a pictorial overview of various programs and activities at the second annual National Information Conference and Exposition. The conference was sponsored by the Information Industry Association and held in April 1978.

39. **"ONLINE '81 Picture Story."** *Online* 6 (January 1982): 66.
Includes three pictures of activities and exhibits at ONLINE '81 held in Dallas. Topics featured are briefly noted. Over 800 people attended the conference.

40. **"ONLINE '79 Picture Story."** *Online* 4 (January 1980): 44-47.
Presents a pictorial overview of the ONLINE '79 conference held in Atlanta in November 1979. The conference was heavily attended, with about 1,500 people. Pictures of speakers, preconferences, poster sessions, and exhibits are included.

41. Oppenheim, Charles. **"Fourth International Online Information Meeting."** *Online Review* 5 (February 1981): 55-60.

Reports on the Fourth International Online Conference. The exhibits, speeches and presentations, products reviews, and social events are briefly summarized. Pictures of attendees and speakers are also included. (See also #36.)

42.   Pemberton, Jenny. **"ASLIB Picture Story."** *Database* 4 (December 1981): 44-48.
Provides a pictorial description of the fifty-fourth annual conference of Aslib, the British Association of Special Libraries. Exhibits and displays of Pergamon's Infoline, Blackwells, DIALOG, and OCLC Europe are illustrated in pictures.

43.   Rugge, Sue. **"IIA Report."** *Online* 2 (January 1978): 53-54.
Summarizes the ninth annual Information Industry Association meeting held October 5-7, 1977. Speakers and workshops at the three-day conference are briefly described.

44.   Sebestyen, Istvan. **"Fifth International Online Information Meeting."** *Online Review* 6 (February 1982): 47-52.
Provides a brief overview of presentations and activities at the Fifth International Online Information Meeting held in London in December 1980. Statistics related to attendees and papers presented are given. Notes the increased attention given to videotex systems.

45.   **"Second International Online Information Meeting. Abstracts of Papers."** *Online Review* 2 (December 1978): 329-36.
Lists abstracts of papers to be presented at the Second International Online Information Meeting. Affiliation of speakers and brief outlines included. (See also #34.)

46.   **"3rd International Online Information Meeting. Abstracts of Papers."** *Online Review* 3 (December 1979): 411-22.
Lists abstracts of papers to be presented at the Third International Online Information Meeting. Indicates speaker's affiliation and summarizes the general topic of each proposed presentation. (See also #47.)

47.   **"The Third International Online Meeting."** *Online Review* 4 (March 1980): 57-60.
Presents a pictorial overview of activities at the Third International Online Meeting held in London in December 1979. Responses to questionnaires completed by delegates are also reported. (See also #46.)

48.   White, Martin S. **"Conference Report. First International Online Information Meeting."** *Online Review* 2 (March 1978): 31-39.
Summarizes the activities and formal sessions of the First International Online Information Meeting held in London in December 1977. Programs and speakers are chronologically recounted. The exhibits, database updates, and group meetings are also noted. (See also #35.)

DATABASES AND DATABASE PRODUCERS

Hundreds of databases are prepared by individual database producers and made readily accessible through the major commercial search services. Selection of which database to search is often difficult. It is important to carefully compare and evaluate those databases which appear to cover the same topic or subject area. Articles which generally discuss database design are included in this section, but comparisons of databases available in a specific subject are generally included in the appropriate section of the "Specialized Subject Areas and Databases in Online Searching" portion of this bibliography.

Related sections in this bibliography include:

Commercial Search Services (Entries 12-32)
Search Aids (Entries 286-295)
Search Strategies (Entries 321-340)

49.   Antony, Arthur. **"The Database Index."** *Database* 2 (December 1979): 28-33.
Examines the DATABASE INDEX or DBI file developed in 1978 by SDC to serve as an online index to their databases. Characteristics of the system available in 1979 are detailed. Four sample topics are searched on DBI and the results analyzed. Limitations due to term ambiguity are noted. Concludes that DBI can be a valuable aid in helping searhers determine which databases to search. Certain weaknesses and negative situations are also discussed. "Database Specifications" are appended.

50.   Bourne, Charles. **"Frequency and Impact of Spelling Errors in Bibliographic Data Bases."** *Information Processing and Management* 13 (1977): 1-12.
Analyzes the extent and effect of spelling errors in bibliographic databases. Eleven different databases were investigated and the results presented in charts and graphs. The effect of these spelling errors was considered for the commercial search services, the database producers, and the end users. Concludes that for most databases, these errors will have minimal impact on search results. BIOSIS and SSCI are cited as examples of outstanding quality control.

51.   Christensen, John E. **"Non-Legal Databases: Selected Information Sources."** *Law Library Journal* 73 (February 1980): 880-81.
Presents a brief, unannotated bibliography of sources of information concerning nonlegal databases. Lists items under the following categories: 1) database vendors; 2) newsletters; 3) journals; 4) directories; 5) bibliographies and literature reviews; and 6) user groups.

52.   **"Databases Online."** See issues of *Online Review* beginning with volume 1, #2.
Provides a regularly updated list of databases available from the major commercial search services. Database name and producer, subject coverage, online suppliers, starting year online, and connect charges are listed for each database. Since 1979, the column has been in the first issue of the year.

53.   Dolan, Donna R. **"The BRS Cross Database."** *Database* 3 (December 1980): 50-55.
Examines the BRS/CROS database, which is a "postings only" file that indicates the number of references on certain searchable terms in all of the online BRS files. Primarily used as an aid in database selection, CROS can also help answer certain ready-reference questions, verify interlibrary loan requests, and aid in training new searchers. CROS is compared to SDC's DATABASE INDEX (DBI) file. Problems in using such files (e.g., false drops) are examined. "Database Specifications" are appended.

54.   Gordon, Helen A. *"Which Database? A Review."* *Database* 5 (June 1982): 48.
Reviews *Which Database?*, a guide to bibliographic databases in the business and social sciences areas. Designed to aid in the selection of databases, the guide also outlines

various search strategy decisions. Concludes that *Which Database?* is "logically outlined, clearly written, and authoritatively presented."

55.   Molster, H. C. **"Restrictions on Database Use: Are They Necessary?"** *Online Review* 3 (March 1979): 85-93.
    Analyzes the various restrictions put on the use of bibliographic databases by database producers. Three types of restrictions (input cooperation, economic, and administrative controls) are individually evaluated. High threshold fees and restrictions on use of output are examples of economic restrictions discussed in some detail. Concludes that two or three standardized agreements will eventually become widely accepted by both users and producers.

56.   Nitecki, Danuta A. **"Reviewing Online Resources."** Guest editor of "Online Services." Edited by Danuta Nitecki. *RQ* 20 (Summer 1981): 335-36.
    Explains the rationale for a new ongoing feature in *RQ*—the review of online databases in the "Sources" section of the journal. Prompted by suggestions from the Machine-Assisted Reference Sections (MARS) of the Reference and Adult Services Division of ALA, these reviews will be written for the generalist and are intended to be a "source for general information on new databases."

57.   Norton, Nancy Protho. **" 'Dirty Data'—A Call for Quality Control."** *Online* 5 (January 1981): 40-41.
    Bemoans the lack of quality control exhibited by both database producers and commercial search services. Numerous examples of errors, including unrelated records with the same accession number and incorrect citations, are presented. Contends that the "time is ripe for consumers of online information to demand that database producers and commercial vendors deliver the product they advertise and for which they are paid." Urges individual users and online users groups to actively express dissatisfaction with the current lack of quality control.

58.   **"On-Line Update."** See issues of *Online Review* in volume 1.
    Presents a "bibliography of recent on-line articles with a search example from a data base producer showing techniques especially useful in searching its data base." ISI, INSPEC, and ORBIT's NTIS and LIBCON were represented in the three columns published in volume 1.

59.   Pemberton, Jeffery K. **"The Linear File—A Column by the Publisher."** See issues of *Database.*
    Presents a variety of personal and editorial opinions by Jeffery K. Pemberton, president and publisher of *Database.* Similar to "The Inverted File" column in *Online.* (See also #179.) This column emphasizes database developments and changes. Included in each issue of *Database.*

60.   **"SDI—The Database News Section."** See issues of *Database.*
    Reports current news about databases—their development, availability, status, etc. Brief notices also indicate title or personnel changes.

61.   Swanson, Rowena Weiss. **"Probing Private Files."** *Database* 3 (June 1980): 70-74. 3 (December 1980): 57-67.
    Defines and provides a general overview of private online files in the initial column. This column was only published in two issues of *Online.* The second column dealt

specifically with the in-house private files of the Library and Information Services Department of the Polaroid Corporation.

62. Teitelbaum, Henry H. and Donald T. Hawkins. **"Database Subject Index."** *Online* 2 (April 1978): 16-22.
Groups 86 databases available as of mid-October 1977 on DIALOG, SDC, BRS, MEDLINE, and New York Times INFORMATION BANK into relatively specific subject areas. Databases are not ranked in order of importance and are indicated in abbreviated form. No additional information about any individual database is provided.

63. Williams, Martha E. **"Database and Online Statistics for 1979."** *Bulletin of the American Society for Information Science* 7 (December 1980): 27-29.
Reports that "records contained in databases and the online use of databases has increased dramatically over the past several years." In 1979, 528 databases containing over 148 million records were available and over four million online searches were conducted through the major American and Canadian systems. Statistics are presented for databases available, their subject coverage, and type of access. Factors accounting for the increase in databases are briefly discussed. (See also #64 and #66.)

64. Williams, Martha E. and Lawrence Lannom. **"Data Bases On-Line in 1979."** *Bulletin of the American Society for Information Science* 6 (December 1979): 22-31.
Lists 149 databases available online as of October 1979. Databases from DIALOG, SDC, BRS, New York Times INFORMATION BANK, and the National Library of Medicine are included. The following information is given for each database: subject coverage, availability, years covered, updating frequency, connect charges, and print costs. (See also #63 and #66.)

65. Williams, Martha E. and Lawrence Lannom. **"Lack of Standardization of the Journal Title Data Element in Databases."** *Journal of the American Society for Information Science* 32 (May 1981): 229-33.
Notes the lack of standardization of data elements even within the same database. Eleven physics journals were searched in eight DIALOG databases (METADEX, INSPEC files, SCI files, and CA files). Results were statistically analyzed in four ways: 1) "Number of forms of an element in a database"; 2) "Percent retrievability by element form"; 3) "Number of noncontiguous entry points in a sorted list"; and 4) "Percent retrievability by best form of an element." Warns searchers to be aware of this problem and urges database producers to fix it.

66. Williams, Martha E. and W. T. Brandhorst. **"Data Bases."** See issues of *Bulletin of the American Society for Information Science.* Volume 1, #1 through volume 5, #6.
Discusses and frequently lists databases available on the major commercial search services. Annual lists were occasionally published as separate articles (see #63 and #64). Columns were written by one or both authors during the period the column was regularly published. Database lists have been published as monographs since 1979. (See #735.)

67. Zamora, Antonio. **"Automatic Detection and Correction of Spelling Errors in a Large Database."** *Journal of the American Society for Information Science* 31 (January 1980): 51-57.
Reports the procedures used to detect and correct spelling errors in the database of Chemical Abstract Service. The large size of the database (one million words per week) to be edited requires an accurate computerized method of error detection. Applications of

hashing techniques and heuristic procedures are described. Notes that automatic corrections are made to words that are known to be misspelled.

DESIGN AND THEORY OF ONLINE SEARCHING

Many articles of a highly technical nature have been written concerning various aspects of online searching. Topics covered include the design of databases and retrieval systems, new applications and techniques, programming languages, and theoretical discussions of the mechanics of online searching. These articles are generally written for the systems specialist or experienced searcher interested in the design of specific systems and databases.

Related sections in this bibliography include:

Commercial Search Services (Entries 12-32)
Databases and Database Producers (Entries 49-67)
History of Online Searching and Future Trends (Entries 189-207)
Search Strategies (Entries 321-340)

68. Atherton, Pauline. **"Standards for a User-System Language in Online Retrieval Systems. The Challenge and the Responsibility."** *Online Review* 2 (March 1978): 57-61.

Argues that there should be more standardization, "user interface commonality," in online searching, especially with regard to technical terms and symbols used. Notes that if this occurred, recommended methods of operations or "a code of practice" could logically be developed. Suggests that a subcommittee of ANSI (American National Standards Institute) be directed to investigate this issue.

69. Bibins, Kathleen T. and Roger C. Palmer. **"REFLES: An Individual Microcomputer System for Fact Retrieval."** *Online Review* 4 (December 1980): 357-65.

Details the design and implementation of an in-house data file known as REFLES. System design and functions are described. Selection and adaptation of both hardware and software are discussed. Experiences from actual online tests are presented and future developments outlined. REFLES (Reference Librarian Enhancement System) was developed at the University of California, Los Angeles, Graduate School of Library and Information Science.

70. Blanken, R. R. and B. T. Stern. **"Planning and Design of Online Systems for the Ultimate User of Biomedical Information."** *Information Processing and Management* 11 (1975): 207-227.

Presents a general discussion of design of online information systems. Describes various operational considerations and the psychology of the user. Findings of a survey of users of EXCERPTA MEDICA are reported and improvements planned for 1976 are noted. The future development of the *Excerpta Medica* thesaurus, *Malimet*, is briefly discussed.

71. Boyle, Stephen O. and A. Patricia Miller. **"Feature Comparison of an In-House Information Retrieval System with a Commercial Search Service."** *Journal of the American Society for Information Science* 31 (September 1980): 309-317.

Demonstrates how a commercially available search service can be used as the standard for the development of a similar in-house system. MASQUERADE (Marathon's

Automatic System for Query and Document Entry) was patterned after system features available on SDC. Certain common features (e.g., truncation) were judged impractical for the in-house system. Notes that an in-house system must primarily meet local conditions and real user needs.

72. Cawkell, A. E. **"Developments in Interactive On-Line Television Systems and Teletext Information Services in the Home."** *Online Review* 1 (March 1977): 31-38.

Provides a technical overview of Teletext and Viewdata. These systems, currently being developed in the United Kingdom, use modified television sets to view actual pages of text. A basic keyboard is used in the viewdata system to send commands. SCITEL, the science news service of ISI, is also briefly described. Future trends and developments for interactive home services are presented.

73. Cawkell, A. E. **"Technical Briefing: Acceptability of Transmission Errors in On-Line System."** *Online Review* 1 (December 1977): 318-20.

Raises the issue of data transmission errors and their potentially harmful effects on search results. Reasons for such problems are enumerated and means of detecting errors are presented. Notes that error detection mechanisms are typically not applied to commercially available databases. Therefore, the problem of transmission errors may become more significant as more numerical and statistical databases become available.

74. Doszkocs, Tamas E. **"AID, An Associative Interactive Dictionary for Online Searching."** *Online Review* 2 (June 1978): 163-73.

Presents a technical discussion of an experimental system designed to automatically display related terms, synonyms, narrower and broader terms, and other semantic associations to aid a searcher in preparing a search strategy. The Associative Interactive Dictionary (AID) can be used on a large free text file and was operational on TOXLINE in 1978. An example of an actual AID terminal session is included.

75. Gordon, Helen A. *"Guidelines for Development of Biology Databanks — A Review."* *Online* 6 (March 1982): 40-41.

Reviews a technical report prepared and published by the Life Sciences Research Office, the Federation of American Societies for Experimental Biology and the National Library of Medicine. *Guidelines for Development of Biology Data Banks* is considered an important publication because it outlines the standard procedures necessary to develop a computerized information system and because it is "systematically and accurately prepared."

76. Hickey, Thomas. **"Searching Linear Files On-Line."** *Online Review* 1 (March 1977): 53-58.

Compares linear and inverted search programs for the same file. A linear search which is conducted character by character is too slow to be practical, but a linear file which uses index keys to select records can be used online. However, the inverted file search is quicker and more convenient. Advantages of linear searches are that they necessitate less file preparation and maintenance, require significantly less storage space, and need less processing time to build indexes. Comparisons were made using a database of 100,000 INSPEC records.

77. Kirtland, Monika; Pauline Atherton; and Shirley Harper. **"Integrating Borrowed Records into a Database: Impact on Thesaurus Development and Retrieval."** *Database* 3 (December 1980): 26-33.

Details an effort by the New York State School of Industrial and Labor Relations at Cornell University to develop a database called LABORLIT by including items previously indexed in the MANAGEMENT CONTENTS database. Merging of records from one file into another presents significant indexing and vocabulary problems. Options include 1) reindexing both files; 2) merging the two vocabularies; or 3) initial standardization. Concludes that in this case it is virtually impossible to integrate the two vocabularies without making major changes in the hierarchy. Problems with the thesaurus used with MANAGEMENT CONTENTS are also detailed.

78.　Levine, Gwen Reveley. **"Developing Databases for Online Information Retrieval."** *Online Review* 5 (April 1982): 109-120.

Summarizes the procedures required in developing a database for online searching. Various similarities between functions in a traditional library and of a database producer are discussed. Six aspects of developing a database are considered: 1) analysis of file format; 2) design of file; 3) conversion to machine-readable form; 4) testing the file; 5) loading of the file; and 6) provision of necessary documentation. Notes that information professionals must take "responsiblity to help shape the future of information retrieval."

79.　Meadow, Charles T. **"Matching Users and User Languages in Information Retrieval."** *Online Review* 5 (August 1981): 313-22.

Discusses how user languages can and should be matched with users, with special emphasis given to computer languages used in online information retrieval. Reviews the literature dealing with the practicality of matching user languages with specific groups of users. No criteria is available to determine accurately which language is the "best fit" for a given user. User behavior and the suitability of language for specific tasks are also considered.

80.　Niehoff, Robert T. and Stan Kwasny. **"The Role of Automated Subject Switching in a Distributed Information Network."** *Online Review* 3 (June 1979): 181-94.

Defines automated subject switching and describes the potential for a "distributed network." Various types of subject switching (e.g., exact matching or partial synonym switching) are identified. Earlier studies are reviewed and ongoing experiments briefly noted. Benefits of automated subject switching are mentioned. Concludes that it is "technologically possible within the foreseeable future."

81.　Niehoff, Robert; Stan Kwasny; and Michael Wessells. **"Overcoming the Database Vocabulary Barrier — A Solution."** *Online* 3 (October 1979): 43-54.

Describes the Vocabulary Switching System (VSS) being developed at Battelle Institute to allow cross-file searching. "Subject switching" is defined and the benefits of automated subject switching presented. Basic operational procedures of VSS are summarized and sample results given. Future plans for VSS are briefly discussed.

82.　Power, D. Lee; Charlene A. Woody; Francis Scott; and Michael Fitzgerald. **"SCORPIO, A Subject Content Oriented Retriever for Processing Information On-line."** *Special Libraries* 67 (July 1976): 285-88.

Discusses the design and implementation of SCORPIO (Subject Content Oriented Retriever for Processing Information Online) for the Library of Congress and U.S. Senate. Users can search four files: 1) Bill Digest file; 2) Major Issues file; 3) National Referral Center Master Resources file; and 4) a bibliographic file of information on current topics and issues. Historical background and potential consequences of the development of SCORPIO are briefly presented.

83.   Preece, Scott E. **"An Online Associative Query Modification Methodology."** *Online Review* 4 (December 1980): 375-82.

Describes the Online Associative Query System (OAQS) designed to aid the searcher in developing and modifying online search strategies. Capabilities and features of OAQS are discussed and their impact on the search process explained. The practicality of implementing such an online system of associative information retrieval is examined. Concludes that OAQS could function directly with other online bibliographic search systems for a modest cost.

84.   Rush, James E. **"Development and Operation of a Database Machine for Online Access and Update of a Large Database."** *Online Review* 4 (September 1980): 237-61.

Describes the technical development of a database processor to replace the conventional file system used by OCLC. Database management systems are briefly explained and the growth of OCLC's database is depicted. Selection of the necessary hardware and software developments are detailed. Explains the need for fault tolerance. Development costs and tentative conclusions based on almost one year of use are also presented.

85.   Smith, Linda C. **"Implications of Artificial Intelligence for End Users of Online Systems."** *Online Review* 4 (December 1980): 383-91.

Proposes the use of artificial intelligence to improve the end user interface with online systems. User-oriented systems are defined and criteria for such systems presented. The use of artificial intelligence in the development of future generations of online systems, e.g., knowledge-based systems, is suggested. Various studies which have been conducted on man-machine communication are also reviewed.

86.   **"Viewdata — A Review and Bibliography."** *Online Review* 2 (September 1978): 217-24.

Reviews the development of teletext and viewdata systems in the United Kingdom. Prestel, the trade name of the British Post Office viewdata system, is described and cost figures presented. Viewdata is compared to existing online bibliographic services and future plans identified. A lengthy bibliography is included.

87.   Williams, Philip W. **"The Use of Microelectronics to Assist Online Information Retrieval."** *Online Review* 4 (December 1980): 393-99.

Details possible uses of microcomputers and microprocessors to dramatically increase the quality of online searches at a low cost. Benefits include: lower search costs, increased convenience and ease of searching, and improved quality of results. Problems in developing such systems involve software and economic factors. Experimental applications have resulted in savings of over 50% in search cost. Suggested improvements are noted.

DOCUMENT DELIVERY AND INTERLIBRARY LOAN

An online search identifies sources of information, but, in most cases, does not supply the actual documents. Therefore, introduction of online searching in most libraries has a significant impact on interlibrary loan. The major commercial search services do, however, make available various services which allow the user to order the documents whose citations have been retrieved.

Related sections in this bibliography include:

Impact of Online Searching (Entries 208-221)
Search Results (Entries 309-320)

88. **"Document Delivery."** See issues of *Online* beginning with volume 2, #1.
Describes how to obtain copies of items retrieved from online searches. Sources of documents and techniques involved in the various online document delivery systems are included in this regular column in *Online*.

89. Faust, Julia B. **"Tailoring On-line Search Retrieval to Match a Library's Journal Collection."** *Bulletin of the Medical Library Association* 70 (April 1982): 241-43.
Details how a hospital library limits results from MEDLINE online searches to those from journals in the library's collection. The list of journals in the library indexed in MEDLINE is entered and stored using the SAVESEARCH feature. This stored search is then executed against the results of a bibliographic search. This solves the problems of document delivery and reliance on interlibrary loan. Disadvantages are also noted.

90. Gibbs, Mary Margaret and George A. Laszlo. **"Document Ordering through Lockheed's DIALOG and SDC's ORBIT—A User's Guide."** *Online* 4 (October 1980): 31-38.
Explains the online document ordering procedures available on DIALOG and SDC in 1980. Instructions prepared by the commercial search services are modified and briefly summarized. Step-by-step guides are presented for ordering documents on both SDC and DIALOG. General instructions are supplemented by additional "hints" for using each system. Notes the practical applications of this capability as a "totally new ILL source."

91. Martin, Jean K. **"Computer-Based Literature Searching. Impact on Interlibrary Loan Service."** *Special Libraries* 69 (January 1978): 1-6.
Investigates the effect online search results have on interlibrary loan requests in a specialized library. Searches conducted during an 18-month period from January 1976 through June 1977 at the Russell Research Center Library, U.S. Department of Agriculture, were statistically compared to the number of interlibrary loan requests processed during the same period. The high number of requests correlated with the number of online searches conducted. Notes that this has both budgetary and staffing implications for libraries.

92. Nitecki, Danuta A. **"Online Interlibrary Services: An Informal Comparison of Five Systems."** Guest Editor of "Online Services." Edited by Danuta Nitecki. *RQ* 21 (Fall 1981): 7-14.
Describes five automated library systems which can be used to locate resources and transmit interlibrary loan requests. Online bibliographic searches frequently retrieve items not owned by the patron's library, and this has forced interlibrary loan services to explore alternative procedures for document delivery. The systems discussed are OCLC, RLIN, UTLAS, CLSI, and LCS.

93. Popovich, Marjorie. **"Online Ordering with Dialorder."** *Online* 5 (April 1981): 63-65.
Outlines the uses of DIALORDER, the online document ordering service available on DIALOG. Factors to consider before ordering online are enumerated and representative cost figures presented. Fast response time, elimination of copyright worries, and

accessibility of conference papers and foreign publications are cited as significant advantages to DIALORDER. Problems are noted involving both inadequate preparation and lack of supplier feedback.

ECONOMICS OF ONLINE SEARCHING

The costs involved in providing online searches are varied and often substantial. The actual costs, including both start-up and ongoing expenditures, must be analyzed and methods of financing an online search service considered. Comparisons of the cost-effective use of the major commercial search services and available databases are also included in this section.

Related sections in this bibliography include:

Manual Versus Online Searching (Entries 230-241)
Search Strategies (Entries 321-340)
Setting Up and Managing an Online Search Service (Entries 345-367)
User Fees (Entries 444-454)

94.   Almond, J. Robert and Charles H. Nelson. **"Improvements in Cost-Effectiveness in Online Searching. I. Predictive Model Based on Search Cost Analysis."** *Journal of Chemical Information & Computer Sciences* 18 (February 1978): 13-15.

Analyzes the various costs involved in performing an online search and presents a formula to predict search costs based on databases to be used and the search strategy developed. Cost factors considered include: terminal speed, turnaround time, number of operators, number of prints, online and telecommunications charges, and operator keystrokes required. Statistical analysis of the formula indicates a validity factor of 83%.

95.   Barwise, T. **"Cost of Literature Searching in 1985."** *Journal of Information Science* 1 (October 1978): 195-201.

Reviews the results of recent studies concerning the future costs of online searching. It is generally accepted that database royalties, which accounted for 20-40% of the direct costs of computer searching in 1978, may "roughly double in real terms by 1985." Other direct costs (i.e., connect charges and telecommunications costs) are expected to drop slightly, as will subscription fees for print indexes.

96.   Burroughs, Barbara E. and Joey Skaff. **"Maximizing Online Use of a Single System — Will It Really Save Big Money?"** *Online* 2 (April 1978): 55-64.

Investigates the potential of cost savings by primarily using only one commercial search service. Similar searches were made on SDC and DIALOG, and the discount rates announced by both applied to the results. Costs and discounts in dollars are presented in various tables. Exclusive use of either SDC or DIALOG was "not found to be practical."

97.   Calkins, Mary L. **"On-Line Services and Operational Costs."** *Special Libraries* 68 (January 1977): 13-17.

Gives the results of a cost analysis of online searches conducted by the U.S. Environmental Protection Agency library at the Research Center in Cincinnati. Searches performed in four major systems (DIALOG, SDC, MEDLINE, and TOXLINE) are compared with regard to cost for similar manual searches. Online searching is found to be very cost-effective. Suggestions for improvement (e.g., more training sessions and revised users' manuals) are presented.

98.   Collier, H. R. **"Long-Term Economics of On-Line Services and Their Relationship to Conventional Publishers Seen from the Database Producers' Viewpoint."** *Aslib Proceedings* 30 (January 1978): 16-24.

Investigates the costs involved in producing a database. Examines the difficulties in obtaining exact cost figures from database producers and in even identifying who the producers are. Statistics and cost figures for ISI are presented and hypothetical costs developed for a typical database. Concludes that the "future is good," but that both users and producers must be aware of the "fragile economics of the immediate future."

99.   Cooper, Michael D. **"Input-Output Relationships in On-Line Bibliographic Searching."** *Journal of the American Society for Information Science* 28 (May 1977): 153-60.

Analyzes the relationship between output variables of a search (e.g., cost and cost-effectiveness) and input variables (e.g., type of request, search strategy elements, and characteristics of the request and searcher). Four statistical measures of cost-effectiveness for online searches are presented and applied to data from actual searches on DIALOG databases. Finds that output variables are not sensitive to changes in input variables. Determines a relationship between cost and value.

100.   Cooper, Michael D. and Nancy A. Dewarth. **"The Cost of Online Bibliographic Searching."** *Journal of Library Automation* 9 (September 1976): 195-209.

Reports the results of a study to determine the actual costs of online searching in four public libraries in the San Francisco Bay Area during August 1974 to May 1976. Time spent and corresponding costs were compiled for the following seven different tasks which make up one complete search: 1) reference interview; 2) originating library preparation; 3) DIALOG library preparation; 4) online search; 5) DIALOG library follow-up; 6) originating library follow-up; and 7) follow-up with patron. Actual cost figures are given for each task. Study was conducted as part of DIALIB project.

101.   Hillman, Donald J. **"A Simulation Model of the ELHILL 3 System of the National Library of Medicine."** *Online Review* 4 (September 1980): 281-88.

Analyzes the possibility of reducing the cost of online searching. Describes models of the ELHILL 3 system of the National Library of Medicine, which were designed to simulate various applications and workloads of the system. The difficulty of describing such a system in "quantifiable components" is noted. Concludes that "distributed processing systems offer promising alternatives."

102.   Jensen, Rebecca J.; Herbert O. Asbury; and Radford H. King. **"Costs and Benefits to Industry on Online Literature Searches."** *Special Libraries* 71 (July 1980): 291-99.

Surveys both industrial clients and NASA—Small Business Administration Technology Assistance Program clients who used the online computerized search service provided by the NASA Industrial Application Center at the University of Southern California. More than half (53%) mentioned cost benefits. Shows a direct relationship between money spent and beneficial results achieved. Statistical findings are presented in various charts.

103.   Koch, Jean E. **"A Review of the Costs and Cost-Effectiveness of Online Bibliographic Searching."** *Reference Services Review* 10 (Spring 1982): 59-64.

Considers all costs involved in providing an online bibliographic service to library patrons. Costs are divided into three general categories: 1) support costs, i.e., all costs not directly related to a given search; 2) production costs, i.e., all costs directly attributable to a specific search; and 3) overhead. Compares costs of manual and online literature searches and identifies several future trends.

104.   Lancaster, F. W. **"The Cost-Effectiveness Analysis of Information Retrieval and Dissemination Systems."** *Journal of the American Society for Information Science* 22 (January-February 1971): 12-27.
Distinguishes between cost-effectiveness analysis and cost-benefits analysis as used to evaluate information retrieval systems. Factors affecting the cost-effectiveness of retrieval systems include: coverage, indexing, index languages, and search procedures. Certain practical "tradeoffs" in developing information systems are noted. Cautions that the human factor must also be considered.

105.   Lynch, Mary Jo. **"Financing Online Services."** Guest editor of "Online Services." Edited by Danuta A. Nitecki. *RQ* 21 (Spring 1982): 223-26.
Summarizes some of the findings of a study completed to discover how prevalent online search services are in public libraries and how they are funded. The survey was conducted by ALA's Office for Research, and complete results are presented in *Financing Online Services in Publicly Supported Libraries* (see #728). Responses to various questions regarding costs and user fees are presented. The availability of online searching was reported to depend most on "level of funding available."

106.   Markee, Katherine M. **"Economics of Online Retrieval."** *Online Review* 5 (December 1981): 439-44.
Analyzes the actual costs of online searching to both the end user and the institution providing the service. Annual statistics compiled at the Purdue University Library's Computer Based Information Service are used to investigate the economics and the overall benefits of online searching. Methods of recovering costs and evaluating user satisfaction are also considered.

107.   Saffady, W. **"Economics of Online Bibliographic Searching: Costs and Cost Justifications."** *Library Technology Reports* 15 (September-October 1979): 567-653.
Investigates the costs and economic factors associated with online searching. Potential cost justifications are examined in some detail. An introductory section provides a general overview of online searching. Specific costs are identified and other related expenses, such as document delivery, are considered. Actual charge structures for DIALOG, BRS, and SDC are appended. A lengthy bibliography is also included.

108.   Shireley, Sherrilynne. **"A Survey of Computer Search Service Costs in the Academic Health Sciences Library."** *Bulletin of the Medical Library Association* 66 (October 1978): 390-96.
Analyzes all costs involved in providing online search services. Contends that indirect costs, e.g., those in addition to direct charges from commercial search services and telecommunication costs, must be accounted for in any attempt to determine actual costs to the library. Costs are divided into three categories: 1) production costs; 2) supporting costs (including start-up and recurring costs); and 3) overhead. Methods to establish a price structure are considered. An outline summarizes all cost factors discussed.

109.   Smith, John Brewster and Sara D. Knapp. **"Data Base Royalty Fees and the Growth of Online Search Services in Academic Libraries."** *Journal of Academic Librarianship* 7 (September 1981): 206-212.

Regards the increasing online royalty fees as an "immediately critical factor" in the overall cost of online search services. Libraries should be especially concerned about increasing royalty fees for the use of many "broad appeal data bases" (e.g., PSYCINFO or BIOSIS). Alternative methods of charging are analyzed, and the viability of low costs resulting in sufficiently high volume to maintain profit levels is considered. Responses of representatives of the major search services and several database producers are appended.

110.   Summit, Roger K. **"The Dynamics of Costs and Finances of On-Line Computer Searching."** *RQ* 20 (Fall 1980): 60-63.

Provides a detailed analysis of the various costs which influence the prices charged by commercial search services such as DIALOG. Four major activities which affect the eventual cost to users are identified: 1) operations; 2) file maintenance; 3) new file loads; and 4) accounting and reporting. These internal costs are combined with two major external expenses (royalties and telecommunication charges) to determine the charge to users. Predicts that personnel and royalty costs will most directly affect user charges in the near future.

111.   Williams, Martha E. **"An Analysis of Online Database Prices and a Rationale for Increasing the Price of MEDLINE."** *Online Review* 6 (February 1982): 7-26.

Uses various statistical analyses of connect hour prices for databases available on seven major commercial search services to justify the proposed price increase for online use of MEDLINE through the MEDLARS search system. Notes that "database size correlates extremely well with price." Reasons for increasing the connect hour price for MEDLINE are given. Concludes that the price increase is "appropriate."

112.   Williams, Martha E. **"Relative Impact of Print and Database Products on Database Producer Expenses and Income — Trends for Database Producer Organizations Based on a Thirteen Year Financial Analysis."** *Information Processing and Management* 17 (1981): 263-76.

Describes in great detail a 13-year statistical study of the finances of a large database producer. Trends are identified and interpreted. Income, expenses, excess of income over expenses, and prices are presented in graphs. Investigates the "migration" from print to online versions and concludes that future price increases for online users appear inevitable.

END USERS

There is some controversy over the effectiveness and efficiency of researchers conducting their own online searches without the use of a trained intermediary. The major commercial search services are not designed for easy use by untrained end users; consequently, the need to provide training for end users is often emphasized.

Related sections in this bibliography include:

History of Online Searching and Future Trends (Entries 189-207)
Search Analysts (Entries 296-308)

113. Barber, A. Stephanie; Elizabeth D. Barraclough; and W. Alexander Gray. **"On-line Information Retrieval as a Scientist's Tool."** *Information Storage and Retrieval* 9 (August 1973): 429-40.

Investigates the practicality of having scientists conduct their own online searches. A training program, known as MEDUSA, was used to allow physicians to learn to perform their own searches of the MEDLARS databases. MEDUSA is briefly described, as is the experiment to test its effectiveness. Search results compiled by the end users were compared with items retrieved by professional searchers on the same topics. Concludes that "search formulation by the users is a practical possibility."

114. Elias, Arthur W.; Nancy Vaupel; and David Lingwood. **"End User Education: A Design Study."** *Online Review* 4 (June 1980): 153-62.

Discusses the role one major abstracting and indexing service, BIOSIS, plays in the education and training of searchers and end users. Results of a study and a workshop conducted in 1979 by BIOSIS with the assistance of Ilium Associates are presented. End users are grouped according to the following "market segments": educators, students, and managers. Objectives and implications of an integrated educational program for end users are described.

115. Lowry, Glenn R. **"Online Document Retrieval System Education for Undergraduates: Rationale, Content and Observations."** *Online Review* 4 (December 1980): 349-56.

Describes an undergraduate course in information retrieval for computer science students taught at Stockton State College in New Jersey. Online experience using DIALOG is required. Differences between this course and graduate library science courses are noted. The course has been considered very successful by students and other faculty.

116. Meadow, Charles T. **"The Computer as a Search Intermediary."** *Online* 3 (July 1979): 54-59.

Describes a research project being conducted at Drexel University to design a computer intermediary for bibliographic online searching and to evaluate its performance. The system, called Individualized Instruction for Data Access (IIDA), is outlined and various "fault types" explained. Future uses of IIDA are discussed, and additional research is strongly suggested.

117. Meadow, Charles T. **"Online Searching and Computer Programming: Some Behavioral Similarities (OR – Why End Users Will Eventually Take Over the Terminal)."** *Online* 3 (January 1979): 49-52.

Presents a general "social history of programming" to provide a basis for predicting increased end user searching in the future. Believes that increased end user training will result in substantially more online search systems and databases and that the role of the search intermediary will be greatly reduced. Concludes this is beneficial because it will result in "less time being devoted to hand-holding and more to problem solving."

118. Moghdam, Dineh. **"User Training for On-Line Information Retrieval Systems."** *Journal of the American Society for Information Science* 26 (May-June 1975): 184-88.

Reviews methods for training end users to use online retrieval systems. The need for training and problems inherent in providing it are discussed. Four types of training (printed instructions, live tutors, and audiovisual and online instruction, and computer-assisted instruction) are examined. Concludes that an online tutorial program which is a part of the actual information retrieval system is the best means of training end users.

119.   Olson, Paul E. **"A Study of the Interaction of Nonlibrarian Searchers with the MEDLINE Retrieval System."** *Bulletin of the Medical Library Association* 63 (January 1975): 35-41.
Analyzes the ability of nonlibrarian searchers to perform and modify online searches. Search strategies and actual searches conducted by 16 nonlibrarians on MEDLINE were examined and the number of online modifications noted. Concludes that these searchers were able to use the various interactive capabilities of MEDLINE to obtain good search results. A general review of the literature dealing with end user online searching is also presented.

120.   Richardson, Robert J. **"End-User Online Searching in a High-Technology Engineering Environment."** *Online* 5 (October 1981): 44-57.
Reports the results of a one-year study to determine the feasibility of having scientists and engineers conduct their own online searches. The Submarine Signal Division of Raytheon Company worked with DIALOG in a project which allowed 20 researchers to have direct online access to three DIALOG databases (NTIS, COMPENDEX, and INSPEC). Results are tabulated and discussed. Notes that "overall system usage was surprisingly low." Implications for online use by end users are considered.

121.   Williams, P. W. and J. M. Curtis. **"Use of Online Information Retrieval Services."** *Program* 11 (January 1977): 1-9.
Compares the results of searches conducted by end users, by users assisted by experienced intermediaries, and by intermediaries after an informational interview with the requester. While 95% of the end users were pleased with their own results, 90% preferred those conducted by the intermediary because they were shorter and retrieved more relevant references. Concludes that "the search by the user alone does not seem an attractive method of on-line searching." Results are statistically analyzed.

FOREIGN AND INTERNATIONAL APPLICATIONS

Online activities in Europe and other areas of the world are expanding rapidly. Difficulties are frequently encountered in trying to use American systems in Europe and vice versa. Communications and economic factors have, until fairly recently, limited foreign use of American commercial search services. Canadian online services are considered foreign.
Related sections in this bibliography include:

History of Online Searching and Future Trends (Entries 189-207)

122.   Anthony, L. J. **"European Notes."** See issues of *Online* beginning with volume 2, #4.
Reports on online activities in Europe. Discusses new developments in European information retrieval and communications.

123.   Bingham, Archie. **"The UKCIS Advisory Service."** *Database* 2 (December 1979): 46-53.
Describes the Advisory Service developed by the United Kingdom Chemical Information Service (UKCIS) to assist both online searchers and potential users of chemical and biological databases in the United Kingdom and Ireland. Questions received fall into the following categories: 1) Terminal and printer selection; 2) Selection of online

training sessions; 3) Usage of various online commercial search services; and 4) Usage of the various chemical and biological databases. Certain very common problems in using registry numbers are explained. The free Advisory Service is available only to users in the United Kingdom or Ireland.

124. **"BLAISE — The British Library Automated Information Service."** *Online Review* 2 (September 1978): 229-32.

Describes BLAISE, the British Library Automated Information Service. Both its catalog and retrieval functions are outlined. Databases available include the MEDLARS files, Library of Congress MARC tapes, and the UK MARC files. General operations of BLAISE, including personnel and document delivery, are briefly presented. Future plans are also noted.

125. Bourne, Charles P. **"Computer-Based Reference Services as an Alternative Means to Improve Resource-Poor Local Libraries in Developing Countries."** *International Library Review* 9 (January 1977): 43-50.

Analyzes various approaches to providing current awareness and retrospective reference services to researchers in developing countries. Suggestions are made to allow implementation of SDI services, retrospective bibliographic searching, and document delivery to these countries. Stresses the ability of computer-based services to supplement local reference sources.

126. Clinton, Marshall. **"Online Searching in Canada — The DATAPAC Interface."** *Online* 2 (July 1978): 41-51.

Notes the impact a Canadian communications network, DATAPAC, will have on both online searching in Canada and Canadian search services. Access procedures are briefly summarized and "System Messages and Meanings" presented in a table. Communiction costs for online searching in Canada are also given. Unique Canadian databases are also identified.

127. Clinton, Marshall and Sally Grenville. **"Using European Systems from a North American Library."** *Online* 4 (April 1980): 22-27.

Considers the possibility of accessing European databases from the United States. The Memorial University of Newfoundland Library's use of the QUEST system operated by the European Space Agency's Information Retrieval service in Italy is described. Difficulties in initially determining what databases are available and arranging access to them are noted. Communication problems encountered are also explained.

128. Collier, Harry R. **"European Online Users: A Mid-1981 Report."** *Online Review* 6 (February 1982): 27-37.

Summarizes the responses to a questionnaire sent in the spring of 1981 to over 7,000 individual users of online services in Europe by *Online Review*. Results were analyzed on an organizational basis and 497 European search organizations were represented. Detailed statistics are reported in the following areas: 1) background information; 2) searcher profile; 3) professional training and education; and 4) search profile. European users primarily use major international commercial search services, with DIALOG being the heaviest used.

129. Corning, Mary E. **"The U.S. National Library of Medicine and International Medlars Cooperation."** *Information Storage and Retrieval* 8 (December 1972): 255-64.

Provides background on the international cooperative aspects of MEDLARS, as in effect in 1972. Notes that the National Library of Medicine has bilateral agreements with seven foreign countries and the World Health Organization. Operational and policy aspects of these arrangements are described.

130. Cribb, J. L. and S. M. Lynn-Robinson. **"You Need Uncle Sam. Information Retrieval from the U.S."** *Australian Library Journal* 26 (June 1977): 166-68.

Discusses the use of DIALOG and SDC in Australia. Difficulties in telecommunications are indicated and the costs involved are given. Dependency of Australia on American commercial search services is justified because of the relatively small number of potential users in Australia. A sample search conducted on AGRICOLA is used to generally explain search procedures.

131. Cuadra, Carlos A. **"U.S.-European Cooperation and Competition in the Online Retrieval Services Marketplace."** *Information Scientist* 12 (June 1978): 45-53.

Discusses the historical development and future trends of European use of American commercial search services. Immediate problems concern telecommunications and pricing. Urges European users to "mount effective opposition to telecommunications charges that are unnecessarily high." A brief overview of online activities in the United States is also presented.

132. **"Euronet Hosts—The Space Documentation Service."** *Online Review* 2 (June 1978): 149-50.

Gives the historical development of the Space Documentation Service (SDS) of the European Space Agency (ESA). Its location in Frascati near Rome is described. The network, ESANET, of the agency and the databases available are briefly discussed. Political and administrative problems are noted and potential future activities presented.

133. Evers, H. and Z. Urbanek. **"Financial Aspects of Information Brokerage in Europe."** *Online Review* 6 (February 1982): 39-46.

Discusses the outlook for independent information brokers in Europe. Goal of financial independence is considered and founded to be feasible "only in rare cases." Factors affecting expenditure, income, and quality of the information provided are identified and analyzed. Quantitative cost analyses are reported and average costs per request presented in tables. Concludes that further cuts in government subsidies to brokers will "lead to their entrepreneurial death."

134. Harley, A. J. **"UK MEDLARS Service: A Personal View of Its First Decade."** *Aslib Proceeding* 29 (September 1977): 320-25.

Comments on the use of MEDLARS in the United Kingdom from 1966 to 1976. A historical summary of the origins of MEDLARS, especially from a British perspective, is provided. The importance of early training courses and workshops is stressed. British contributions to the continual development of MEDLARS is also noted. Future developments are predicated on the availability of EURONET.

135. Holmes, P. L. **"The British Library Automated Information Service (BLAISE)."** *Online Review* 3 (September 1979): 265-74.

Describes the services provided by the British Library's BLAISE (British Library Automated Information Services) system. Primarily a bibliographic utility, BLAISE concentrates on technical processing applications. Hardware, software, and communication requirements are discussed. Services provided are summarized and future plans briefly noted.

136. **"InfoLine — A New European Online Service."** *Online Review* 2 (December 1978): 325-27.

Describes INFOLINE, a European online service which became operational in 1978. The system, ownership, and management are briefly discussed. Notes that INFOLINE is a "commercial operation set up to develop profitably services in the online marketplace." Databases to be made available and availability of INFOLINE on various telecommunications networks are also presented.

137. Janke, Richard V. and Maureen Wong. **"Online in Canada."** *Online* 5 (July 1981): 12-29.

Details the operation of the Computer Search Service at the University of Ottawa. Contends that it represents a typical online search service in a Canadian university library in 1980. Some of the service elements discussed include: 1) budget and fee structure; 2) administrative organization; 3) physical facility; 4) publicity; and 5) databases available. Particular emphasis is given to four Canadian online systems (QL Systems, CAN/OLE, Informatech France-Quebec, and the International Development Research Centre's IDRC/MINISIS System).

138. Lopes da Silva, Gabriela and Carlos Pulido. **"Starting Online Information Services in Portugal."** *Online Review* 5 (June 1981): 225-58.

Assesses the first two years' operation of the Centro de Documentacao Cientifica e Técnica (CDCT), the documentation service of the Portuguese National Institute for Scientific Research. Operational experiences and promotional activities are described. Connect hours and the databases used most heavily are given in tables. Future plans are briefly noted.

139. Martin, Peter. **"Predicasts in Europe."** *Online Review* 2 (September 1978): 233-35.

Describes the experiences of Predicasts Inc. in introducing their databases to European users. Complaints that Predicasts databases were biased towards American sources were justified, and increased emphasis was placed on including more European statistics and information. Feels the databases were enhanced by having "Europeans abstracting European information." Communication costs within Europe and the lack of adequately trained intermediaries are the most significant problems.

140. Mauerhoff, Georg R. **"Distribution of SDC Search Service in Canada by INFOMART."** *Online Review* 1 (June 1977): 137-41.

Details the history and background of INFOMART, a Canadian service which provides access to SDC in Canada. Marketing and sales procedures are described, and the company's emphasis on user education and training is noted. The importance of effective communication between SDC and INFOMART is stressed. Concludes that INFOMART provides a beneficial service to Canadians conducting online searches.

141. **"Online Visits England."** *Online* 3 (January 1979): 54-55.

Provides a pictorial view of a trip to England in the fall of 1978 by Jeff and Jenny Pemberton of *Online*. Views of database producers, online system operators, and exhibits of teletext systems are presented.

142. Pelissier, Denise. **"PASCAL Database File Description and Online Access on ESA/IRS."** *Online Review* 4 (March 1980): 13-31.

Introduces PASCAL, the database version of the French abstract journal *Bulletin Signalétique*. Primary sources, coverage, and description of record are presented. Availability of PASCAL on ESA/IRS (European Space Agency/Information Retrieval System) is also described. Examples of sample searches and formats available are appended.

143. Pelissier, Denise. **"Pascaline on Questel."** *Online Review* 5 (June 1981): 241-54.

Discusses how to search the PASCAL database with MISTRAL software on QUESTEL, the French host system. Content and coverage of PASCAL is briefly presented. Sample searches are used to demonstrate search techniques and file format. Appendices list language codes, document type codes, role indicators, output formats, user aids, and document sources.

144. Phillips, Dorothy. **"A Review of Telidon Development."** *Online Review* 4 (June 1980): 169-71.

Summarizes the planning and testing of Telidon, a second-generation videotex system being developed by the Canadian Federal Government's Department of Communications. The technical features of Telidon are described, and the results of various field tests are discussed. The role of the Canadian Videotex Consultative Committee in coordinating national development of videotext in Canada is noted. Concludes that "future developments await only the economic impetus of demand and less expensive components."

145. Rao, M. K. Dhirendra. **"Computerized Bibliographical Information Handling: Status and Modern Trends."** *Herald of Library Science* 19 (January-April 1980): 33-37.

Summarizes the developments and trends in computerized information retrieval and emphasizes their impact on libraries and information centers in India. The advantages and disadvantages of online searching are presented. Concludes that increased use of such computerized capabilities in India depends on "the availability of finance and computer."

146. Shahdad, B. **"Iranian Library of Medicine Local Computer Network."** *Online Review* 5 (April 1981): 133-35.

Covers the introduction of online searching by the Iranian Library of Medicine to improve biomedical information retrieval in Iran. Difficulties in establishing the necessary computer and communications facilities are described. Access to MEDLINE was initially provided and search statistics are given. Use of CATLINE is discussed in some detail.

147. **"Spotlight on a Training Centre."** *Online Review* 5 (August 1981): 342-43.

Presents a brief view of the SOVIN online training center in operation in Holland. Summarizes the types of courses offered and the physical facilities available. The background of SOVIN is discussed and its impact on online searching in the Netherlands noted. Concludes that SOVIN has "an important educational function."

148. Tedd, L. A. **"Education, Training, and Marketing for Online Information Retrieval Systems."** *Online Review* 3 (June 1979): 205-212.

Analyzes how twelve information services in seven European countries utilize online searching to satisfy patron requests. Six information centers are individually discussed. General education and marketing techniques are also summarized. Notes that pricing structures directly affect the amount of promotion needed.

149. Tomberg, Alex. **"The Development of Commercially Available Databases in Europe."** *Online Review* 3 (December 1979): 343-53.

Recounts the phenomenal growth in the number of databases available, particularly in Europe, in the 1970s and notes the change in emphasis from bibliographic databases to "files of information." An "impasse" is seen between the existence of many databases and their availability to users. Hopes that new technologies like viewdata and the European Communication Satellite will resolve this problem.

150. Tomberg, Alex. **"On-line Services in Europe."** *Online Review* 1 (September 1977): 177-93.

Analyzes statistically the use of online services in Europe. Notes the dependency in 1977 on American databases and services. Three "urgent requirements" are presented: 1) co-networking of databases with bibliographic files; 2) an export drive; and 3) improved reliability and marketing. Stresses that Europeans must find a means of reducing "Europe's information trade imbalance."

151. Van der Meer, K.; L. M. Koster; and D. L. Brand-de-Heer. **"National Courses in Online Retireval in the Netherlands."** *Online Review* 5 (October 1981): 405-407.

Describes the development of an online training course organized and presented by VOGIN, the Online User Group in the Netherlands. The content of the course is outlined and problems encountered in providing the course are detailed. Notes that the course "was probably the world's first training course arranged and given by a user group."

152. Van Slype, Georges; Eric Laudet; Claude Machgeels; and Yves Vander Auwera. **"A Mini-Euronet Standard Command Set at Université Libre de Bruxelles (ULB)."** *Online Review* 4 (March 1980): 41-53.

Describes the search commands and features of an online bibliographic search system, called SERIDU, developed by the Brussels Free University Information and Documentation Science Department. Commands are based on the standard command language being developed by various DIANE hosts. A sample search is included. Problems and future developments are also presented.

153. Verheijen-Voogd, C. **"Is EURONET C.C.L. a 'Common' Command Language?"** *Online Review* 5 (October 1981): 399-401.

Presents a chart which lists equivalent commands for common search operations for three retrieval languages used in Europe. Actual examples are presented and significant differences noted. Two versions of the EURONET Common Command Language (C.C.L.) are compared with the IRS/ESA-QUEST retrieval language. Concludes that EURONET C.C.L. is not yet a "common" command language.

154. Weitzel, Rolf. **"Medline Services to Developing Countries."** *Bulletin of the Medical Library Association* 64 (January 1976): 32-35.

Details the MEDLINE services provided by the World Health Organization MEDLINE Center in Geneva, Switzerland, to the Third World countries in Africa, Asia, and Oceania. Difficulties in promoting the service and completing the searches because of the lack of direct contact with the requesters are noted. However, user delivery is also discussed.

155. Williams, Philip. **"Access to Information in Europe."** *Computer Communications* 1 (December 1978): 290-94.

Details developments in online searching and telecommunications in Europe. Notes that while most of the major commercial search services are in the United States, there has been increasing expansion of online access in Europe. Factors affecting cost and availability are discussed. Advantages of Euronet are described and administrative and technical problems examined.

156.   Wilmot, C. E. **"Online Opportunity: A Comparison of Activities in America and the United Kingdom."** *Aslib Proceedings* 28 (April 1976): 134-43.

Compares the use and acceptance of online searching in the United States and the United Kingdom in the mid-1970s. Types of usage and factors such as reliable telecommunications networks in the United States are discussed. British use of commercial online search services is judged to be "gathering momentum," but not yet substantial. Some doubts about the online usage are expressed. Implementation of EURONET should eliminate many of the technical problems.

GENERAL AND MISCELLANEOUS

The major journals which deal with online searching, i.e., *Database, Online*, and *Online Review*, include various editorial and informational columns. These journals also occasionally contain general articles beyond the scope of online searching, e.g., discussions of OCLC or UTLAS (University of Toronto Library Automation Systems). Literature reviews, reports of surveys, and articles which provide a general overview of online searching are included in this section.

Related sections in this bibliography include:

History of Online Searching and Future Trends (Entries 189-207)

157.   Archer, Mary Ann E. **"The 'Make or Buy' Decision. Five Points to Consider."** *Online* 2 (July 1978): 24-25.

Offers advice for deciding when to acquire magnetic tapes for in-house use, when to search databases available from commercial search services, and when to contract with an information broker. Five guidelines are presented: 1) availability of information in the most useful form; 2) computer support — both in hardware and software terms; 3) response time; 4) security needs; and 5) price.

158.   Blue, Richard I. **"Directory of U.S. Full-Text System Vendors."** *Online Review* 3 (July 1979): 175-79.

Lists organizations which "sell or lease software or provide subscription service for online information retrieval from the full text of documents in user-provided databases." Suppliers for various systems are identified and addresses and telephone numbers of contact persons provided. List was compiled in early 1979.

159.   **"Book Reviews."** See issues of *Online Review* beginning with volume 2, #1.

Provides brief reviews of books, conference proceedings, search aids, and other publications of interest to online searchers. A regular feature in *Online Review* beginning with volume 5, #2. (See also #160.)

160.   **"Books Received."** See issues of *Online Review* beginning with volume 2, #4.

Lists books received by *Online Review*, but not yet reviewed. Brief annotation and availability information are given for each book. (See also #159.)

161.   **"Calendar."** See issues of *Online Review* beginning with volume 1, #4.

Presents for the forthcoming year a calendar of events of interest to online searchers. Events are listed chronologically, and the name and address of a contact person is noted. This is a regular column in *Online Review*.

162.   Clay, Katherine. **"Byte My Baud: A Day in the Life of an Information Center."** *Online* 2 (April 1978): 31-35.

Depicts an allegedly typical day at the San Mateo Educational Resources Center. Self-described as "a piece of fluff," this article presents a chronological record of one day's activity at an information center.

163.   Clinton, Marshall. **"PHOENIX: An Online System for a Library Catalogue."** *Database* 5 (February 1982): 52-65.

Describes the online catalog system introduced in late 1980 at the University of New Brunswick. Called PHOENIX, the system provides access to the library's catalog and various other databases (e.g., serials lists and special holdings). Describes the eleven system commands, but emphasizes two basic commands: SEARCH and DISPLAY. An update describing changes and modifications in the system after six months of operation is also included. Notes that location of the terminals is extremely important.

164.   Dolan, Donna R. **"ONLINE Humor."** *Online* 4 (January 1980): 55-57.

Lists, somewhat facetiously, "mistakes to avoid on your first job as an online searcher." Some suggestions are accompanied by cartoon illustrations.

165.   Doyle, Frances M. **"ONLINE Humor."** *Online* 5 (January 1981): 69.

Offers numerous laws and maxims for dealing with various aspects of managing an online search service. These are presented in a humorous fashion and include Doyle's Fourth Law: "Just when you learn one system, a more sophisticated one will be introduced."

166.   Evans, John Edward. **"Jobline."** See issues of *Online* beginning with volume 4, #2, and ending with volume 6, #2. See issues of *Database* beginning with volume 3, #1, and ending with volume 5, #1.

Lists job placement announcements in the field of online searching and information retrieval. Includes notices by both employers and job seekers. Replaced with an expanded and more current version available only online in the ONLINE CHRONICLE.

167.   Fenichel, Carol Hansen. **"The Process of Searching Online Bibliographic Databases: A Review of Research."** *Library Research* 2 (1980-1981): 107-127.

Reviews the studies that have been published dealing with the problems of the user interface in online systems. Studies analyzed are divided into the following sections: 1) theoretical perspectives and models; 2) observations of operating systems; 3) studies of individual cases; 4) controlled experiments; and 5) questionnaire surveys and interviews. Results are summarized and compared. Bibliography is included.

168.   Ferguson, Patricia. **"Chronicles of an Information Company."** *Online Review* 1 (March 1977): 39-42.

Details the growth and development of a small information company which offers online services to government agencies, graduate students, and others. Documentation Associates, founded in 1971 by two librarians, is a money-making custom information service. The financial investment needed to start such a service, as well as basic policies, are described. Future trends and possibilities are also presented.

169. **"First Annual Online Salary and Budget Survey."** *Online* Part I (January 1978): 55-59. Part II (April 1978): 23-25.

Reports the results of a survey conducted of *Online* readers to determine representative salaries and institutional budgets for online services. Figures for expenditures, budgets, and salaries are provided for different types of libraries or information centers. Part I provides American figures. Part II reports foreign statistics. (See also #183.)

170. Greenfield, L. W. **"How the Searcher Saved Christmas."** *American Libraries* 11 (December 1980): 653.

Presents a short, humorous poem detailing the successful efforts of an online searcher to enable Santa Claus to determine why his reindeer wouldn't fly: "My reindeer aren't neurotic—They are simply underpaid."

171. Hawkins, Donald T. **"Online Information Retrieval Bibliography."** *Online Review* 1 (Supplement 1977) S1-S55. First Update 2 (March 1978): 63-106. Second Update 3 (March 1979): 37-73. Third Update 4 (March 1980): 61-100. Fourth Update 5 (April 1981): 139-82. Fifth Update 6 (April 1982): 147-208.

Provides an exhaustive, unannotated bibliography of online information retrieval. Items are arranged into seven sections: 1) Books, Reviews, Conferences; 2) Descriptions of Online Systems, Databases and Services; 3) Man-Machine Studies, the User Interface, User Attitudes, System Design and Evaluation; 4) Profile Development, Searching Techniques, Indexing, Manual vs. Machine Searching; 5) Usage Studies, Economics, Promotion and Impact of Online Retrieval Systems, Management; 6) User Education and Training; and 7) General, Miscellaneous. Permuted title and author indexes are included. *Online Information Retrieval Bibliography, 1964-1979* (see #737) reproduced the items contained in the original supplement issue and the first three updates.

172. Hawkins, Donald T. and Carolyn P. Brown. **"What Is an Online Search?"** *Online* 4 (January 1980): 12-18.

Defines an online search and identifies various types of searches. The need for standard definitions to allow for collecting of comparable search statistics is stressed. Definitions are given for basic terms (e.g., online searching and database access) and also for search types (e.g., citation, demo, and training searches) and people or groups involved (e.g., vendor and search intermediary). Methods of quantifying a "search session" are also suggested.

173. Hillman, Donald J. **"Model for the On-line Management of Knowledge Transfer."** *Online Review* 1 (March 1977): 23-30.

Distinguishes between information retrieval and knowledge transfer. Notes that the latter is much more difficult and necessitates a greater degree of conceptual organization. The LEADERMART information system is presented as an example of a potential knowledge-transfer system. Discusses various ways to convert information flow into knowledge-transfer activities. Notes that enhanced online capabilities will facilitate future advances in knowledge-transfer. A new procedure, QUANSY, which analyzes questions, is also briefly described.

174.　Huber, Wolfgang. **"Referral, A Tool to Increase the Use of Available Information Resources."** *Online Review* 1 (December 1977): 289-94.

Stresses the need for appropriate referral services and projects to aid online searchers. Distinguishes between and gives examples of referral service projects and referral within the framework of a network. The basic aim of referral projects is to develop aids to facilitate the selection of the best sources of information. Benefits from referral services include cost savings, easier access to information, and unbiased assistance.

175.　Kilgour, Frederick G. **"Shared Cataloging at OCLC."** *Online Review* 3 (September 1979): 275-79.

Summarizes the operations and activities of OCLC. The various online subsystems and the online union catalog are described. The technical aspects of the system, including the OCLC computer-communications system, are also explained. Future plans are briefly noted.

176.　Klugman, Simone. **"Conversations with MELVYL: Translated from the MELVYLIAN Language."** *Database* 5 (February 1982): 43-51.

Describes the prototype online patron-accessed catalog (MELVYL) being used experimentally at the University of California, Berkeley, in 1981. Sample screens demonstrating the initial introduction to the system, subject searching, browsing, and limiting searches are reproduced. Stresses that MELVYL is only a sample database and is constantly being evaluated and improved. Plans for future implementation are briefly discussed.

177.　**"News."** See issues of *Online Review*.

Presents brief news items about "on-line retrieval of all kinds." International news about commercial search services, databases and diatabase producers, communications, and other aspects of online information retrieval are covered in this regular column in *Online Review*.

178.　Nitecki, Danuta and Mary Pillepich. **"A Road Map to Basic Sources of Information."** Guest Editor of "Online Services." Edited by Danuta Nitecki. *RQ* 19 (Summer 1980): 319-22.

Identifies various sources of basic information about online databases and commercial search services. Items are included because "they offer a unique access to nonspecialized information or because they are readily available." Journals, manuals, guidebooks, directories, and newsletters are listed. The value of human resources is also stressed. Specialized sources for researchers are specifically excluded.

179.　Pemberton, Jeffery K. **"The Inverted File—A Column by the Publisher."** See issues of *Online*.

Presents a variety of personal and editorial opinions by Jeffery K. Pemberton, president and publisher of *Online*. Topics vary widely and the column is included in each issue of *Online*. Similar to the "Linear File" column in *Database* (see also #59), this column discusses general issues in online searching and information retrieval.

180. Pemberton, Jeff. **"A Layman's Guide to Computers."** *Online* 1 (January 1977): 9 + .

Describes briefly how a computer works and what the binary code is. The sequence of actions that occur when a computer is in operation is presented. Defines core, binary notation, modem, and other computer terms.

181. **"Printout — News from the World of Online Information."** See issues of *Online*.

Presents brief news items in every issue of *Online*. Includes general items and current news concerning commercial search services, databases and database producers, and communications.

182. Rinewalt, J. R. **"Feature Evaluation of a Full-Text Information-Retrieval System."** *Online Review* 1 (March 1977): 43-52.

Describes a series of experiments conducted to evaluate various features of a full-text information retrieval system. Three factors were considered: 1) cost; 2) system load; and 3) user performance. The system used was a minicomputer-based experimental retrieval program known as EUREKA. Three groups of students — one using a complete version of EUREKA, one a limited version, and one using the primary documents — took part in the experiments to evaluate various online features. The value of individual features and the results of various tests to prove their validity are statistically presented.

183. **"Salary and Budget Survey."** *Online* 3 (July 1979): 51-53.

Shows the results of a survey distributed to *Online* subscribers concerning salary and budget allocation for online searching. This is the second annual survey (see also #169), and differences from the initial survey are noted. Statistics were reported for various types of libraries and information centers.

184. Thomson, Jan and Jennifer Hartzell. **"RLG's Research Libraries Information Network: Bibliographic and Information Services."** *Online Review* 3 (September 1979): 281-96.

Presents an overview of the operations of the Research Libraries Information Network (RLIN). One of the primary programs of the Research Libraries Group, RIN provides a computerized bibliographic and technical processing network for member libraries. The content of RLIN and its various applications are described. Hardware and software requirements and general future plans are also briefly discussed.

185. Velazquez, Harriet. **"University of Toronto Library Automation Systems."** *Online Review* 3 (September 1979): 253-64.

Describes the historical development and organization of the University of Toronto Library Automation Systems (UTLAS). Hardware requirements are noted. The Catalogue Support System (CATSS) is presented in some detail. Special facilities and cost figures are briefly noted. Future plans involve the implementation of decentralized minicomputer-based systems.

186. Williams, Martha E. **"Networks for On-Line Data Base Access."** *Journal of the American Society for Information Science* 28 (September 1977): 247-53.

Provides a general discussion of networks and why networks are necessary for online searching. Further describes the uses of online systems, including retrospective searching, current awareness, and bibliometric studies, and lists the physical and personnel requirements for online search service. Advantages and costs of online searching are also discussed.

187. Williams, Martha E. and Sandra H. Rouse. **"On-Line Use of Databases in Illinois."** *Illinois Libraries* 60 (April 1978): 429-35.

Presents an overview of the use of online search services in Illinois in 1978. Conclusions are based on a survey of organizations belonging to the Chicago OnLine Users Group (COLUG). Statistics are given for number of searches, fees charged, types of users, staffing, and search services used. The general impact of online searching on other library services is also discussed.

188. Woods, Richard. **"The Washington Library Network Computer System."** *Online Review* 3 (September 1979): 297-330.

Provides an overview of the Washington Library Network Computer System. The historical development and rapid growth of this automated library system are documented. System features and applications are discussed. The online union catalog and COM catalog capabilities are cited as particularly valuable features.

HISTORY OF ONLINE SEARCHING AND FUTURE TRENDS

An awareness of the historical development of computerized information retrieval is useful in understanding both the present state of the art and potential future applications of online searching. Factors affecting future developments and their possible impact on librarianship must also be considered.

Related sections in this bibliography include:

Commercial Search Services (Entries 12-32)
Databases and Database Producers (Entries 49-67)
General and Miscellaneous (Entries 157-188)

189. Bezilla, Robert. **"Online Messages, Files, Text and Publishing."** *Online* 6 (March 1982): 51-55.

Describes present and future applications of "electronic information exchange" technologies. Specific examples are demonstrated using the Electronic Information Exchange Service (EIES) of the Computerized Conferencing and Communications Center of the New Jersey Institute of Technology. Current users are identified and problems caused by this new technology for both the information industry and the general public are identified. Concludes that the potential opportunities "seem well worth the effort."

190. Bourne, Charles P. **"On-line Systems: History, Technology, and Economics."** *Journal of the American Society for Information Science* 31 (May 1980): 155-60.

Provides a historical overview of the development of computerized information retrieval. The early need for low-cost telecommunications and time-shared computers is documented. Brief backgrounds are provided for the major commercial search services. The economics of online services is discussed in detail. Pricing practices and future trends are identified.

191. Clayton, Audrey. **"Factors Affecting Future Online Services."** *Online Review* 5 (August 1981): 287-300.

Predicts the impact various social, economic, and political factors will have on users and providers of online services. Distinguishes between situational factors (i.e., system momentum, technological influences, and impacts upon areas of user concern) and environmental factors (i.e., reactive policies and exogenous factors). Examples of these influences are presented. Offers little hope that "integration and interconnection" of online systems will occur.

192. Cochrane, Pauline. **"Improving the Quality of Information Retrieval Online to a Library Catalog or Other Access Service ... or ... Where Do We Go from Here?"** *Online* 5 (July 1981): 30-42.

Predicts significant changes in information retrieval in the 1980s. Suggests that by 1985 a majority of users of online systems will be end users and will not "be using the assistance of an information professional." Emphasis of the information industry will be on the home market. Changes to improve the quality of information retrieval are proposed and the importance of search strategy is emphasized.

193. Cuadra, Carlos A. **"Commercially Funded On-Line Retrieval Services—Past, Present and Future."** *Aslib Proceedings* 30 (January 1978): 2-15.

Presents a historical overview of commercial search services and makes various predictions about their role in information retrieval in the future. A general description of online searching and the kinds of databases and search services available is given and the phenomenal growth of such services documented. Notes that the future will be "more of the same," with more emphasis given to quality service and added services. An "On-Line KWIC Index" is given as an example of possible system improvements.

194. Cuadra, Carlos A. **"On-Line Systems: Promises and Pitfalls."** *Journal of the American Society for Information Science* 22 (March-April 1971): 107-114.

Provides a historical overview of the development of online systems up to 1970. Advantages and disadvantages of online systems are discussed. Problems identified are in the areas of time-sharing, interface, and user acceptance. Notes that organizational changes and not technical advances are needed to dramatically increase use of online systems.

195. Doszkocs, Tamas E.; Barbara A. Rapp; and Harold M. Schoolman. **"Automated Information Retrieval in Science and Technology."** *Science* 208 (April 4, 1980): 25-30.

Describes the rapid development of online bibliographic databases in the 1970s. Statistics are presented for databases available, and the NLM databases are summarized in some detail. Examples from various databases and search services are presented. Future development of "knowledge bases" is predicted. Limited use of online searching is blamed on lack of public awareness, uneven quality of searches and searchers, and the use of intermediaries to perform the search.

196. Gardner, Jeffrey J. and David M. Max. **"Online Bibliographic Services."** *Library Journal* 102 (September 15, 1976): 1827-32.

Summarizes the history and development of online search services. Particular attention is paid to the governmental and commercial involvement in a process which should have more library input. Problems frequently encountered by libraries in offering online services are presented. Notes that online searching is one of the "fastest growing services in academic and research libraries" and predicts that this growth will continue.

197. Hawkins, Donald. **"Bibliometrics of the Online Information Retrieval Literature."** *Online Review* 2 (December 1978): 345-52.

Studies the bibliographic characteristics of the professional literature dealing with online information retrieval. Notes that the amount of citations grew rapidly between 1964 and 1975, with the fastest growth occurring between 1974 and 1975. Relevant articles are found to be widely dispersed among a variety of journals. Nineteen journals which included more than five articles are identified.

198.   Josephine, Helen B. **"Electronic Mail: The Future Is Now."** *Online* 4 (October 1980): 41-43.
Examines various electronic message systems and suggests ways they can be used in libraries and information centers. Descriptions of some systems currently available are given, and potential uses for document delivery and information transfer are discussed. In selecting an electronic message system, it is important to consider "who makes up the network, and secondarily, how versatile the system is."

199.   Kiechel, W. **"Everything You Always Wanted to Know May Soon Be Online."** *Fortune* 101 (May 5, 1980): 226-28.
Discusses the various companies, including numerous book publishers, that are entering a "new industry" developing around the creation and marketing of large databases. Distinguishes between online information retrieval and bibliographic databases. Major commercial search services and some individual databases are presented as examples of this new business trend.

200.   Lancaster, F. W. and Linda C. Smith. **"On-line Systems in the Communication Process: Projections."** *Journal of the American Society for Information Science* 31 (May 1980): 193-200.
Analyzes the role of online systems within the entire communication process. Implications for publishers, librarians, library administrators, and library educators are discussed. Labels online systems as "value-added information sources" and provides various examples. Future developments are predicted. Concludes that the "librarian of the electronic age should be more valuable and more valued than the librarian of today."

201.   Lindguist, Mats G. **"An Explanation of the Coming Stagnation of Information Services."** *Online Review* 1 (June 1977): 109-116.
Analyzes the potential future market for online search service retailers, labeled "information search services (ISS)." States that the expected long-range growth of these services has been greatly overestimated. It is also possible that immediate expansion of these ISSs will be much less than expected. Notes that this decline in growth rate is not inevitable, but quite likely.

202.   Nielsen, Brian. **"Online Bibliographic Searching and the Deprofessionalization of Librarianship."** *Online Review* 4 (September 1980): 215-24.
Examines sociological theories that predict deprofessionalization of some professions, possibly librarianship, because of technological advances, especially in the area of computerization. Various survey results are cited to partially refute these ideas and to demonstrate that online searching may actually be "status-enhancing." However, the long-range outlook for librarianship is debatable. Continuing technological advances and increased end user interaction will greatly affect the role of librarians in the future.

203.   Nyren, Karl. **"The Online Revolution in Libraries."** *Library Journal* 103 (February 1978): 439-41.
Reports on the three-day conference on "The Online Revolution in Libraries" held at the University of Pittsburgh in November 1977. Summaries of presentations on the following topics are included: 1) fees; 2) "stewardship of the revolution"; 3) role of the

intermediary; and 4) repositioning of library resources. Other issues raised and reactions to them are also noted.

204. Rogers, Frank B. **"Computerized Bibliographic Retrieval Systems."** *Library Trends* 23 (July 1974): 73-78.

Provides a historical overview of the development of online services and their use in the National Library of Medicine. The background of MEDLARS is presented and its decentralization beginning in 1965 is noted. Other databases and search services available in 1974 are briefly mentioned. Typical questions received and the impact of online searching on medical libraries are also given.

205. Williams, Martha E. **"Data Bases—A History of Developments and Trends from 1966 through 1975."** *Journal of the American Society for Information Science* 28 (March 1977): 71-78.

Recounts the changes and developments in databases from 1966 through 1975. Brief comments and general statistics are given for such factors as number and size of databases, number of searches and users, funding sources, subject coverage, retrospective coverage, standards, file design, and networking. Examples of ongoing research and prospects for the future are also presented.

206. Williams, Martha E. **"Online Problems: Research Today, Solutions Tomorrow."** *Bulletin of the American Society for Information Science* 3 (April 1977): 14-16.

Details trends in database development and information retrieval. Five problems caused by the expansion of database use are noted: 1) economic problems; 2) legal problems; 3) document delivery problems; 4) education/training/familiarization problems; and 5) standardization problems. Research aimed at solving these and other problems is identified. Stresses the need to "progress beyond the state of the art and into the next generation of on-line retrieval systems."

207. Williams, Martha E. **"Online Retrieval—Today and tomorrow."** *Online Review* 2 (December 1978): 353-66.

Projects the future of online retrieval. The following factors are identified and discussed: 1) technological developments; 2) financial considerations; and 3) political, legal, and psychological restrictions. Advocates research into the development of "transparent systems" for information retrieval and notes that eventually consideration must be given to "fact retrieval" and then to "knowledge retrieval."

IMPACT OF ONLINE SEARCHING

Online searching has a tremendous impact not only on the library, but also on the users of the information retrieved. Changes in how researchers use the library after being exposed to online searching have been noted, and the "migration" from print indexes to online sources is an issue of great concern to index publishers.

Related sections in this bibliography include:

Academic Libraries and Online Searching (Entries 1-11)
Economics of Online Searching (Entries 94-112)
History of Online Searching and Future Trends (Entries 189-207)
Public Libraries and Online Searching (Entries 267-278)
Special Libraries and Online Searching (Entries 368-374)

208. Baldinger, Esther L.; Jennifer P. S. Nakeff-Plaat; and Margaret S. Cummings. **"An Experimental Study of the Feasibility of Substituting Chemical Abstracts On-Line for the Printed Copy in a Medium-Sized Medical Library."** *Bulletin of the Medical Library Association* 69 (April 1981): 247-51.

Reports the results of an experiment conducted in the Washington University School of Medicine Library to determine if the online version of *Chemical Abstracts* could be substituted for the printed index. All patrons using the printed index for a 13-week period were offered free online searches. Only 39.6% of them accepted a computerized search, and 62% of these indicated they planned on also using the printed index. Concludes that no substitution for the printed index was feasible with this group of users.

209. Bayer, Alan E. and Gerald Jahoda. **"Effects of Online Bibliographic Searching on Scientists' Information Style."** *Online Review* 5 (August 1981): 323-33.

Describes a study conducted to investigate the effect that access to online searching by both academic and industrial researchers has on the use of traditional print sources. Reports that there was "generally no consistent effect of online searching on the time spent in other information dissemination and gathering activities." However, online users utilized librarians more than they had previously. Various findings are statistically analyzed and presented in tables.

210. Blick, A. R. and D. S. Mogrill. **"Effect of the Introduction of Online Facilities on the Choice of Search Tools."** *Information Scientist* 12 (March 1978): 25-31.

Compares the use of print search tools by information scientists in the Brockham Park information unit of Beecham Pharmaceuticals Research Division before and after online searching was made available. Notes that the introduction of online searching resulted in "substantial changes in the choice of search tools in the information unit." The search process was also completed faster, and researchers used online databases instead of print equivalents when they were available. Concludes that print indexes, such as *Index Medicus*, will "become of questionable value."

211. Childs, Susan and Michael Carmel. **"Effect of Online Services on Purchases of a Printed Index."** *Aslib Proceedings* 33 (September 1981): 351-56.

Analyzes the impact online access to MEDLINE has on the use and need for the print *Index Medicus*. A survey was conducted of 20 post-graduate medical libraries in Great Britain. Results indicate substantial increase in the use of the printed index as more searches are conducted online on MEDLINE. Concludes that, instead of lessening the need for *Index Medicus*, the availability of MEDLINE has "had a positive effect on its use."

212. Cogswell, James A. **"On-Line Search Services: Implications for Libraries and Library Users."** *College and Research Libraries* 39 (July 1978): 275-80.

Analyzes the impact online searching services has on both libraries and users. Specific examples are given from the experiences of the University of Pennsylvania's Van Pelt Library. Library users are found to be increasingly willing to pay for such services and to be more aware of the difficulties in providing information. Libraries must face the issues of rising costs and user fees. A trend in academic libraries toward more personalized and individualized service is noted.

213. Doll, Russell. **"Information Technology and Its Socio-Economic and Academic Impact."** *Online Review* 5 (February 1981): 37-46.

Offers a theoretical discussion of the impact information technology may have on society, with special emphasis on changes in library and academic settings. Distinguishes between manifest and latent functions and presents examples. Both general applications of information technology and specific uses of online searching are described. Development of a "technologically trained elite" will have a significant effect on library schools and education in general.

214.   Hawkins, Donald. **"Impact of On-Line Systems on a Literature Searching Service."** *Special Libraries* 67 (December 1976): 559-67.
  Recounts experiences in using online searching during 1975 in the Bell Laboratories Libraries and Information Systems Center. Search statistics and database costs are analyzed and presented in charts and graphs. The following advantages of online searching are given: completeness, modest cost, speed, expanded resources, print copies of results, Boolean logic capabilities, and increased productivity.

215.   Jahoda, Gerald. **"Comparison of On-Line Bibliographic Searches in One Academic and One Industrial Organization."** *RQ* 18 (Fall 1978): 42-49.
  Reports the results of an experiment funded by the National Science Foundation to investigate "what changes occur in the information-gathering habits of scientists (specifically chemists) when a technological innovation — on-line searching of bibliographic data bases — is introduced and made available to them." Free and subsidized searches were conducted for researchers at the Florida State University Chemistry Department and the Monsanto Textiles Company. Search characteristics, problems encountered, users' opinions, and differences between academic and industrial users are statistically presented.

216.   Lancaster, F. W. and Herbert Goldhor. **"The Impact of Online Services on Subscriptions to Printed Publications."** *Online Review* 5 (August 1981): 301-311.
  Discusses the results of a survey sent to 200 libraries (50 large university, 50 smaller university, 50 U.S. government special libraries, and 50 private industry special libraries) to investigate the effect of online availability on subscriptions to corresponding print indexes. Although many cancellations were reported, few were directly attributed to online access. Reasons for this are presented, and the relatively little effect of online access to cancellation decisions is emphasized.

217.   Nitecki, Danuta A. **"Attitudes toward Automated Information Retrieval Services among RASD Members."** *RQ* 16 (Winter 1976): 133-41.
  Reports the results of a survey sent to a sampling of ALA Reference and Adult Service Division members in 1975 to determine their attitudes toward automated information retrieval services. The methodology and objectives are summarized. Characteristics of respondents are presented, and opinions concerning their libraries' involvement in automated information retrieval are discussed and statistically given in tables. Potential barriers are also identified.

218.   Pfaffenberger, Ann and Sandy Echt. **"Substitution of SciSearch and Social SciSearch for Their Print Versions in an Academic Library."** *Database* 3 (March 1980): 63-71.
  Details a study conducted at the Mary Couts Burnett Library at Texas Christian University which measured the use of *Science Citation Index* and *Social Science Citation Index* for six months and then free computer searches were provided for the last three months. *Science Citation Index* was found to be searched almost exclusively by citation, but patrons used a subject approach for *Social Science Citation Index*. Projected costs and user satisfaction are detailed in tables. As a result of this study, the library maintained a

subscription to the print *Social Science Citation Index*, but went online with SCISEARCH. Evaluation form and sample log sheet are appended.

219. Seba, Douglas B. and Beth M. Forrest. **"Using SDI's to Get Primary Journals – A New Online Way."** *Online* 2 (January 1978): 10-15.
Demonstrates how the results of SDI searches can be used to evaluate the relevancy of a library's periodical collection. Search profiles were developed and run retrospectively and limited by update periods. Results were statistically analyzed using a formula to determine relevancy. Possible savings from cancelling subscriptions to journals identified and a potential "purchasing model" are described.

220. Trubkin, Loene. **"Migration from Print to Online Use."** *Online Review* 4 (March 1980): 5-12.
Considers the potential problem of "migration" from the use of print indexes to the use of online databases. Economic consequences for publishers are examined. Notes that publishers will probably continue to experiment with different types of charges for online use. Reports results of surveys, conducted periodically by Data Courier, of its subscribers. Inflation, new technology, and database enhancements are also cited as causes of price changes.

221. Williams, Martha E. **"The Impact of Machine-Readable Data Bases on Library and Information Services."** *Information Processing and Management* 13 (1977): 95-107.
Provides a general overview of the impact online search services have and will have on libraries. Growth and development of databases, technical apsects, database characteristics, and search services are briefly summarized. The potential of the National Program for Library and Information Service, proposed by the National Commission on Library and Information Science (NCLIS), is emphasized.

INFORMATIONAL INTERVIEW

It is essential that a thorough informational interview be conducted prior to undertaking an online search. The search analyst must communicate effectively with the requester and determine precisely what information is desired. The postsearch interview is also important in completing the entire search process.
Related sections in this bibliography include:

Search Analysts (Entries 296-308)
Search Strategies (Entries 321-340)
Search Results (Entries 309-320)

222. Auster, E. and S. B. Lawton. **"Negotiation Process in Online Bibliographic Retrieval."** *Canadian Journal of Information Science* 4 (December 1979): 86-98.
Reviews the traits of a good reference interview and adapts certain points in developing a proposed model for the informational interview conducted prior to an online search. A review of the literature related to reference interviews is used to describe the normal "structure of negotiations," and various findings regarding nonverbal behavior and role relationships are applied to the informational interview process.

223. Dommer, Jan M. and M. Dawn McCaghy. **"Techniques for Conducting Effective Search Interviews with Thesis and Dissertation Candidates."** *Online* 6 (March 1982): 44-47.

Stresses the importance of performing a thorough informational interview before conducting an online search. This is especially true when dealing with thesis and dissertation candidates. Interview techniques and suggestions are presented for two broad categories: user education and search strategy. Stages of a thesis proposal are identified and appropriate types of online searches discussed.

224. Kolner, Stuart J. **"Improving the MEDLARS Search Interview: A Checklist Approach."** *Bulletin of the Medical Library Association* 69 (January 1981): 26-33.

Provides checklists for both the pre- and postsearch interviews. Reviews literature on the search interview and distinguishes between two approaches: "Flow chart analyses" and "guided practice." Since the former relies on nonverbal cues, it is rejected. The latter is recommended when a checklist of items to be covered in the interview is followed. Screening topics for appropriateness, completing a request form, and analyzing the request are also discussed.

225. Knapp, Sara D. **"The Reference Interview in the Computer-Based Setting."** *RQ* 4 (Summer 1978): 320-24.

Notes that the informational interview conducted prior to performing an online search is "not radically different from interviewing at the reference desk." Suggestions are made to improve the communication between the requester and the search analysts. The presense of the requester when the search is conducted online is recommended. Effective communication and analytical skills are prerequisites for a good informational interview.

226. Knox, Douglas R. and Marjorie M. K. Hlava. **"Effective Search Strategies."** *Online Review* 3 (June 1979): 148-52.

Outlines three steps to be used in conducting an informational interview to allow the requester to define the topic properly: 1) discuss the general topic of the search; 2) explain relevant search aids and the use of descriptors; and 3) formulate a tentative search strategy. A sample search is formulated utilizing these steps. Stresses the need to "work closely with the researcher."

227. Markey, Karen. **"Levels of Question Formulation in Negotiation of Information Need during the Online Presearch Interview: A Proposed Model."** *Information Processing and Management* 17 (1981): 215-25.

Analyzes the presearch interview as it differs from the normal question negotiation involved in the reference process. Considers the applicability of R. S. Taylor's theory of question formulation and concludes that an alternative model is needed to describe the procedures involved in question negotiation in the online presearch interview. Such a model is proposed, and tests to judge its validity are demonstrated.

228. Somerville, Arleen N. **"The Place of the Reference Interview in Computer Searching: The Academic Setting."** *Online* 1 (October 1977): 14-23.

Lists the components of the basic information interview conducted prior to doing an online search. Discusses 10 basic points to be covered and provides a step-by-step approach. Stresses the need for a postsearch interview. Dialogue from a hypothetical interview is presented and a list of "Do's and Don'ts" is appended.

229. Somerville, Arleen N. **"The Pre-Search Reference Interview—A Step by Step Guide."** *Database* 5 (February 1982): 32-38.

Reviews the steps necessary in performing an effective interview prior to conducting an online search. Distinguishes between the presearch interview needed for new or infrequent users, experienced requesters, and when the patron is going to be present when the search is executed. Elements common to all presearch interviews are also enumerated. Discusses various factors which affect the content of the interview and provides examples of searches that have been "adversely affected" by poor interviews. Concludes with a list of "Do's and Don'ts."

MANUAL VERSUS ONLINE SEARCHING

Comparisons are often made between manual and online searches for information of the same topic. However, no definitive conclusions are typically drawn because of the many variables involved in such comparisons. Articles generally comparing manual and online searches are included in this section, but articles comparing approaches within specific subject areas appear in the appropriate section of the "Specialized Subject Areas or Databases" portion of this bibliography.

Related sections in this bibliography include:

Impact of Online Searching (Entries 208-221)

230. Bivans, Margaret M. **"A Comparison of Manual and Machine Literature Searches."** *Special Libraries* 65 (May/June 1974): 216-22.

Compares manual and online searches. Six topics were investigated, and manual searches were found to be very time-consuming and to require persons with subject backgrounds. Online searches were much quicker, but retrieved a higher degree of unrelated items. Nevertheless, online searches are recommended, especially when qualified searchers are unavailable to perform manual searches.

231. Datta, V. **"Coverage of Specialized Biological Information by On-Line Databases and Comparison of the Coverage with an In-House Manual System of a Special Library/Information Unit."** *Program* 12 (April 1978): 55-63.

Compares the coverage of specialized biological information, specifically the field of vegetable insecticides, by three databases (AGRICOLA, BIOSIS, AND CHEMCON) and an in-house manual system. Search terms are listed and the number of items retrieved from each source given. Total number of relevant citations and the overlap between both the online databases and the online and manual searches are presented. Concludes that online searches cover the field "much more extensively from the subject, geographical and language point of view."

232. East, H. **"Comparative Cost of Manual and Online Bibliographic Searching: A Review of the Literature."** *Journal of Information Science* 2 (1980): 101-109.

Reviews published studies which compare the cost of manual and online searches. Most research indicates that the costs are approximately equal, although difficulties in making valid comparisons are typically enumerated. Many published reports predict future reductions in telecommunications and hardware, but also expect increases in database royalties to eliminate any real decrease in cost to users. Notes that the effectiveness of manual and online searching depends on a wide range of factors that are not easily controlled.

233. Elchesen, Dennis R. **"Cost-Effectiveness Comparison of Manual and On-Line Retrospective Bibliographic Searching."** *Journal of the American Society for Information Science* 29 (March 1978): 56-66.

Presents the results of a study to compare the cost-effectiveness of manual and online bibliographic searching. Forty topics were searched in seven print indexes and their corresponding databases available on SDC. Analyzes costs for a variety of factors, including labor, equipment, and telecommunications. Concludes online searching is faster, less expensive, and generally more effective. However, manual searches offer some advantages in precision and turn-around time.

234. Elman, Stanley A. **"Cost Comparisons of Manual and On-Line Computerized Literature Searching."** *Special Libraries* 66 (January 1975): 12-18.

Attempts to statistically compare the time and costs involved in conducting manual and online literature searches. A formula is used which combines all online cost factors (e.g., labor, telephone, second service, equipment, and citations) into one figure. Cost figures are presented in charts and compared. Concludes that DIALOG online searching is both cost-effective and efficient.

235. Flynn, T.; P. A. Holohan; M. S. Magson; and J. D. Munro. **"Cost Effectiveness Comparison of Online and Manual Bibliographic Information Retrieval."** *Journal of Information Science* 1 (May 1979): 77-84.

Presents a model designed to be used to measure the cost-effectiveness of online searching. Cost components are identified and methods of collecting the data explained. Statistical formulae are given to analyze the various cost elements. Concludes that online searching is "considerably more cost-effective than traditional library manual searching, and online searching also offers many additional qualitative advantages."

236. Johnston, Susan M. and D. E. Gray. **"Comparison of Manual and Online Retrospective Searching for Agricultural Subjects."** *Aslib Proceedings* 29 (July 1977): 253-58.

Investigates differences between online and manual searches of the same topics. Searches were performed by the British Ministry of Agriculture, Fisheries and Food on a variety of databases and equivalent print indexes. Finds that online searches took one-sixth of the staff time required for identical manual searches and costs were almost equal. Manual searches are more precise, but have lower relative recall. Differences in access points partially account for conflicting results between manual and online searches.

237. de Jong-Hofman, M. W. **"Comparison of Selecting, Abstracting and Indexing by COMPENDEX, INSPEC and PASCAL and the Impact of This on Manual and Automated Retrieval of Information."** *Online Review* 5 (February 1981): 25-36.

Compares the indexing and abstracting of the same journal by COMPENDEX, INSPEC, and PASCAL. First identifies articles on one topic in various volumes of one journal indexed by all three databases, then searches both manually and online. Selection and indexing were found to differ widely. Results are statistically presented in tables and Venn diagrams. Concludes that "the manual search appears more trustworthy."

238. de Jong-Hofman, M. W. **"Research into the Practical Results of On-Line Retrieval: An Extensive Analysis."** *Aslib Proceedings* 29 (May 1977): 197-208.

Considers the effect indexing procedures has on both manual and online searching. Two factors have the greatest impact on retrieval: 1) selection process of index terms by indexers and 2) degree of conformity applied to indexing similar articles. Performs two extensive searches manually and online, and statistically analyzes the items retrieved. Concludes that the "practical efficiency" of assigned key words is very low.

239. Kochen, Manfred; Victoria Reich; and Lee Cohen. **"Influence of Online Bibliographic Services on Student Behavior."** *Journal of the American Society for Information Science* 32 (November 1981): 412-20.

Reports the results of an experiment conducted in 1979 in which graduate education students were asked to compile a bibliography on assigned topics. Half of the students received assistance in using ERIC manually and half were provided free online searches. The online group spent less time, but questioned the completeness of the search and also felt they had learned less about conducting research. Concludes that online searches will not make a "major difference" in scholarly production.

240. Santadonato, Joseph. **"A Comparison of Online and Manual Modes in Searching Chemical Abstracts for Specific Compounds."** *Journal of Chemical Information & Computer Sciences* 16 (August 1976): 135-37.

Compares manual searching of *Chemical Abstracts* with online searching of CA CONDENSATES and the CBA (Chemical-Biological Activities) database available through the National Library of Medicine's TOXLINE system. Maximum retrieval is achieved by manual searching when the search requires broad coverage of a specific compound. Concludes that "major reliance" will continue to be placed on manual retrieval of information.

241. Smith, Roger Grant. **"Compare Retrieval Systems."** *Online* 1 (April 1977): 26-27, 51-59.

Presents a step-by-step method for comparing a manual retrieval system and its online version. Seven criteria were used to evaluate each retrieval process: 1) coverage; 2) recall; 3) precision; 4) response time; 5) user effort; 6) form of output; and 7) cost. Presents actual figures compiled in an evaluation of a database used in the Patent Information Center of Merck & Co., Inc. Describes how to interpret the results.

MULTIPLE DATABASE SEARCHING

More and more online searches involve the use of more than one database. Such multiple database searches require knowledge of the databases available and an understanding of the differences involved in their use on the various commercial search services.

Related sections in this bibliography include:

Databases and Database Producers (Entries 49-67)
Search Strategies (Entries 321-240)

242. Angier, Jennifer J. and Barbara A. Epstein. **"Multi-Database Searching in the Behavioral Sciences; Part 1: Basic Techniques and Core Databases."** *Database* 3 (September 1980): 9-15.

Concentrates on the basic search techniques used in searching the major databases in the behavioral sciences. PSYCHOLOGICAL ABSTRACTS and SOCIAL SCIENCE CITATION INDEX are judged to be the "two top titles," but significant differences in their currency and access points are noted. Topics dealing with social aspects of psychology are best searched in SOCIOLOGICAL ABSTRACTS, while subjects more oriented to the "physical" side of psychology (e.g., biofeedback) should be searched in BIOSIS, MEDLINE, and EXCERPTA MEDICA. ERIC is not considered a major psychological source. (See also #243.)

243.   Angier, Jennifer J. and Barbara A. Epstein. **"Multi-Database Searching in the Behavioral Sciences; Part 2: Special Applications."** *Database* 3 (December 1980): 34-40.
Stresses the importance of multiple database searching in the behavioral sciences. Discusses various special purpose databases which cover a broad range of subject areas (e.g., NTIS and numerous audiovisual files). Interdisciplinary searches for behavioral science materials in the humanities, business, and physical science are also summarized. Emphasizes the necessity of searching more than one database for most behavioral topics. Popular databases (e.g., MAGAZINE INDEX) and their usefulness in retrieving behavioral sciences information are also reviewed. (See also #242.)

244.   Brand, Alice A. **"Searching Multiple Indexes and Databases in the Behavioral Sciences: Which and How Many?"** *Behavioral & Social Sciences Librarian* 1 (Winter 1979): 105-112.
Presents a theoretical discussion of the "behavioral sciences as an abstract system." Applies this to the two problems of analyzing a search request and selecting appropriate databases. Five steps are identified: 1) determine the interdisciplinary nature of the user's question; 2) determine the comprehensiveness of the user's needs; 3) determine the type of material relevant to the user's request; 4) determine the currentness of the literature relevant to the user's request; and 5) analyze the efficiency of the search.

245.   Conger, Lucinda D. **"A Comparison of Basic Index Fields in Multiple System Searching."** *Online* 4 (July 1980): 25-30.
Presents a chart detailing differences in the basic index fields of the major commercial search services. Databases are listed alphabetically and content of the basic index fields noted for all commercial search services providing access to the file. General differences between DIALOG, SDC, and BRS are also briefly noted.

246.   Evans, John Edward. **"Database Selection in an Academic Library: Are Those Big Multi-File Searches Really Necessary."** *Online* 4 (April 1980): 35-43.
Questions the value of multiple database use and presents statistical analysis of retrieved references to demonstrate that in many cases searching a single database may be sufficient. Advocates the concept of the "principle database," the searching of the one database identified as the best source. Implications for service procedures and database selection policy are noted. Argues against a policy of "uninhibited database selection."

247.   Hawkins, Donald T. **"Multiple Database Searching: Techniques and Pitfalls."** *Online* 2 (April 1978): 9-15.
Investigates the need for multiple database searches and presents suggestions for both selecting databases and performing the searches. Problems encountered include indexing differences and required variations in search strategies. Variant spellings and chemical formulae are cited as other problem areas. A list of "Do's and Don'ts" is included.

248.   Onorato, E. S. and G. Bianchi. **"Automatic Identification of Duplicates after Multidatabase Online Searching."** *Online Review* 5 (December 1981): 445-51.
Examines the need and practicality of identifying and eliminating duplicates retrieved as a result of multidatabase searches. Several rationales for not eliminating duplicates are

noted, but practical needs to merge retrieved references are also presented. The technical feasibility of using a host computer to automatically identify and eliminate duplicates is explained. Such a system could also provide an online editing capability.

249. Wanger, Judith. **"Multiple Database Use: The Challenge of the Database Selection Process."** *Online* 1 (October 1977): 35-47.

Addresses the problems inherent in trying to determine which of many available databases is the best suited for a particular topic. Identifying potential databases as either primary or secondary sources is generally the first step in database selection. Then primary databases are evaluated concerning subject coverage, source document coverage, and searchable and printable elements. An outline of the basic search strategy process is appended.

NUMERIC AND NONBIBLIOGRAPHIC DATABASES

Nonbibliographic and numeric databases are becoming increasingly available from the major commercial search services. These databases have most commonly dealt with business, economic, scientific, or statistical information, but as more reference sources, e.g., *Encyclopedia of Associations*, become available online, nonbibliographic databases will play a significantly more important role in online searching. General articles are included in this section, but articles dealing with a specific nonbibliographic database or with such databases available in a certain field are included in the appropriate section in the "Specialized Subject Areas or Databases" portion of this bibliography.

Related sections in this bibliography include:

Databases and Database Producers (Entries 49-67)

250. Cronin, Blaise. **"Databanks."** *Aslib Proceedings* 33 (June 1981): 243-50.

Stresses the growing importance of nonbibliographic databases. Distinguishes between "reference databases" (bibliographical) and "source databases" (numerical or factual). Differences between the two are discussed and methods of evaluating nonbibliographic databases are also summarized. Urges more evaluative studies be conducted and that nonbibliographic searching be emphasized more in library schools.

251. Cubillas, Mary M. **"Nonbibliographic Databases in a Corporate Health, Safety and Environment Organization."** *Special Libraries* 72 (July 1981): 243-48.

Describes nonbibliographic databases used in Shell Oil Company's Health, Safety and Environment Organization. Systems described include TOXIN, CHEMFILE, the Product Profile Information System (PPIS) and the Health Surveillance System (HSS). Composition of the various files is briefly presented. Notes that such nonbibliographic databases are very important components of the overall search operations.

252. Fried, John E.; James A. Luedke; Stephen A. Rubin; and Helen C. Pestel. **"Numeric Databases."** See *Online* volume 1, #3 and #4.

Discusses numeric database systems. Only included as a column in two issues of *Online*.

253. Hawkins, Donald T. **"The ManLab—NPL Materials Databank."** *Online* 3 (April 1979): 40-52.

Describes ManLab—NPL Materials Data Bank, a highly specialized numeric database useful to chemists and metallurgists. A detailed subject knowledge of thermodynamics is "crucial" in the utilization of this database and, consequently, thermodynamics is generally discussed before the applications of the database are presented. The value of the file as a source of thermodynamics information is stressed.

254. Luedke, James A., Jr. **"Numerical Data Bases On-line."** *On-Line Review* 1 (September 1977): 207-215.

Estimates the number of numeric databases available in 1977. Databases are grouped according to accessibility (e.g., online, batch, and remotely accessible) and availability (e.g., public, restricted, and in-house). Notes the need for more extensive user training. Except for the general business and financial databases, few users exist for most numeric files. Predicts future expansion in the availability and use of numeric databases.

255. Mignon, Edmond. **"Numeric Data Bases in the Professional Librarianship Curriculum: Implications for Behavioral and Social Sciences Librarians."** *Behavioral & Social Sciences Librarian* 1 (Spring 1980): 181-87.

Describes a course dealing with numeric databases developed and offered by the University of Washington School of Librarianship. The relationship between these files and bibliographic databases is stressed. The course concentrates on socioeconomic databases, and four types of search exercises are identified: 1) convenience search; 2) aggregate search; 3) reorganized data search; and 4) cross-tabulation tables. Importance of numeric databases in the social sciences is emphasized.

256. **"Nonbibliographic Databases Online."** See issues of *Online Review* beginning with volume 1, #4.

Covers nonbibliographic databases. Name of the database, database producer, subject area, and online vendor are indicated for each database listed in this irregular column in *Online Review*.

257. Tyzenhouse, Joanne. **"Econometric and Statistical Bases for the Non-Econometrician."** *Online* 2 (April 1978): 48-54.

Describes the nonbibliographic business databases available from four major suppliers: 1) Data Resources Inc.; 2) General Electric Information Services Division; 3) Interactive Data Corporation; and 4) Predicasts. Sample searches are presented from each and general comparisons made. The reluctance of some librarians to use nonbibliographic databases is recognized.

258. Tyzenhouse, Joanne. **"The Pleasures and Pitfalls of the Predicasts Computational System."** *Online* 4 (January 1980): 26-29.

Evaluates the Predicasts Computational System available on four DIALOG files in 1980. The lack of comprehensive statistics and the availability of much of the information in standard print sources (e.g., *Statistical Abstract of the U.S.*) are cited as examples as why the "system falls far short of expectations." Three actual search examples are presented to demonstrate how the system works and what it can do. Urges Predicast to expand the coverage and content of these statistical databases.

259. Wanger, Judith. **"Introduction to Non-Bibliographic Online Databases."** *Law Library Journal* 73 (February 1980): 871-80.

Provides an overview of nonbibliographic databases, especially as they can be used by law librarians. Distinguishes between "reference databases" and "source databases" and indicates their general availability from the major commercial search services. Output from numeric files is described and examples given. Stresses the "challenges posed by non-bibliographic databases" and urges librarians to become more familiar with them.

260.   Wanger, Judith and R. N. Landau. **"Nonbibliographic On-Line Data Base Services."** *Journal of the American Society for Information Science* 31 (May 1980): 171-80.

Notes that the majority of databases available are actually nonbibliographic. An overview of the types and sources of these nonbibliographic databases is provided. Databases available in business, economics, science, and technology are specifically identified. Two major questions are addressed concerning nonbibliographic databases: 1) who should use them? and 2) what part should they play in library and information services?

PROMOTION AND MARKETING OF
ONLINE SEARCH SERVICES

Online search services must be publicized and promoted to ensure their use. Traditional public relations techniques need to be adapted to market online services. The importance of online demonstrations and a visible terminal are typically stressed.

Related sections in this bibliography include:

Impact of Online Searching (Entries 208-221)
Search Analysts (Entries 296-308)
Setting Up and Managing an Online Search Service (Entries 345-367)

261.   Crane, Nancy B. and David M. Pilachowski. **"Introducing Online Bibliographic Service to Its Users: The Online Presentation."** *Online* 2 (October 1978): 20-29.

Outlines a presentation designed to introduce online searching to new user groups. The actual program is summarized and suggestions for choosing sample search topics are provided. Examples of graphic materials and handouts are included. A list of "Do's and Don'ts" and a "Summary of Steps" are appended.

262.   Elias, Art. **"Marketing for Online Bibliographic Services."** *Online Review* 3 (March 1979): 107-117.

Uses the marketing of BIOSIS *Previews* by BioSciences Information Service (BIOSIS) to examine the overall marketing of online bibliographic products within the information retrieval industry. Diagrams various multilevel marketing structures and summarizes some of the basic market conditions. Distribution and extent of organizations, institutions, and individuals using online services are discussed. Suggests that other database producers should "share useful marketing characteristics that all can utilize."

263.   Ferguson, Douglas. **"Marketing Online Services in the University."** *Online* 1 (July 1977): 15-23.

Identifies the need to "market" online services; outlines various promotional methods for introducing computer searching in a large university. Stresses the need to first analyze what the benefits actually are and what potential groups of users exists. Posters, personalized approaches, and brochures are cited as examples of effective publicity. Notes that pricing and user fees are an important aspect of any successful marketing of online services.

264.   Jankowski, Terry Ann. **"Use of Thermal Image Film for Demonstrations of Computer-Assisted Searching."** *Bulletin of the Medical Library Association* 67 (April 1979): 254-55.

Describes a method of using thermal image film with a standard thermal-printing terminal to produce instant transparencies for use in a large demonstration. Equipment requirements, cost, and availability of the film are provided. Ease of use and other advantages are given.

265.   Schmidt, Janet A. **"How to Promote Online Services to the People Who Count the Most ... Management ... End Users."** *Online* 1 (January 1977): 32-38.

Describes various ways to announce the availability of online services and to promote their use within a business organization. Discusses the key elements in any publicity effort and notes the effectiveness of a highly visible terminal. Receptions at the search center, presentations to special groups, and free searches are other suggestions given. Stresses that timing is critical and that promoting online services is not easy.

266.   Schmidt, Janet A. **"Outline for an Online Public Relations Program."** *Online* 2 (October 1978): 47-50.

Discusses various public relations techniques that can be used to introduce and promote online services. The need to initially determine attitudes toward the library is stressed. Specific techniques to promote a new service are given and examples described. A sample questionnaire to survey patrons of the library is appended.

PUBLIC LIBRARIES AND ONLINE SEARCHING

Public libraries are becoming increasingly involved with online searching. As more general indexes, e.g., *Magazine Index*, and reference sources, e.g., *Encyclopedia of Associations*, become available online, more and more public libraries are implementing online search services. Public libraries use online searches not only as a means of providing bibliographies for their patrons, but also as a source of answers to many types of ready-reference questions.

Related sections in this bibliography include:

Impact of Online Searching (Entries 208-221)
Reference Uses of Online Searching (Entries 279-285)
Setting Up and Managing an Online Search Service (Entries 345-367)

267.   Byrd, Gary D.; Mary Kay Smith; and Norene McDonald. **"Minet in K.C."** *Library Journal* 104 (October 1, 1979): 2044-47.

Reports on the Kansas City Libraries Metropolitan Information Network (MINET) during its first year of search activity. Background and reasons for developing MINET are discussed. Tables provide statistics on databases searched, status of patrons, commercial search services used, referring library, and type of patrons. Concludes that MINET is successful and is providing its member libraries with significant benefits.

268. Firschein, Oscar; Roger Summit; and Colin K. Mick. **"Planning for Online Search in the Public Library."** *Special Libraries* 69 (July 1978): 255-60.

Summarizes a three-year experiment in introducing online searching to four public libraries in California. The following nine "Key Requirements" were identified: 1) establishing scope and limits of service; 2) staff time requirements; 3) staff attitudes and support; 4) funding; 5) need for promotional planning; 6) need for ongoing staff training; 7) need for a critical mass of searches; 8) document support; and 9) management and evaluation.

269. Firschein, Oscar; Roger K. Summit; and Colin K. Mick. **"Use of Online Bibliographic Search in Public Libraries: A Retrospective Evaluation."** *Online Review* 2 (March 1978): 41-55.

Describes the results of a three-year experiment in utilizing online searching in public libraries. Known as the DIALIB project, it involved four public libraries in the San Francisco Bay Area. Evaluations were conducted that dealt with use of the various databases available, user characteristics, librarian reactions to the capability, and cost-effectiveness of providing online searching in a public library. Objectives and study design are also presented. Particular emphasis is given to the issue of charging for online services in a public library.

270. **"In Online Searching, Business Questions Predominate."** *American Libraries* 11 (March 1980): 159.

Describes the Computer-Assisted Reference Center (CARC) established by the Chicago Public Library's Business/Science/Technology Division. Funding for the service and the impact of user fees are briefly presented. Users are generally described as having "personal, business, and school/university demands." Stresses the need for searchers to be professional reference librarians, and increasing requests for nonbibliographic information are noted.

271. Johnson, Robert A. **"Planning for Online Searching at San Jose: A Design for Public Libraries of the 1980s."** *Science and Technology Libraries* 1 (Fall 1980): 117-32.

Outlines the experiences of San Jose Public Library in introducing online searching as part of the DIALIB Project. The entire process from determining the need for such a service to evaluating patron satisfaction is described. The commitment of the library administration is essential to the success of such a service. Concludes that "any medium-sized public library with a sound financial base can and should be offering online reference to its patrons."

272. Keenan, Stella; Nick Moore; and Anthony Oulton. **"On-line Information Services in Public Libraries."** *Journal of Librarianship* 13 (January 1981): 9-24.

Describes two British projects to introduce online search services in public libraries. The BIROS (Bibliographic Information Retrieval On-Line Service) project involved the use of online services at the Lancashire County Library in 1978 and 1979 and its subsequent evaluation. Another project in which four public libraries participated resulted in a set of guidelines for the introduction of online services. Both projects found a "genuine demand for on-line services amongst the general public."

273. Kusack, James M. **"Online Reference Service in Public Libraries."** *RQ* 18 (Summer 1979): 331-34.

Reports the results of a survey conducted in July 1978 of 34 of the largest public library systems in the United States concerning their use of online searching. Less than half offered such services. Financial considerations and the nontraditional nature of online searching are the two main reasons for public libraries not providing online services. Benefits and potential uses are identified and a statistical analysis of the survey's results are presented. Concludes that the policy of public libraries in this area is in a "state of flux."

274.   McClure, Charles R. **"A Planning Primer for Online Reference Service in a Public Library."** *Online* 4 (April 1980): 57-65.

Provides a planning outline for public libraries which are considering implementing an online search service. The importance of planning is stressed and seven "basic planning steps" identified and discussed: 1) goals and objectives; 2) needs assessment; 3) "political environment"; 4) project description; 5) time schedule; 6) preliminary budget; and 7) evaluation. Additional issues concerning policies, funding, and training are briefly presented.

275.   Raedeke, Amy. **"Machine Assisted Reference Service in a Public Library: A One Month Test Period."** *Online* 2 (October 1978): 56-59.

Summarizes the use of free online searches during a one-month trial at the Minneapolis Public Library and Information Center in November 1977. Statistics are presented for a wide variety of search factors (e.g., databases used and amount of online time), and tentative conclusions about online searching in a public library are reached. The possible effect of user fees is briefly considered.

276.   Summit, Roger and Oscar Firschein. **"On-Line Reference Retrieval in a Public Library."** *Special Libraries* 67 (February 1976): 91-96.

Describes the initial part of a project to introduce online services to public libraries. The first year of an experiment to use public libraries as a "linking agent" between the public and online databases in four public libraries in California is described. Effects on the libraries after one year of the service include new patrons, increased workload, and increased visibility of the library. Preliminary evaluations indicate the service will be accepted.

277.   Summit, Roger and Oscar Firschein. **"Public Library Use of Online Bibliographic Retrieval Services: Experiences in Four Public Libraries in Northern California."** *Online* 1 (October 1977): 58-64.

Presents an overview of the three years of the DIALIB Study. Summarizes the experiences of public libraries in California in introducing online searches. The intent of the project was to investigate the potential of public libraries as "linking agents" between online information and the public. The effects of user fees are discussed and the predicted growth of such services is noted. Stresses the need for support of both the library staff and administration.

278.   Waters, Richard L. and Jane Mann. **"Online Search Service at the Dallas Public Library."** *Science & Technology Libraries* 1 (Fall 1980): 109-115.

Describes the administrative decisions made at the Dallas Public Library in implementing an online search service in 1974. Staffing considerations, fee structure, and record keeping are discussed in some detail. Future predictions concerning facilities and type of services to be offered are briefly stated. Notes that while online searching at the Dallas Public Library has not been "trouble free," it has been "a challenging and rewarding endeavor."

REFERENCE USES OF ONLINE SEARCHING

More and more librarians consider online searching "just another reference tool." As nonbibliographical databases continue to proliferate, online searches will be used more often to answer specific reference questions. Examples of standard reference works that are now available as databases include *Books in Print, Encyclopedia of Associations*, and *American Men and Women of Science*. The currency of databases also makes them valuable reference tools. The interaction between traditional reference services and online search services is a key factor in the successful utilization of the capabilities of online searching.

Related sections in this bibliography include:

Impact of Online Searching (Entries 208-221)
Search Strategies and Techniques (Entries 321-340)

279. Gardner, Trudy A. **"Effect of Online Databases on Reference Policy."** *RQ* 19 (Fall 1979): 70-74.

Analyzes the effect online searching has on the traditional philosophy of reference service as provided by most librarians. The ongoing debate over the appropriate level of reference service is being exacerbated by the development and availability of computerized information retrieval. Argues that the function of reference is to provide information and not simply to direct patrons to sources. Therefore, online searching has "subtly but directly revolutionized the practice of reference service."

280. Klugman, Simone. **"Online Information Retrieval Interface with Traditional Reference Services."** *Online Review* 4 (September 1980): 263-72.

Considers the necessary interaction between traditional reference service and online information services in a large academic library. Discusses both the library environment and the background of online searching and demonstrates how the two services must merge. Five problems are identified: 1) human problems; 2) administrative and economic problems; 3) problems of the user; 4) document delivery problems; and 5) hardware problems. Future developments are also considered.

281. Kusack, James M. **"Integration of Online Reference Service."** *RQ* 19 (Fall 1976): 64-69.

Argues that online searching is not a "special and exotic service only tangentially related to the reference process," but an essential reference tool which should be integrated with traditional reference service. Describes four administrative methods for providing an online search service in a library and then presents a case for integration. Recommendations to maximize benefits from such an integration are presented.

282. Nitecki, Danuta. **"Online Services."** See issues of *RQ* beginning with volume 19, #4.

Covers topics related to automation as it affects reference and other public services. Columns are written by guest editors and are intended to "meet the need for easily accessible information on developments in automated information services to help nonspecialists stay abreast in this area." Topics are generally covered in nontechnical language and do not require previous knowledge. (Relevant columns have been individually annotated in this bibliography.)

283. Ojalla, Mary Portes. **"Using BALLOTS as a Reference Tool."** *Online* 2 (October 1978): 11-19.

Demonstrates how BALLOTS (Bibliographic Automation of Large Library Operations using a Time-sharing System), primarily a bibliographic file to aid in cataloging and acquisitions, can be used as an online reference tool. Access points are noted and possible applications described. Compiling bibliographies and searching for organizational names are given as two potential reference uses of BALLOTS. Examples of searches are provided and "Database Specifications" are included.

284. Snow, Susan. **"Computerized Cooperative Reference."** *RQ* 18 (Summer 1979): 364-66.

Describes the hazards and rewards of "computerized cooperative reference." Stresses that the keyword is cooperative, not computerized. Successful use of online searching as part of a cooperative reference network depends on human cooperation and communications. Problems of inappropriate searches and financial restraints are considered. Concludes that more and more libraries and librarians will make use of online cooperative reference networks.

285. Sweetland, James H. **"Using Online Systems in Reference Work."** *Online* 3 (July 1979): 10-19.

Identifies ways online systems can be used cost-effectively as basic reference tools. Examples are provided which describe how various types of online services can be used for acquisitions, interlibrary loan and name/address verification, and identification of a group or field of study. Search statistics and cost figures are included. Suggestions for efficiently using online databases in reference are summarized.

SEARCH AIDS

Manuals, guides, thesauri, and other types of search aids are available from the major commercial search services and many of the individual database producers. Directories of available user aids and evaluations of them are often published in the major online journals. These search aids and materials are frequently referred to as "file documentation."

Related sections in this bibliography include:

Databases and Database Producers (Entries 49-67)
Search Strategies and Techniques (Entries 321-340)

286. Alvey, Celine H. *"Guide to DIALOG Databases* — A **Review."** *Online* 2 (July 1978): 21-23.

Evaluates the *Guide to DIALOG Databases* made available by DIALOG in 1978. Stresses that all searchers, both beginners and advanced search analysts, can benefit from using this manual. Highly recommends the manual and concludes that it is "a boon to all searchers of DIALOG databases and a model for writers of manuals to emulate."

287. Casey, Michael. **"Euronet-DIANE: A Study on the Harmonization of User Manuals."** *Online Review* 4 (March 1980): 33-40.

Presents the recommendations made in a study of user manuals funded by the Commission of the European Communities as part of the Euronet-DIANE project.

Stresses the need for the "harmonization" of the user manuals for the databases to be available on Euronet — DIANE. Intention was to develop a "set of guidelines for an agreed harmonized format" for all user manuals. Contends that such harmonization of user manuals is essential for proper user education and training.

288.   Dempsey, Tim. **"Write Your Own User's Manual."** *Online* 6 (March 1982): 11-19.
Details how the free online search time offered by commercial search services can be used to investigate the database systematically and to prepare a homemade user's manual. Steps are outlined which will produce a useful guide for future reference. Examples of searches conducted when half-hour free time was available on DIALOG's NCJRS file are appended.

289.   Foreman, Gertrude. **"Online Search Aids."** See issues of *Online* beginning with volume 1, #3.
Lists available search aids for both databases and commercial search services. Titles, price, availability, and source are noted for each. Only included in volumes one and two of *Online*.

290.   Lawrence, Gerri G. **"Searchaid Review — *BRS Reference Manual.*"** *Online* 3 (April 1979): 55.
Reviews the *BRS System Reference Manual and Database Search Guides* available in early 1979. The preface by Jan Egelad and the "Directory of Search Aids for BRS Databases" are judged to be very useful. Concludes that the manual provides "a solid basis for the inexperienced user and a good reference tool for the experienced searcher."

291.   Morrow, Deanna I. **"A Generalized Flowchart for the Use of ORBIT and Other On-Line Interactive Bibliographic Search Systems."** *Journal of the American Society for Information Science* 27 (January 1976): 57-62.
Presents a four-page series of generalized flowcharts to depict the process of performing an online search on SDC. It is intended for new or occasional users. It is designed to help searchers answer three basic questions when preparing or conducting a search: 1) What do I want to do? 2) How am I going to do it? and 3) What do I do now?

292.   Nitecki, Danuta A. and Mary Pillepich. **"A Road Map to Basic Sources of Information."** Guest editor of "Online Services." Edited by Danuta Nitecki. *RQ* 19 (Summer 1980): 319-22.
Profiles the various sources of basic information about different aspects of online databases and search services. Examples and necessary bibliographic citations are provided for relevant journals, guidebooks, directories, newsletters, and professional organizations and their committees and publications. The value of personal contacts and attending workshops is also stressed.

293.   Nolan, Maureen P. **"How to Handle the Avalanche of Online Documentation."** *Online* 5 (July 1981): 51-55.
Describes a filing system developed by NPM Information Services Ltd. to handle the printed documentation associated with online searching services. Materials are divided into three main files: 1) database files; 2) system files; and 3) network files. Subject and database indexes are used to link related items and provide access to specific items. Numerous advantages of the system are noted.

294.   Smith, Linda C. **"Data Base Directories: A Comparative Review."** *Reference Services Review* 8 (October/December 1980): 15-21.
    Reviews and compares six database directories published in 1979 and 1980. Each directory is briefly described and the following characteristics are evaluated: basic features, coverage, content of entries, and indexes. Directories produced by ASIS, Cuadra Associates, CSG Press, Learned Information, MIDLNET, and Aslib are compared. No overall qualitative rankings are presented.

295.   Unruh, Betty. **"Database User Aids and Materials—A Study."** *Online Review* 5 (February 1981): 7-24.
    Investigates various assumptions about the user aids and materials available for the databases searchable on DIALOG and/or SDC in March 1979. considers both cost and availability factors, but no qualitative judgments are presented. Notes the number of commercial search services on which a database is available. Databases are also distinguished by subject coverage and type of producer. The value of newsletters and training sessions is also noted.

SEARCH ANALYSTS

Online searches are typically performed by trained intermediaries, known as search analysts. Traits of a good search analyst have been identified and the issue of quality control raised. The role of such an intermediary in providing information has been debated. Search analysts are usually professional reference librarians who have been specifically trained in online search techniques.
    Related sections in this bibliography include:

End Users (Entries 113-121)
Informational Interview (Entries 222-229)
Search Strategies and Techniques (Entries 321-340)
Training and Education of Search Analysts (Entries 400-435)

296.   Baker, Christine and Kenneth D. Eason. **"An Observational Study of Man-Computer Interaction Using an Online Bibliographic Information Retrieval System."** *Online Review* 5 (April 1981): 121-32.
    Describes an experimental attempt to measure and statistically analyze the man-computer interaction required when an online search is performed. Procedures used to acquire the data are discussed and the results are presented in tables and briefly summarized. Notes that the interaction is a "computer dominated process." Attempts to minimize time on the computer, for both economic and psychological reasons contribute to users' fears of the system.

297.   Chapman, Janet L. **"A State Transition Analysis of Online Information-Seeking Behavior."** *Journal of the American Society for Information Science* 32 (September 1981): 325-33.
    Employs a "transition analysis of state occurrences" to analyze differences in the search commands used by different types of searchers in performing similar searches. Three classes of users (library science students, engineers, and research scientists) were further divided into groups based on their online experience and exposure to a training system, Individualized Instruction for Data Access (IIDA). Results indicate that searchers

tend to follow the advice of their trainer, whether human or computer. Differences between groups of searchers are statistically analyzed.

298.   Dolan, Donna R. and Michael Kremin. **"The Quality Control of Search Analysts."** *Online* 3 (April 1979): 8-16.
    Assesses the effectiveness of programs to train online searchers and attempts to establish a pretest to identify potentially good searchers. The following traits of a good search analyst are given: 1) concept analysis; 2) flexibility of thinking; 3) ability to think in synonyms; 4) anticipation of variant word forms and spelling; and 5) self-confidence. Limitations of the proposed pretest and problems in attempting to certify searchers are noted. The pretest is appended.

299.   Ericson, Linda. **"Of Jobs and Seekers."** *Online* 5 (April 1980): 62.
    Summarizes some of the information about the ONLINE '80 Job Clearinghouse. Most employers sought someone with either a science or engineering degree, but most job seekers had backgrounds in history or education. All 60 job seekers had online experience. Sample job titles, location, and salaries are also listed.

300.   Fenichel, Carol Hansen. **"An Examination of the Relationship between Searching Behavior and Searcher Background."** *Online Review* 4 (December 1980): 341-47.
    Reports the results of a study which investigated the relationship between a searcher's experience and background and the actual search techniques and strategies used. Subjects were familiar with ERIC online searching to different degrees. Results are briefly presented for five different groups of searchers. Beginning searchers were found to do "surprisingly well." The effects of different background variables are statistically analyzed.

301.   Fenichel, Carol H. **"Online Searching: Measures That Discriminate among Users with Different Types of Experiences."** *Journal of the American Society for Information Science* 32 (January 1981): 23-32.
    Investigates the assumption that online "skill is strongly related to experience." Searchers with varying levels of experience and expertise performed searches on selected topics using ONTAP, the training file for ERIC on DIALOG. Few significant differences were found between the various groups. In fact, beginning searchers scored quite well. A possible correlation between search effort and recall was noted for experienced ERIC searchers.

302.   Girard, Anne and Magdeleine Moureau. **"An Examination of the Role of the Intermediary in the Online Searching of Chemical Literature."** *Online Review* 5 (June 1981): 217-25.
    Examines the need for a trained intermediary when conducting online searches in the field of chemistry. Intermediaries and end users are defined and the knowledge necessary to conduct a good search discussed. Five search topics in the chemical field are investigated to determine whether they can be searched by the end user directly or whether the skills of an intermediary are needed. Concludes that some searches need an intermediary, but some can be performed by the end user.

303.   Goldstein, Charles M. and William H. Ford. **"The User-Cordial Interface."** *Online Review* 2 (September 1978): 269-75.
    Considers the appropriateness of referring to the "user-oriented interface (UOI)" when discussing online retrieval systems. Contends that the phrase is often used in a contradictory fashion and argues that the user interface is simply "a matter of format."

Technology is available which can separate retrieval operations from the format or interface presented to the searcher. An attempt to deal with this problem practically is described.

304. Hlava, Marjorie M. K. **"Online Users Survey 1980."** *Online Review* 4 (September 1980): 294-99.
Reports the results of a survey of SDC online users conducted in January of 1980. Analyzes responses to 11 questions concerning the background experience, salary, and affiliation of searchers. The questionnaire is included and some results presented in graph form.

305. Krentz, David M. **"Online Searching: Specialist Required."** *Journal of Chemical Information & Computer Sciences* 18 (February 1978): 4-9.
Stresses the importance of having online searches performed by trained specialists. Notes the increasing complexity of databases and concludes that a specialist is needed to differentiate between online and print sources, deal with the variety of indexing conventions, and apply appropriate Boolean logic in developing a search strategy. A trained searcher is seen as a "key factor" in the success of any online search service.

306. Lawrence, Gerri G. **"C.M.L.: Clinical Medical Librarian."** *Online* 3 (July 1979): 60-63.
Profiles the role of a clinical medical librarian in providing information to physicians and medical students at the University of Missouri—Kansas City Medical School. The direct involvement of the librarian, including participating in "rounds" is emphasized. Benefits of online searching in this medical setting are described.

307. Slusar, Vernon G. **"Research Information Technician."** *Science & Technology Libraries* 1 (Fall 1980): 75-80.
Describes the position of "Research Information Technician" used at the Information Services Division of the Amoco Research Center to designate those information specialists trained in online searching. Development of the position and the requirements and guidelines for selecting the technicians are described. The training received and the actual work environment are also presented. Notes the technicians have been very successful in meeting the information needs of most clients.

308. Van Camp, Ann. **"Effective Search Analysts."** *Online* 3 (April 1979): 18-20.
Identifies the following 10 traits of a good search analyst: 1) self-confidence; 2) logical mind; 3) people-oriented; 4) exploits successes; 5) knows subject areas; 6) goes beyond formal training; 7) retentive memory; 8) perseverance and patience; 9) efficient work habits; and 10) shares knowledge. Stresses the need to also consider other factors such as previous experience.

SEARCH RESULTS

Search results must be analyzed to determine the efficiency of the search and to consider its cost-effectiveness. Processes are being developed to eliminate duplicate references when conducting searches in more than one database and to obtain the results in a machine-readable form for further manipulation. It is possible to edit and format results to suit the needs of individual users. Other unconventional uses of search results, e.g., bibliometric studies, have also been attempted.

Related sections in this bibliography include:

Search Strategies and Techniques (Entries 321-340)
User Evaluation and Attitudes (Entries 436-443)

309. Boyce, Bert R. and Edward J. Gillen. **"Is It More Cost-Effective to Print On- or Offline?"** Guest editor of "Online Services." Edited by Danuta A. Nitecki. *RQ* 21 (Winter 1981): 117-20.

Presents a formula which can be used to compare online print costs with offline print charges. The equation was tested on three databases searched on both DIALOG and SDC. Results indicate "a clear cost savings in printing online" when using a 1200 baud terminal. Describes a method for determining the maximum citation length at which online printing is no longer economical. Concludes that "the conventional wisdom that it is always cheaper to print offline is nonsense."

310. Brooks, Kristina M. **"The Online Transfer Machine Readable Data: A Pandora's Box."** *Database* 5 (February 1982): 18-21.

Summarizes the technical, legal, and procedural problems in attempting to obtain data in machine readable form directly and then reusing the material locally. An actual project attempted by the Oregon State University library staff beginning in 1975 is described. Reports "mixed" reactions to the direct transfer of machine readable data by search services and database producers. Concludes that the technical problems are most easily solved and offers suggestions for eliminating the legal and procedural problems.

311. Conger, Lucinda. **"CLAIMS/CITATION."** *Online* 6 (January 1982): 28-34.

Describes a technique which can be used to eliminate duplicate citations in the same file and thereby reduce printing costs. CLAIMS/CITATION is used as an example of a very expensive file which also imposes online print charges. The technique involves comparing accession numbers and works best in databases which have sequential accession numbers. Notes that the need for such search techniques will increase as more files require fees for online record displays.

312. Cooper, William S. **"On Selecting a Measure of Retrieval Effectiveness. Part I. The 'Subjective' Philosophy of Evaluation. Part II. Implementation of the Philosophy."** *Journal of the American Society for Information Science* Part I, 24 (March-April 1973): 87-100; Part II, 24 (November-December 1973): 413-24.

Attempts to develop an ideal measure of retrieval effectiveness. Based on the assumption that the best evaluation would be a quantified interpretation by the user of the actual utility of the search results, a theoretical methodology using an elicitation procedure is outlined. Objections to the methodology are discussed and the procedure modified. The practical difficulties encountered in trying to quantify "utility" are analyzed. Further research is suggested.

313. Hawkins, Donald T. **"Machine-Readable Output from Online Searches."** *Journal of the American Society for Information Science* 32 (July 1981): 253-56.

Describes a process by which machine-readable output (MRO) is acquired as the product of an online search and used to compile large bibliographies. A magnetic tape, instead of normal offline prints on paper, is purchased from the search service. The computer program needed to process the data is described and a procedure to eliminate duplicate references explained. Notes that the use of MRO has proved to be very cost-effective.

314. Hawkins, Donald T. **"Unconventional Use of On-Line Information Retrieval System: On-Line Bibliometric Studies."** *Journal of the American Society for Information Science* 28 (January 1977): 13-18.

Describes how the information available in most bibliographic databases can be used for bibliometric studies. Such studies statistically analyze the bibliographic features of the literature written in a certain field. Examples of "on-line bibliometrics" involving corporate source searches, journal searches, statistical studies, journal comparisons, and author searching are provided.

315. Hitchingham, Eileen E. **"Selecting Measures Applicable to Evaluation on On-Line Literature Searching."** *Drexel Library Quarterly* 13 (July 1977): 52-66.

Investigates various ways to measure and evaluate the performance of online search services provided by libraries. Reasons for such evaluations are also discussed. Suggestions for measuring both costs and quality of results are presented. Two statistical measures for performance evaluation are provided—unit cost in dollars per relevant citation and recall. Factors influencing the decision concerning whether to continue such services are also given.

316. Huleatt, Richard S. **"Finishing the Online Search."** *Online* 3 (April 1979): 24-31.

Details a technique for editing and formatting the offline results from computer searches. The equipment needed, specifically a terminal with an editing capability, is described and a format for production of the results suggested. Copyright complications are considered and comparisons made with normal printouts. Examples of completed search results are included.

317. Marshall, Doris B. **"To Improve Searching, Check Search Results."** *Online* 4 (July 1980): 32-47.

Stresses the need for searchers to evaluate the actual results of their online searches to improve recall and precision. Examples are given which demonstrate that "sometimes extra effort in searching is required." Problems in using truncation, abbreviations, acronyms, homonyms and colloquial expressions are presented. A list of 32 checkpoints to use in preparing search strategies and in evaluating results is also given.

318. Riley, Connie; Margaret Bell; and Tom Finucane. **"Elimination of Duplicate Citations from Cross Database Searching Using an 'Intelligent' Terminal to Produce Report Style Searches."** *Online* 5 (October 1981): 36-41.

Details the equipment and programming necessary to produce report-style search results and to eliminate duplicated references. Demonstrates how a Hewlett Packard CRT terminal with the BASIC Interpreter option linked with an Anderson Jacobson floppy disc can be used to store the results of searches in a machine-readable form for offline editing. The computer program to eliminate duplicates is appended. Benefits of such edited search results are noted.

319. Stibic, Vlado. **"Influence of Unlimited Ranking on Practical Online Search Strategy."** *Online Review* 4 (September 1980): 273-79.

Examines the practicality of ranking retrieved documents in descending order of their direct relationship to the request. Examples of unlimited ranking used in an in-house retrieval system are given. Advantages are presented and differences between unlimited ranking and Boolean systems are described. Stresses that ranking cannot function as the only method of retrieval in a system.

320.   White, Howard D. **" 'Bradfordizing' Search Output: How It Would Help Online Users."** *Online Review* 5 (February 1981): 47-54.
Proposes sorting bibliographic items retrieved by an online search by journal title and then by the number of items in each issue. The procedure is referred to as "Bradfordizing" since its application is related to Bradford's law. Advantages predicted include: 1) immediate awareness of journals retrieved and how many articles are contained in each; 2) ability to selectively receive results by journal; 3) capability to analyze retrieval bibliometrically; and 4) printouts alphabetically arranged by journal for ease of locating on periodical shelves.

SEARCH STRATEGIES AND TECHNIQUES

A search analyst must make a variety of decisions in preparing a search strategy, ranging from the basic decision of which database to search first to the specific techniques to be used in conducting the search online. Innovative methods, search options, the use of controlled vocabulary, and techniques of restricting the results are all important factors which must be considered in developing a search strategy. This process is complicated by differences in actual search techniques among the commercial search services and the various databases available.
Related sections in this bibliography include:

Informational Interview (Entries 222-229)
Search Aids (Entries 286-295)
Search Analysts (Entries 296-308)
Search Results (Entries 309-320)

321.   Adams, Arthur L. **"Planning Search Strategies for Maximum Retrieval from Bibliographic Databases."** *Online Review* 3 (December 1979): 373-79.
Proposes various techniques that can be used to increase search recall. Stresses the importance of the presearch interview and properly outlining the search strategy. Other factors that influence search output include: minimizing the number of concepts to be combined, adapting the strategy to a specific database, planning in advance ways to narrow or broaden the search, and minimizing problems with search techniques.

322.   Ashton, Paul. **"How to Search 'Same-Word' Double Terms on DIALOG."** *Online* 5 (October 1981): 58-59.
Distinguishes between the W and X operators used in proximity searching on DIALOG. Attempts to clarify the explanation provided by DIALOG in their *Chronolog* newsletter. Additional examples are presented and differences between databases noted. The technique described allows searching for adjacent words that are exactly the same, e.g., Johnson & Johnson.

323.   Bates, Marcia J. **"Idea Tactics."** *Journal of the American Society for Information Science* 30 (September 1979): 280-89.

Discusses "idea tactics" which are defined as attempts to create new ideas or possible solutions to problems in information searching. Tactics presented are primarily psychological in nature and are applicable to both manual and online searching. Seventeen idea tactics are defined and examples of their possible applications are given. Tactics are divided into "idea generation" and "pattern-breaking" tactics. (See also #324.)

324.   Bates, Marcia J. **"Information Search Tactics."** *Journal of the American Society for Information Science* 30 (July 1979): 205-214.

Summarizes the literature on human information search strategy and then presents 29 theoretical "search tactics" used to further or continue a search. The 29 tactics are named and listed in a chart and discussed individually. They are grouped into the following four categories: 1) monitoring; 2) file structure; 3) search formulation; and 4) term tactics. Notes that this model of search strategy is viewed primarily as a "facilitation model," but can also be considered a potential "teaching model." The theory applies to both manual and online searching. (See also #323.)

325.   Buntrock, Robert E. **"The Effect of the Searching Environment on Search Performance."** *Online* 3 (October 1979): 10-13.

Assesses the effect of various environmental factors on the quality of online searches. The value of the presence of the requester when the search is being conducted depends on the various circumstances of the request (e.g., need immediate information). Three search concepts are defined and explained: 1) Building Blocks; 2) Successive Fractions; and 3) Pearl Growing. Stresses that searchers must know their users and suggests a searcher's motto should be "STAY LOOSE."

326.   Calkins, Mary L. **"Free Text or Controlled Vocabulary? A Case History Step-by-Step Analysis—Plus Other Aspects of Search Strategy."** *Database* 3 (June 1980): 53-67.

Considers the decisions involved in preparing a search strategy. Using a case study approach involving an actual search request, decisions made by the searcher in the following areas are individually examined: 1) scope; 2) concepts; 3) selection of databases; 4) development of the search strategy; 5) changing tactics during the search; and 6) deciding on print format. Controlled vocabulary searching is also compared with free text searching. Concludes that using both approaches results in the most comprehensive search. Two databases, COMPENDEX and ENVIROLINE, available on DIALOG were used for this study. Sample search strategies are appended.

327.   Conger, Lucinda D. **"Restricting Searches in DIALOG."** *Online* 1 (October 1977): 68-77.

Describes how to limit or restrict searching in DIALOG. These search techniques are briefly summarized. Provides a list that gives examples of various restricting options for individual DIALOG databases. The list is arranged by DIALOG file number. Methods to update this ever-changing list are also pointed out.

328.   Dolan, Donna R. **"Offlines."** See issues of *Database* beginning with volume 2, #2.

Concentrates on "searching and survival." Brief and nontechnical articles discuss search techniques and unconventional uses of databases. Written for both the beginning and experienced searcher.

329.   Hartwell, Ieva O. **"Searchguide: Points to Remember about Searching.... "** See issues of *Online* volume 1, #3 and #4; volume 2, #1.

Identifies specific search techniques that are useful in searching a given database on a specific commercial search service. Three databases (ASI, INSPEC, and EIS PLANTS) were studied indepth in this column in *Online*. The column only appeared in three issues of *Online*.

330. **"I Learned about Searching from That...."** See issues of *Online* beginning with volume 3, #4.

Presents items submitted by readers of *Online* which demonstrate innovative methods of search technique. Topics vary widely. Offers searchers an opportunity to "exchange ideas and information on shortcuts, pitfalls, and so on which have become part of our profession."

331. de Jong-Hofman, M. W. **"Computer-Aided Searching in the INSPEC Database. Analysis of Subject Indexing by INSPEC and the Resulting Cost and Efficiency as Related to Various Search Strategies."** *Online Review* 2 (June 1978): 175-98.

Details the results of an in-depth study of the accuracy and consistency of indexing completed by human indexers and abstracters. Concludes that the efficiency of using assigned descriptors is very low because of the large number of synonyms and because of the inaccuracy of the indexers. Given this difficulty, alternative search strategies are proposed and compared. Results are presented in tables. Concludes that the best search uses both assigned terms or codes and selected free text terms.

332. Markey, Karen; Pauline Atherton; and Claudia Newton. **"An Analysis of Controlled Vocabulary and Free Text Search Statements in Online Searches."** *Online Review* 4 (September 1980): 225-36.

Reports on a series of studies conducted in 1978 and 1979 by the ERIC Clearinghouse on Information Resources Special Project Staff to determine how experienced ERIC searchers used both free and controlled vocabulary terms in their search strategies. Over 650 different ERIC searches were analyzed and 68% were found to use controlled vocabulary terms. Closely examines free text terms used and presents tables summarizing various comparisons between free text and controlled vocabulary searching. Concludes that free text has higher recall, but controlled vocabulary yields more precise results.

333. Oldroyd, Betty K. and Charles L. Citroen. **"Study of the Strategies Used in Online Searching."** *Online Review* 1 (December 1977): 295-310.

Studies the approaches taken in preparing and conducting searches by experienced online searchers. Three important "decision areas" are identified: 1) Selecting the appropriate database or databases; 2) Using suitable vocabulary; and 3) Developing proper logic in the search strategy. Strongly suggests that commercial search services and database producers standardize as much as possible, especially in spelling, vocabulary, basic commands, and indexing procedures.

334. Oldroyd, Betty K. and J. J. Schroder. **"Study of Strategies Used in Online Searching: 2. Positional Logic — An Example of the Importance of Selecting the Right Boolean Operator."** *Online Review* 6 (April 1982): 127-33.

Analyzes the use of positional logic to retrieve the most relevant items with the least amount of inappropriate citations. Results of searches on three databases (NASA, NTIS, and INSPEC) on the topic of "microwave integrated circuits" are presented. Notes advantages and disadvantages of various search strategies and difficulties in switching files. Concludes that in most cases the searcher "will be safer making judicious use of the (F) operator in preference to the (W) operator."

335.   Padin, Mary Ellen. **"Computer Ease."** See issues of *Online*.
Discusses specific aspects of online searching in a column regularly included in *Online*. Tricky aspects of searching a particular database or answers to questions submitted by readers are frequently discussed. Comments are brief and typically deal with practical applications of search techniques.

336.   Quinn, Karen Takle. **"STAIRS Search Strategy: Ideas and Opinions."** *Online Review* 4 (June 1980): 163-68.
Presents a practical guide to formulating search strategies for STAIRS users. Lists the steps in a good search strategy and stresses the importance of being familiar with the database to be searched. Search options and techniques are both described and depicted in various tables. Practical guidelines for increasing search efficiency are listed.

337.   Sabatine, Alicia and Arthur Antony. **"Break Even Points on Dialog ... Or ... What Are the Tradeoffs between Expand and Super Select, Plus Format Impact on Printing Costs."** *Online* 5 (July 1981): 46-49.
Examines possible cost benefits from two search options: 1) online versus offline printing and 2) EXPAND versus SELECT STEPS. Actual sample searches were conducted and the results analyzed. Costs were not reduced by having online prints in a bibliographic format. However, certain cases in which the EXPAND command was comparable in price to the SELECT STEPS command are identified. All searches and cost comparisons were conducted on DIALOG.

338.   **"Search Corner."** See issues of *Online Review*.
Presents "tips on online searching, sample searches on various data bases, and search problems that our readers have found particularly challenging." Encourages reader contributions. Regular column in *Online Review*.

339.   Smith, Sallye Wrye. **"Venn Diagramming for On-Line Searching."** *Special Libraries* 67 (November 1976): 510-17.
Suggests the use of rectangular Venn diagrams in planning search strategies for online searching. Contends that such diagrams aid in both profile construction and the actual search. They also allow the retention of the strategy for future use. Various examples are provided. Concludes that Venn diagrams may be most appropriate in an academic setting.

340.   Wolf, Barbara J. **"Creative Searching in a Current Affairs Database."** *Online Review* 4 (June 1980): 173-75.
Presents basic suggestions and "tips" for users of large, general-interest databases. Specific examples are taken from the New York Times INFORMATION BANK. Emphasizes the importance of adequate preparation before going online. Three basic ways of modifying online retrieval are distinguished and described: 1) terms; 2) modifiers; and 3) logic. Notes the value of searcher experience and creativity.

SELECTIVE DISSEMINATION OF INFORMATION

Selective dissemination of information, often abbreviated SDI, is the regular use of current awareness searches to provide end users with the most current references to items of potential interest. General articles describing SDI systems are included in this section, but most articles discussing SDI deal with a specific subject area and are, consequently, contained in the "Specialized Subject Areas or Databases in Online Searching" portion of this bibliography. The subject index can be used to identify these other articles.

Related sections in this bibliography include:

Search Results (Entries 309-320)

341. Brandili, Michael J. **"Current Awareness Services — Observations of the Past and Present, and Implications for the Future."** *Special Libraries* 67 (January 1976): 40-44.

Presents a brief history of the SDI service developed and offered by the College of Medicine and Dentistry of the New Jersey Library. Progression from a manual current awareness service to an online system, eventually including access to MEDLARS, is described. Discusses results of a user survey to evaluate the service. Stresses the "obligation" medical librarians have to provide such service.

342. Cole, Elliot. **"Examining Design Assumptions for an Information Retrieval Service: SDI Use for Scientific and Technical Databases."** *Journal of the American Society for Information Service* 32 (November 1981): 444-50.

Investigates why SDI systems have not been as widely accepted and implemented in the areas of scientific and technical research as expected in the 1960s and 1970s. This "failure analysis" questions the basic assumptions upon which SDI systems were designed. Notes that SDI was not intended to serve as a source of background information, but this is how it has typically been used. Concludes that SDI remains a "valuable system," but a wider audience of users must be sought.

343. Kaminecki, Ron. **"Comparison of Selective Dissemination of Information Systems."** *Online Review* 1 (September 1977): 195-206.

Compares batch and online SDI services. Three different types of online SDI procedures ("Rekeyed SDI," "Saved SDI," and "Vendor-Supplied SDI") are detailed and compared. Various equations are used to determine actual costs involved. Costs are broken down by "person-time" and "system costs." Notes that any methodology, whether batch or online, may be the best in a given situation.

344. Warden, Carolyn L. **"Industrial Current Awareness Service: A User Evaluation Study."** *Special Libraries* 69 (December 1978): 459-67.

Presents the benefits users of the General Electric Whitney Library Current Awareness Service expressed concerning their involvement with an SDI service using CA CONDENSATES and COMPENDEX. Results of a user study indicated that most users were highly satisfied with the service and appreciated its convenience, level of coverage speed, and time-saving aspects. Further benefits identified included avoiding duplication of research and more free time for reading or research.

SETTING UP AND MANAGING AN ONLINE SEARCH SERVICE

Guidelines and suggestions for planning and implementing an online search service have been developed. Initial considerations include needs assessment, commercial search service selection, impact of service, and costs involved.

Continued operation of a search service requires administrative and financial management, as well as overall evaluation of the service.

Related sections in this bibliography include:

Economics of Online Searching (Entries 94-112)
Impact of Online Searching (Entries 208-221)
User Evaluation and Attitudes (Entries 436-443)

345. Atherton, Pauline. **"Introduction: Planning for Online Search Services in Sci-Tech Libraries."** *Science & Technology Libraries* 1 (Fall 1980): 3-5.

Introduces a series of articles in this issue of *Science & Technology Libraries* which concern planning for the introduction of online services in various types of libraries that specialize in science and technology (see also #271, 278, 307, 346, 351, 359, 361, 362, 371, 454). Emphasizes the need for planning and identifies three aspects of the planning process: 1) strategic planning; 2) operational planning; and 3) task programming.

346. Berger, Patricia W. and Elsie Cerutti. **"The Management of Online Reference Search Services in Federal Libraries."** *Science & Technology Libraries* 1 (Fall 1980): 81-107.

Outlines how online search services have been established in various science and technology libraries which serve the executive branch of the federal government. Differences within federal libraries because of geographic and statutory restrictions are noted. Discusses general aspects of establishing a search service, including selection of databases, service policies, staffing, training, and physical facility. Includes a glossary of federal agency acronyms.

347. Blue, Richard I. **"Questions for Selection of Information Retrieval Systems."** *Online Review* 3 (March 1979): 77-84.

Provides an extensive list of potential questions to be asked when considering which information retrieval system to select. Questions concern all aspects of the selection process, ranging from database creation to service reliability. Suggests ways to acquire this information and notes that a needs analysis should be undertaken before attempting to answer the questions.

348. Daniels, Linda. **"A Matter of Form."** *Online* 2 (October 1978): 31-39.

Provides examples of various forms typically used in an online search service to evaluate the service and to compile necessary statistics. Examples of search request forms, an evaluation form, and a search log are given. Suggestions for developing specific forms are presented.

349. Drinan, Helen. **"Financial Management of Online Services—A How to Guide."** *Online* 3 (October 1979): 14-21.

Presents a detailed financial management methodology for analyzing the economic impact of online services. Three tasks are identified: 1) budgeting for online services; 2) pricing online services; and 3) controlling costs of online services. Examples are presented for each, and gradual improvement of forecasting is predicted.

350. Echt, Sandy; Ann Paffenberger; and M. Glenn Crouch. **"Save Time, Simplify Procedures, Get Better Statistics."** *Online* 5 (April 1981): 21-35.

Describes an automated bookkeeping program designed and implemented by the Texas Christian University Library's Automated Information Retrieval Service (AIRS).

Objectives of the system are briefly presented and then the mechanics are detailed. Generation of monthly statistical reports is completed faster and more accurately using AIRS, and virtually all manual bookkeeping records have been eliminated.

351. Goodemote, Rita L. **"Planning Online Search Service for a Pharmaceutical Company."** *Science & Technology Libraries* 1 (Fall 1980): 69-73.

Justifies the need for online searching in a pharmaceutical library. The following basic planning stages in implementing a search service in a specialized library are discussed: 1) the proposal; 2) equipment and suppliers; 3) staffing; 4) operational decisions; 5) promotion of the service; and 6) evaluation. Stresses the need for preliminary and ongoing planning.

352. Halperin, Michael. **"Preparing Online Service Reports with Packaged Programs."** *Online* 5 (October 1981): 62-69.

Explains how packaged computer programs can be used to prepare the necessary statistical reports for auditing and managing an online search service. Two specific programs for analyzing data are described: SPSS (Statistical Package for the Social Sciences) and SAS (Statistical Analysis System). Three types of management reports are defined using examples from an online search service. Advantages to computer processing of search data include sortability, legibility, and immediate availability.

353. Haygarth Jackson, A. R.; P. A. Holohan; and M. J. Shether. **"Online Retrieval of Bibliographic Information: Its Introduction and Evaluation Based on the First Year's Experience."** *Information Scientist* 12 (March 1978): 9-24.

Outlines the experiences of the library at ICI Pharmaceuticals Division in introducing online searching in 1976. Discusses unique difficulties encountered because of the specialized environment and the need for librarians to serve as "information intermediaries." General overview of the steps in implementing an online service are given, and several suggestions for improving databases are noted.

354. Heinlen, W. F. and M. A. Midbon. **"Data Base Management on a Budget."** *RQ* 18 (Fall 1978): 50-52.

Provides guidelines to aid small or medium-sized academic libraries in implementing online searching. Criteria for selecting search services are discussed and the training available is generally considered to be "deficient." Start-up costs and other financial considerations are also considered. Examples from California State University, Fresno, are used to further clarify the procedures and suggestions presented.

355. Hoover, Ryan E. **"Computer Aided Reference Services in the Academic Library: Experiences in Organizing and Operating an Online Reference Service."** *Online* 3 (October 1979): 28-41.

Describes the development and implementation of the Computer-Aided Reference Services (CARS) division of the University of Utah Library's Reference Department. Discusses the historical background and organizational structure. Other initial considerations (e.g., equipment and training requirements) are dealt with. Statistics and patron evaluation of the service are briefly noted. Suggests "pitfalls to avoid" in establishing an online service.

356. Knapp, Sara D. and James Schmidt. **"Budgeting to Provide Computer-Based Reference Services: A Case Study."** *Journal of Academic Librarianship* 5 (March 1979): 9-13.

Describes the implementation and evolution of an online search service at the library at SUNY/Albany. Free searches were provided from 1972 to 1977 and then fees were imposed. Discusses the effects charging had on use of the service. Number of searches performed and their costs are presented in tables. Administrative and organizational aspects are also noted.

357. Landau, Herbert B. **"Can the Librarian Become a Computer Data Base Manager?"** *Special Libraries* 62 (March 1971): 117-24.

Contends that librarians must be directly involved in managing large databases. However, librarians must first become knowledgeable and skilled in the development and utilization of such machine-readable files. Formal education in database management needs to be developed. An annotated bibliography is appended.

358. Lewis, D. A. and R. Adkins. **"The Management of Online Resources: Problems and Opportunities."** *Online Review* 5 (October 1981): 367-76.

Identifies both "old problems as well as new problems" faced by managers of online services. Stresses that good management involves two simple concepts: control and development. Control is concerned with daily operations, while development involves planning for the future. Discusses various methods for dealing with typical problems, such as reduced motivation or negative attitudes. Briefly describes Project Radius, which stands for "Rapid Access to Data and Information by Untrained Scientists," and its development by ICI Plastics Division.

359. Martin, Jean K. **"Preparation of Proposals for Online Bibliographic Services in Academic, Government, and Industrial Libraries."** *Science & Technology Libraries* 1 (Fall 1980): 7-15.

Outlines the steps necessary in preparing a formal proposal for the implementation of online searching in a library. Key factors to be identified in the planning stage are: 1) needs assessment; 2) anticipated usage; 3) comparison with manual searching; 4) database and vendor selection; 5) terminal selection; 6) impact of online services; 7) alternatives to online searching; and 8) charging for the services. A basic outline for a proposal is also provided.

360. Mourreau, Magdeleine L. **"Problems and Pitfalls in Setting Up and Operating an Online Information Service."** *Online Review* 2 (September 1978): 237-44.

Provides a checklist of the problems typically encountered in setting up an online search service. Decisions which must be made concerning database producers, search services, and telecommunications networks are individually discussed. Other considerations (e.g., physical, economic, technical, and social factors) are also presented. Solutions are presented from the perspective of both the end user and the search intermediary.

361. Pensyl, Mary E. and Susan E. Woodford. **"Planning and Implementation Guidelines for an Academic Online Service: The MIT Experience."** *Science & Technology Libraries* 1 (Fall 1980): 17-45.

Uses the experiences of the Massachusetts Institute of Technology Libraries in providing online search services to develop guidelines that can be used by other libraries for planning and implementing a search service. Considers the following areas in some detail: 1) planning for online services; 2) staffing; 3) training and service implementations; 4) financial aspects; 5) marketing and publicity; and 6) monitoring, evaluating, and planning for future growth. Urges librarians to "keep pace with the major developments and trends that are emerging nationally and internationally."

362. Piermatti, Patricia Ann and Shirley W. Bolles. **"Planning Online Search Services in a State University."** *Science & Technology Libraries* 1 (Fall 1980): 47-50.

Details the philosophy and principles developed by the Rutgers University Library of Science and Medicine when it initiated online searching in 1973. The planning procedure is explained and decisions reached concerning the following areas are outlined: 1) integration of service with reference; 2) staffing and administration; and 3) fees and costs. Basic philosophy is to consider online searching simply "an extension of reference service."

363. Plosker, George R. and Roger K. Summit. **"Management of Vendor Services. How to Choose an Online Vendor."** *Special Libraries* 71 (August 1980): 354-57.

Describes a systematic approach to evaluating and selecting a commercial search service. A step-by-step method for comparing services is given. Questions to ask are listed and possible acceptable answers discussed. Brief overview of the major issues to be considered is presented.

364. Potter, William. **"An Online Search Log."** *Online* 3 (January 1979): 27-35.

Presents an online search log developed and used on a mini-computer to monitor search activity. Requirements and criteria for such an online log are established and the various necessary data elements defined. The different system modules are briefly explained. Sample outputs are included.

365. Ruhl, Mary Jane and Elizabeth J. Yeates. **"Introducing and Implementing On-Line Bibliographic Retrieval Services in a Scientific Research and Development Organization."** *Journal of Chemical Information & Computer Sciences* 16 (August 1976): 147-50.

Describes the experiences of the National Bureau of Standards Library in introducing online searching to its patrons. Methods and materials used to promote and educate users are presented. Discusses results of user evaluations regarding success of searches, purposes of requests, and impact on future library use. Notes the implications, especially financial requirements, that introducing such a service will have on the library.

366. Seba, Doug. **"Management Outpost."** See issues of *Online* beginning with volume 2, #3.

Deals with the management of online search services. This regular column in *Online* discusses the managing and marketing aspects of administering an online service.

367. Selman, Sharon and Marcia J. Meyers. **"Use of an On-line Bibliographic Search Service in Chemistry."** *Special Libraries* 71 (May 1980): 270-75.

Describes the introduction of online computer searching to the chemistry department at Florida State University. A three-phase approach was used to gradually expose users in the chemistry department to free computer searches. Describes initial problems, frequency of use, reasons for searches, and results of searches conducted. Fewer than three search requests were typically received per day. Concludes that online searching was "readily accepted."

SPECIAL LIBRARIES AND ONLINE SEARCHING

Special libraries were early users of online searching and contributed much to the development of both individual databases and the major search services. The use of databases by both research and industrial libraries remains very high and, as more nonbibliographical and statistical databases become available, this use should increase even more. Since special libraries tend to deal with a specific field or area of research, other appropriate articles concerning the use of online searching by special libraries can be found in the "Specialized Subject Areas or Databases in Online Searching" portion of this bibliography.

Related sections in this bibliography include:

Databases and Database Producers (Entries 49-67)
Numeric and Nonbibliographical Databases (Entries 250-260)

See also appropriate sections in the "Specialized Subject Areas or Databases in Online Searching" portion of this bibliography.

368.   Brown, Carolyn P. **"Online Bibliographic Retrieval Systems Use."** *Special Libraries* 68 (April 1977): 155-60.
Stresses the need for continual publicity and promotion of online search services. Surveys were conducted of both users and nonusers of the computerized information service offered since 1974 in the library at the National Bureau of Standards. Number of searches conducted, frequency of use, cost of searches, and reasons for use and nonuse are presented in various charts.

369.   Colthurst, J. P. and M. E. Shilling. **"On-line Searching in a Research Environment."** *Online Review* 1 (December 1977): 311-17.
Discusses all aspects of introducing online searching in a scientific research laboratory. Topics covered include uses of online services, cost-effectiveness, operating considerations, choice of databases, and customer reactions. Notes that substantial savings can result from the use of online searching in such a specialized setting.

370.   Dawling, K. and J. Kirsch. **"Online Information Retrieval in a Local Education Agency."** *School Media Quarterly* 6 (Fall 1977): 33-38.
Reports on the use of computer searching in the Montgomery County (Maryland) Public Schools. Historical evolution of the program is briefly described and use statistics are provided. The Educational Materials Laboratory, the central library for the school system, provides online services to school staff, students, and county residents. Foresees the day when all school media centers will have computer terminals.

371.   Hawkins, Donald T. **"Six Years of Online Searching in an Industrial Library Network."** *Science & Technology Libraries* 1 (Fall 1980): 57-67.
Describes the use of online searching in the Bell Laboratories Network. Notes various changes in information retrieval patterns during the six-year period from 1974 through 1979. Statistics for this period are presented to demonstrate the growth in searching activity and to classify the types of searches conducted. Average search times and costs are also given. Notes the "spectacular growth of online searching at Bell Laboratories" during this period.

372.   Jacob, Mary Ellen; Ann T. Dodson; and Nancy Finnegan. **"Special Libraries and Databases. A State-of-the-Art Report."** *Special Libraries* 72 (April 1981): 103-112.
Reviews the use of bibliographic and nonbibliographic databases, especially those available through commercial search services and online support services. Trends are identified concerning database coverage, vocabulary, printed index use, client use of online services, and standardization. Emphasis is on the use of databases by special libraries. A

bibliography, including annotated references of selected journals and directories, is appended.

373. Kodac, Sarah T. and Rhoda Mancher. **"Online Services in the Executive Office of the President."** *Online Review* 3 (December 1979): 361-66.

Describes the use of both internal and external databases in the Executive Office of the President (EOP). The Office of Administration within the EOP is responsible for overseeing these online systems. External databases and commercial search services accessed include DIALOG, SDC, BRC, SCORPIO, and the New York Times INFORMATION BANK. Internal systems described concern correspondence and legislative tracking systems, electronic mail, and internal documents indexing.

374. Lawrence, Barbara; Ben H. Weiljand; and Margaret H. Graham. **"Making On-Line Search Available in an Industrial Research Environment."** *Journal of the American Society for Information Science* 25 (November-December 1974): 364-69.

Describes the introduction of online searching at the Research Center of Exxon Research and Engineering Company. Emphasizes the importance of recognizing differences both between commercial search services and databases. Search quality is best when the scientist and searcher work together in conducting the search. Cost and user acceptance are also discussed. Includes statistics for searches done in 1973 and 1974.

TELECOMMUNICATIONS

The transmission of digital information between a terminal and the computer of a commercial search service through a communications network, such as TELENET, TYMNET, or UNINET, is an essential component of online searching. One special application that has been reported is the use of conference calls to conduct an interactive online search.

Related sections in this bibliography include:

Terminals and Microcomputers (Entries 384-399)

375. Brimmer, Karl W. **"Telecommunications Regulations and Policy."** *Online Review* 5 (December 1981): 481-86.

Examines four current issues related to telecommunications regulations: 1) shifts in common carrier regulatory policies; 2) technological and economic reasons for these changes in policy; 3) major regulatory actions that have occurred recently; and 4) implications that alternatives to local telephone service have on online services. Significant decisions of the FCC are discussed and barriers to competition in providing local telecommunications services are noted.

376. Brown, Fran and John Walsh. **"New Wrinkles in Conference Call Searching."** *Online* 6 (March 1982): 30-33.

Describes an innovative technique which allows "conference searching." This involves two searchers at different locations conducting and interacting with an online search. In this instance it was used as a means to allow an experienced searcher to oversee the searches of a newly trained search analyst who was searching in a different location. Technical explanations are simply presented and other possible applications briefly noted.

377. Clinton, Marshall. **"Packet Switching Networks. Their Technology and Costs."** *Online* 2 (July 1978): 51-53.

Summarizes how packet switching networks such as TYMNET and TELENET actually operate. Figures are used to illustrate the workings of such a communications network. Advantages of packet switching networks include low cost, flexibility, and accuracy.

378. Graham, Deborah L. **"Simultaneous Remote Search: A Technique of Providing MEDLARS Services to Remote Locations."** *Bulletin of the Medical Library Association* 68 (October 1980): 370-71.

Describes a service offered by the Tucson Medical Center (TMC) to provide instantaneous access to MEDLINE to medical personnel at remote locations. Requesters phone the TMC search center and the information interview is conducted. Terminals at both the remote site and search center are then jointly used via a conference call to perform the search. The actual search and online results are received on both terminals. Benefits and problems encountered are described.

379. Huber, W. **"Recent Developments within Euronet."** *Computer Communications* 1 (April 1978): 79-84.

Presents a historical overview of the development of EURONET and predicts possible future expansions of the system. Distinguishes between EURONET as a telecommunications network and an information network. Need for the service and reasons for its success are outlined. Telecommunications costs are also briefly discussed.

380. Kallenbach, P. A. **"Introduction to Data Transmission for Information Retrieval."** *Information Processing and Management* 11 (1975): 137-45.

Presents a general overview of data communication principles and theories. Data signals, modulation, communications, network configuration, and terminal equipment are discussed. Examples used are for the ESA/RECON network.

381. **"Telecommunication Terminology."** *Online Review* 1 (March 1977): 11-14.
Presents definitions of 34 telecommunications terms.

382. Warden, Carolyn L. **"Update on Conference Call Searching."** *Online* 3 (July 1979): 34.

Describes the use of conference calls to allow for direct interaction between a searcher and a remote requester. Experience has identified certain optimum procedures (e.g., searching in half duplex via TELENET provides the best results). Differences in the informational interview when dealing with a remote patron are also noted.

383. Witiak, Joanne L.; Barbara G. Prewitt; and Allen R. Deschere. **"Online Database Searching via Telephone Conferencing."** *Online* 3 (April 1979): 21-23.

Presents techniques for using telephone conferencing to allow direct patron interaction with an online search from a remote location. Two phone lines are utilized to provide verbal communication between the requester and the searcher and to provide duplicate online printouts on terminals at both locations. Problems generally include securing a good signal at both terminals. Concludes that conference searching can be a "real advantage."

TERMINALS AND MICROCOMPUTERS

A terminal is needed in an online search to transmit data to and from the computer of a commercial search service. Terminals can be either print or CRT, and criteria for selecting a terminal for online searching have been developed. Current interest is centered on the use of microcomputers in online retrieval and the cost-effectiveness of searching at 1200 baud.

Related sections in this bibliography include:

Setting Up and Managing an Online Search Service (Entries 345-367)
Telecommunications (Entries 375-383)

384. Blair, John C. **"Database Designs."** *Database* 5 (June 1982): 72-79.
Lists various software products available for use on Apple computers. Programs are summarized and hardware requirements noted. Future articles are proposed to deal with other software and other microcomputers.

385. Blair, John C., Jr. **"Micro Magic."** See issues of *Online* beginning with volume 5, #4.
Discusses various applications and uses of microcomputers in libraries, especially in online searching. Certain items are written for intermediate and expert level users.

386. Blair, John C. **"Micros, Minis and Mainframes — A Newcomers Guide to the World of Computers — Especially Micros."** *Online* 6 (January 1982): 14-26.
Presents a practical overview of computers, with special emphasis on the possible uses of microcomputers in libraries. Distinguishes between mainframes, minicomputers and microcomputers. Also discusses available programs, communication requirements, advantages of disks, librarians as programmers, and future applications of videodisks. A brief list of references and a glossary of computer terms are included.

387. Blair, John C., Jr. **"Utilization of 1200 Baud for On-Line Retrieval in a Health Sciences Library."** *Bulletin of the Medical Library Association* 63 (July 1980): 294-97.
Considers the benefits and drawbacks to using a 1200 baud terminal for online searching. Discusses selection of an appropriate modem and terminal for efficient 1200 baud searching. Differences in search techniques at the faster speed are noted. The effects of 1200 baud searching on health science libraries is specifically considered. Increased benefits must be balanced against the additional effort required for 1200 baud searching.

388. Bonn, Jane H. and Philipp R. Heer. **"Terminal Equipment for Online Interactive Information Retrieval Using Telecommunications."** *Special Libraries* 67 (January 1976): 30-39.
Provides a basic overview of telecommunications equipment and terminals. Techniques of transmitting data through the various data communications networks are briefly described. Types of terminals, both print and display, are discussed and compared. An appendix provides a survey of equipment and manufacturers, as of August 1975.

389. Crawford, W. C. **"CRT Terminal Checklist."** *Journal of Library Automation* 13 (March 1980): 36-44.
Presents a checklist for selecting cathode ray tube (CRT) terminals developed by the Technical Standards for Library Automation Committee (TELSA) of the Information Science and Automation Section in the Library and Information Technology Association

of ALA. After identifying particular institutional needs, three steps are suggested: 1) consult advertisements and literature; 2) actually use and observe use of possible terminals; and 3) talk to other users. Specific items to examine and questions to ask are also noted.

390.   **"Holug's Online Equipment Fair."** *Online* 5 (July 1981): 56-57.
Presents a pictorial look at an online equipment fair presented by the Hudson-Valley Online Users Group (HOLUG) on March 11, 1981. Fourteen different exhibitors displayed equipment and services to over 130 people.

391.   Kazlauskas, Edward John. **"Selecting a Computer Terminal for the Library."** *Special Libraries* 68 (January 1977): 24-27.
Summarizes the questions to ask when selecting a computer terminal for a library. Topics covered include CRT versus print terminals, type of formats and character fonts available, size of screen or display, system compatibility, storage and editing capabilities, and cost. Notes that future use of terminals in other areas of the library should also be considered.

392.   Monsen, Gordon L., Jr. **"Computer Terminals and Minicomputers in On-line Retrieval."** *Online Review* 1 (September 1977): 217-29.
Investigates the advantages and disadvantages of using minicomputers when performing online searches. Various benefits are given. Increased user acceptance of the online product is cited as the major benefit. The major difference involves the higher speeds at which minicomputers can operate. Stresses that the decision to use minicomputers for online searching depends on projected use, availability of qualified staff, and estimated costs involved.

393.   Radwin, Mark S. **"The Intelligent Person's Guide to Choosing a Terminal for Online Interactive Use."** *Online* Part I, 1 (January 1977): 11-19; Part II, 1 (April 1977): 61-73.
Indicates various factors which must be taken into account when choosing a terminal. Part I provides answers to the following five questions: 1) printing terminal or CRT? 2) low speed or high speed access? 3)portable or stationary unit? 4) lease or buy? 5) obtain from a broker or manufacturer? Other terminal qualities to be considered include: maintenance, reliability, simplicity of operation, clarity of printing, and noise. Part II is a table listing and describing terminals commonly used for online searching. (See also #394.)

394.   Radwin, Mark. **"List of Terminal Manufacturers."** *Online* 1 (July 1977): 81-83.
Provides a list of terminal manufacturers inadvertently not included with an earlier two-part article (see #393). Manufacturers are identified and addresses given. Brokers or leasing companies offering terminals which can be used for online searching are also listed.

395.   Shenton, Kathleen and M. Karen Landsberg. **"Conference Searching at 1200 Baud."** *Online* 5 (January 1981): 42-43.
Describes a method of conferencing searching using 1200 baud terminals developed by the Linden Information Center of Exxon Research and Training Company. Technical requirements are explained and a step-by-step outline of the entire procedure given. Difficulties encountered are noted and possible solutions explained. Considers such conference searching to be invaluable for certain types of rush requests for information.

396.   Steffenson, Martin B. and Kathryn L. King. **"Prerecord Your Online Bibliographic Searches for Time and Money Savings."** *Online* 5 (January 1981): 47-49.

Describes a method for storing searches on cassette tape prior to conducting the actual search online. The stored search statements can then be quickly and accurately transmitted to the computer without any additional typing. Besides saving online time and money, recorded searches can be used to maintain SDIs and as demonstration tools. An appendix details how to record a search using a Texas Instruments Silent 700 Series, Model 733 ASR Data Terminal.

397. Stewart, Alan K. **"The 1200 Baud Experience."** *Online* 2 (July 1978): 13-18.

Examines the benefits of 1200 baud searching. Factors to be considered before switching to a 1200 terminal are discussed, and the faster searching is found to have a "definite advantage." Differences in online time and offline charges are depicted in graphs. Notes that searching at 1200 baud requires certain changes in search style.

398. Tyner, Sue. **"Checklist for Printing Terminals."** *Journal of Library Automation* 13 (June 1980): 108-119.

Presents a checklist for selecting print terminals. The checklist covers the following: model, printer, keyboard, paper, acoustic coupler, line communications, and reliability, warranty, and maintenance. User requirements, how to obtain and install a terminal, and costs involved are also discussed. Stresses the need to analyze specific requirements for the terminal before beginning the actual selection process.

399. Wish, John; Craig Collins; and Vance Jacobson. **"Terminal Costs for On-Line Searching."** *College and Research Libraries* 88 (July 1977): 291-97.

Offers a methodology for choosing a terminal. Estimates are given for cost-per-minute connect time, estimated time of average search, the ratio of input to output time, and the cost per month for a two-year lease of a terminal. Terminals of speeds ranging from 10 to 120 characters-per-second are compared. The slowest and least expensive terminals are recommended when less than 25 searches are performed per month.

TRAINING AND EDUCATION OF SEARCH ANALYSTS

Online searching is a relatively new area of librarianship which requires librarians to acquire new skills and techniques. The necessity of providing some sort of formal training to enable librarians to function as search analysts has been clearly demonstrated and such training is widely available. In some cases, a distinction is made between "training" selected librarians in the mechanics of computer searching and "educating" all librarians about the potential benefits of online reference services.

Related sections in this bibliography include:

Informational Interview (Entries 222-229)
Search Analysts (Entries 296-308)
Setting Up and Managing an Online Search Service (Entries 345-367)

400. Bellardo, Trudi; Gail Kennedy; and Gretchen Tremoulet. **"On-line Bibliographic System Instructions."** *Journal of Education for Librarianship* 19 (Summer 1978): 21-31.

Describes an online biblioigraphic systems course taught at the University of Kentucky's College for Library Science. Three practitioners each taught five-week sections of the course which covered three different bibliographic utilities: OCLC, MEDLINE, and

DIALOG. Objectives for each section are explained and difficulties encountered are noted. Major problems involved class size, scheduling, theft of equipment and required readings. Students and instructors judged the course to be a success.

401. Berk, Robert A. and Rebecca W. Davidson. **"MEDLINE Training within the Library School Curriculum: Quality Control and Future Trends."** *Bulletin of the Medical Library Association* 66 (July 1978): 302-308.

Reports the results of a survey of schools of library science in 1976-1977 to determine the current availability of MEDLINE training. Concludes that library schools should increase their efforts in this area. Specific suggestions are directed at library schools, health science librarians, and the National Library of Medicine. Summarized information is given for such aspects of library school courses as instructor's background and experience, the course structure, and the amount of online time provided to students.

402. Borko, Harold. **"Teaching On-Line Retrieval Systems at the University of California, Los Angeles."** *Information Processing and Management* 14 (1978): 477-80.

Reports on the teaching of online retrieval at the University of California, Los Angeles. Applications of computer searching should be demonstrated in both cataloging and reference courses, but separate advanced courses should be offered to train students in searching the major search services. Various aspects of teaching (e.g., length of class, textbooks used, and amount of individual online experience) are also enumerated. Problems include cost and time involved in conducting such a course.

403. Bourne, Charles P. and Jo Robinson. **"Education and Training for Computer Based Reference Services: Review of Training Efforts to Date."** *Journal of the American Society for Information Science* 31 (January 1980): 25-35.

Discusses who is to be trained, what the training needs are, and who is responsible for training in the area of computer-based reference services. Summarizes the training available (as of June 1979) from commercial search services, database suppliers, library schools, library cooperatives and professional organizations. Supporting training manuals and search aids available are also discussed. Concludes that library schools will be more directly responsible for such training in the future.

404. Byerly, Greg. **"Training without Education: A Lost Cause."** Guest editor of "Online Services." Edited by Danuta Nitecki. *RQ* 20 (Spring 1981): 229-31.

Differentiates between the "training" of searchers in the mechanics of online searching and the "education" of the entire library staff about the potential uses of computer searching. While the need for training is well established, the need to educate all librarians concerning online reference services must be emphasized. Summarizes problems encountered in trying to integrate computer searching into reference service and gives examples of questions easily answered by online searches.

405. Caruso, Elaine. **"Hands On Online: Bringing It Home."** *Online Review* 2 (September 1978): 251-68.

Describes the problems a new user faces in trying to learn to use a bibliographic database. Current methods of training are summarized and found to be deficient. Introduces a new training program, the "Hands on Online Multisystem Multidatabase Trainer," developed at the University of Pittsburgh. Designed to allow a trainee to be instructed at his own terminal, this system uses emulators to "mimic" the actual commercially available search services. Training goals, future plans, and evaluation methods are also presented.

406.　Caruso, Elaine. **"TRAINER."** *Online* 5 (January 1981): 36-38.

　　Provides information concerning the availability and capabilities of the University of Pittsburgh's TRAINER. TRAINER is a computer-based tutorial system which introduces users to basic search commands and techniques. System emulators also provide practice on both DIALOG and SDC. The system is designed for individual use and is available via EDUNET/TELENET. Examples of actual uses are detailed and sources of additional information are noted.

407.　Caruso, Elaine and John Griffiths. **"A TRAINER for Online Systems."** *Online* 1 (October 1977): 28-34.

　　Describes an online training program being developed at the University of Pittsburgh in 1977. TRAINER utilizes programmed instruction to familiarize new searchers with basic aspects of online searching. Emulators which can imitate or respond like larger systems such as DIALOG and SDC are an important part of TRAINER. Several practice files, which typically represent one issue or update of a database, are also used in the TRAINER program.

408.　Crampon, Jean E. **"Training Backup Searchers or How 'Reluctant Ralph' Deals with 'Terrified Tess.' "** *Online* 4 (October 1980): 25-29.

　　Details the problems encountered in training backup searchers, i.e., searchers who have been trained but who do not normally perform searches unless other primary searchers are unavailable. Three factors are identified that determine training methods: 1) Institution as a problem; 2) Trainee as a problem; and 3) Trainer as a problem. Stresses the need for preliminary planning and considers whether the training should be conducted in-house or by external suppliers. Various types of institutions, trainees, and trainers (e.g., Terrified Tess and Careful Cathy) are examined.

409.　Duncan, Elizabeth E.; Patricia J. Klingensmith; and Nina M. Ross. **"An Exercise in Utility; Training in Search and Seizure at the University of Pittsburgh."** *Online* 4 (January 1980): 64-67.

　　Describes the online training sessions which have been conducted every month at the University of Pittsburgh since April 1978. Details the difficulties in designing such a course to meet the needs of a wide variety of students. A general overview of the entire training schedule is briefly provided. Emulators of the major commercial search systems are used heavily in the training. Stresses that systems, not individual databases, are taught.

410.　Faibisoff, Sylvia and John L. Bennett. **"On-line Reference Retrieval Training for Effective Use."** *Bulletin of the American Society for Information Science* 3 (August 1979): 35.

　　Summarizes the activities at a full-day workshop held prior to the 1977 ASIS Mid-Year Meeting dealing with the training of online searchers. Group discussions generated opinions concerning the following: 1) distinctions between education and training; 2) levels of training needed; 3) costs of training; 4) training aids available; and 5) searcher performance evaluation. Notes that the increased need for trained searchers is a real "challenge for library schools."

411.　Haggerty, Thomas M. **"Education of On-Line Users."** *Bulletin of the American Society for Information Science* 3 (August 1977): 20-21.

　　Discusses how the Washington Area On-line Users Group attempts to provide various types of training sessions for both beginning and experienced searchers. Two types of training are described. "Piggyback training" utilizes an experienced searcher at another library to train a new searcher over a period of several months and "rehabilitative training" involves the retraining of an experienced, but not proficient, searcher in a similar fashion.

412. Hardin, Mary and Danuta Nitecki. **"A New Breed of Online Speciality: The Remote Profiler."** *Online* 2 (July 1978): 31-38.

Details an approach taken to train library personnel in "profiling" search requests which would be performed by a trained searcher at a different location. A training workshop for such "remote profilers" was conducted in September 1977 as part of a statewide information network, OTIS/OIL (Oklahoma Teletype Interlibrary System/Oklahoma Information Lines). Lectures and other aspects of the workshop are summarized.

413. Harter, Stephen P. **"An Assessment of Instruction Provided by Library Schools in Online Searching."** *Information Processing and Management* 15 (1979): 71-75.

Summarizes the results of a survey conducted of 64 accredited library schools in January 1977 to determine the extent to which instruction is available in online searching. Figures indicate a "strong movement" by library schools towards the integration of such instruction in other courses and the establishment of separate courses dealing with online information retrieval. Amount of online experience varies widely from school to school. The course developed at the University of South Florida is outlined.

414. Heyer, John. **"In-house Training for Online Searching at a Special Library."** *Online Review* 4 (December 1980): 367-74.

Sketches the in-house training programs developed and used in the U.S. General Accounting Office Library. Outlines for courses on DIALOG, SCORPIO, ORBIT, and the New York Times INFORMATION BANK are given. Individualized courses are offered based on the experience of the students. Continued contact between instructor and students and the integration of online searching into normal reference procedures are cited as advantages of in-house training.

415. Jackson, William J. **"ONTAP-ERIC: A Critical View."** *Online Review* 5 (December 1981): 335-38.

Criticizes ONTAP ERIC, an online training file developed by DIALOG. Of four stated purposes, only one is successfully met by this file. ONTAP ERIC does allow users to practice various features of the DIALOG system, but it does not adequately demonstrate refined search capabilities and it does not allow self-evaluation as proclaimed by DIALOG. Recommendations for improvement are enumerated. Agrees that low cost files for online training are valuable but should be improved.

416. Knapp, Sara D. and Jacquelyn A. Gavryck. **"Computer Based Reference Service—A Course Taught by Practitioners."** *Online* 2 (April 1978): 65-76.

Summarizes a wide variety of teaching methods (e.g., guest lectures, role-playing, Venn diagramming, etc.) and search techniques (e.g., Boolean logic, free text searching, stop words, etc.) used in a two-week course taught by the State University of New York at Albany's School of Library and Information Science since 1975. Objectives, costs, and problems of maintaining currency and of evaluating search results are also discussed.

417. Kuroki, Kristyn. **"Online Regional and On-Site Training Opportunities in Lockheed, SDC and BRS System and Their Databases."** *Online* 3 (July 1979): 36-49.

Details the training sessions available from the three major commercial search services (BRS, DIALOG, and SDC) in 1979. Describes the content of the training, length of the session, types of training offered (e.g., Beginner, Advanced, Subject, or Custom), cost involved, and contact information. Similar information is given for over 25 database suppliers that provide some sort of training. Briefly discusses the factors involved in deciding where to get training. Since this information rapidly becomes dated, it is suggested that commercial search services or database producers be contacted directly for current information.

418.   Lowry, Glenn R. **"Training of Users of Online Services: A Survey of the Literature."** *Science & Technology Libraries* 1 (Spring 1981): 27-40. ⌐

Reviews the literature published from 1976 to 1979 dealing with the education and training of users of online services. References are divided into the following categories: 1) general articles; 2) promotion of online services; 3) education of professional search analysts; and 4) the training of end users. Future trends are also noted.

419.   Markee, Katherine M. **"Online User Training: A 'Team' Approach."** *Science & Technology Libraries* 1 (Spring 1981): 21-25.

Advocates the "team approach" to train and educate users about online searching. The team includes the commercial search service, database producer, search analyst, and end user. Stresses the need for "communication to flow in all directions" and the importance of having search analysts who are well trained and able to explain search operations to end users.

420.   **"Online Training Sessions: Suggested Guidelines."** *RQ* 20 (Summer 1981): 353-57.

Outlines suggested guidelines for various types of online training sessions. General introduction is given and appropriate definitions provided. Guidelines are presented for five types of training sessions: 1) Search Service—Beginning; 2) Search Service—Advanced; 3) Search Service—Subject; 4) Database Producer; and 5) Independent Introductory Workshop. Developed by the Education and Training of Search Analysts Committee of the Machine-Assisted Reference Section, Reference and Adult Services Division, ALA.

421.   Ress, Alan; Lydia Holian; and Ann Schaap. **"An Experiment in Teaching MEDLINE."** *Bulletin of the Medical Library Association* 64 (April 1976): 196-202.

Describes the development and implementation of a MEDLINE module within a health sciences communications course at the Case Western University School of Library Science. Eight weeks are devoted to lectures, demonstrations (both videotape and online), and online exercises concerning MEDLINE. Course design, equipment used, and student performance and evaluation are discussed. Concludes that such a mini-course is expensive but "feasible" within a library school curriculum.

422.   Robinson, Jo. **"Education and Training for Computer-Based Reference Services: A Case Study."** *Journal of the American Society for Information Science* 31 (March 1980): 97-104.

Details a training program for online searching used by the University of California's Computerized Information Services. The training program concentrated on DIALOG, BRS, and SDC and had five parts: 1) confidence building sessions; 2) initial and advanced search system training sessions; 3) retrieval exercises; 4) database workshops; and 5) database seminars. The latter two are discussed in detail. Costs involved are briefly discussed. Concludes that database seminars and workshops are cost-effective and effective.

423. Sewell, Winifred. **"Use of Medline in a Medical Literature Course."** *Journal of Education for Librarianship* 15 (Summer 1974): 34-40.

Describes student use of MEDLINE as a component of a medical literature course at the University of Maryland College of Library and Information Services in the early 1970s. Actual assignments and student feedback are reported. Concludes that students can, after a few hours of instruction, independently use MEDLINE to perform sample online searches.

424. Simmons, Peter. **"Satellite Television and Training for On-Line Computer Searching."** *Journal of Education for Librarianship* 19 (Spring 1979): 312-17.

Describes an eight-week experimental continuing education program involving various Canadian organizations and universities which used interactive educational television to teach online searching to librarians located in various remote areas of British Columbia. Course was taught in a series of weekly sessions and transmitted using the Canadian Communications Technology Satellite. Although the program resulted in successful learning, technical and teaching problems are detailed.

425. Slavens, Thomas P. and Marc E. Ruby. **"Teaching Library Science Students to Do Bibliographical Searches of Automated Data Banks."** *RQ* 18 (Fall 1978): 39-41.

Outlines the topics covered in a course on computer searching given to approximately 450 graduate library science students in a three-year period at the School of Library Science at the University of Michigan. These lecture topics include qualifications of a search analyst, selection of equipment, choice of search services, and impact of computer searching on the library. After completing the series of lectures, small groups of two or three students were allowed a minimal amount of "hands-on" experience. Concludes that having students actually perform a basic search must be an essential part of any course such as this one.

426. Swanson, Rowena Weiss. **"An Assessment of Online Instruction Methodologies."** *Online* 6 (January 1982): 38-53.

Presents a comparison of nine available training programs in four major areas: 1) purposive documentation; 2) education program; 3) resources; and 4) evaluation/feedback mechanisms. Notes that most programs do not adequately state overall goals and that costs in program preparation can be considerable. Two essential elements are printed materials and hands-on practice. Computer-assisted instruction and videotape presentations can also be very effective. No qualitative judgments are made concerning the specific training programs studied.

427. Tedd, Lucy A. **"Teaching Aids Developed and Used for Education and Training for Online Searching."** *Online Review* 5 (June 1981): 205-216.

Describes various teaching aids available for the education and training of search analysts. Examples given are primarily from British schools of librarianship and information science. Training aids are divided into the following categories: 1) audio and digital recording devices; 2) computer-assisted instruction; 3) audiovisual aids; and 4) printed materials. Viewdata is also briefly discussed. Cost, choice of instructor, and suitable facilities are problems also encountered in conducting an online training course.

428. Tedd, Lucy A. and E. Michael Keen. **"Methods of Teaching On-Line Bibliographic Searching: Experience at the College of Librarianship Wales."** *Information and Processing and Management* 14 (1978): 453-63.

Presents an outline for a course on online bibliographic searching used at the College of Librarianship Wales. Five main components of such a course are detailed: 1) general introduction; 2) specific introduction; 3) demonstration search; 4) live search; and 5) assessing search results. Compares the cost-effectiveness of various types of demonstrations (e.g., videotape, audio cassettes, digital cassettes, and live demonstrations). Cites several advantages to recording a search for demonstration purposes.

429.   Triolo, Victor. **"Continuing Education in On-Line Searching. An Instructional Module for Special Librarians."** *Special Libraries* 68 (May/June 1978): 189-200.
Details a two-day seminar for special librarians in online bibliographic searching developed by the Division of Library Science and Instructional Technology at Southern Connecticut State College. Four objectives are examined in detail: 1) planning and program development; 2) cost analysis; 3) environmental and equipment requirements; and 4) evaluation instruments. Suggestions are also made to improve the training sessions.

430.   **"User Education and Training."** See issues of *Online Review* in volume 1.
Describes the content and availability of training sessions obtainable from database producers. BIOSIS, INSPEC, ISI, and COMPENDEX are represented in three columns, which were published in volume 1 of *Online Review*.

431.   Vickery, Alina and Angela M. Batten. **"Development of Multimedia Teaching Packages for User Education in Online Retrieval Systems."** *Online Review* 2 (December 1978): 267-74.
Discusses a multimedia training device, known as Mediatron, which attempts to demonstrate the basic concepts of online searching and to illustrate certain search techniques commonly used in conducting a search. Developed by the Central Information Service of the University of London, Mediatron displays previously recorded searches on a video display screen, with appropriate voice commentary and accompanying slide display. Contends that self-teaching aids, such as Mediatron, increase the confidence of beginning searchers.

432.   Waldstein, Robert. **"DIATOM—A DIALOG Simulator."** *Online* 5 (July 1981): 68-71.
Describes DIATOM, a DIALOG simulator designed by the author and used at Syracuse University. Used not only in teaching library science students online searching, it also is demonstrated as a research tool and as an aid in producing local databases. Compares DIALOG and DIATOM features and examines certain ones available only on DIATOM. Information on the availability and distribution of DIATOM is given.

433.   Williams, Martha E. **"Education and Training for On-Line Use of Data Bases."** *Journal of Library Automation* 10 (December 1977): 320-34.
Stresses the need for both the education and training of the users of search services and databases. Various types of users are identified, and the different information requirements of searchers, patrons, service managers, and database processors are listed. Details problems and possible solutions associated with the education and training of those involved in searching.

434.   Wood, Frances E. **"Online Teaching Aids from the Department of Information Science, University of Sheffield, England."** *Online Review* 5 (December 1981): 487-94.

Describes four online simulations used to introduce students to online searching at the University of Sheffield's Department of Information Studies. No databases are actually stored and only the prepared searches can be performed online. Simulations are available for DIALOG, SDC, BLAISE, MARC, and BLAISE MEDLINE. Development of the files is discussed and the transferability of the programs to other computers is noted.

435. **"Workshop Calendar—An International Listing of Online Workshop Sessions."** See issues of *Online* beginning with volume 1, #2.

Presents a current listing of online workshops or training sessions to be conducted in the near future. Includes those conducted by commercial search services, database producers, online user groups, and independent organizers.

USER EVALUATION AND ATTITUDES

Evaluations of the value of an online search can theoretically be best done by the requester of the information. Methods to determine user satisfaction and difficulties in interpreting the results of user surveys are discussed in the articles included in this section. User attitudes toward online searching and why certain people do not use such services are also considered.

Related sections in this bibliography include:

End Users (Entries 113-121)
Search Results (Entries 309-320)

436. Bayer, Alan E. and Gerald Jahoda. **"Background Characteristics of Industrial and Academic Users and Nonusers of Online Bibliographic Search Services."** *Online Review* 3 (March 1979): 95-105.

Reports the results of a study investigating both users and nonusers on online bibliographic search services. Free online searches were provided to academic chemists and industrial scientists, then their satisfaction with and acceptance of the service evaluated. Very few differences were found between users and nonusers, but variations of usage did exist between the academic and industrial settings. Notes that prior search techniques, satisfaction with traditional sources, and attitude toward automation did affect slightly the likelihood of using online services.

437. Hoover, Ryan E. **"Patron Appraisal of Computer-Aided On-Line Bibliographic Retrieval Services."** *Journal of Library Automation* 9 (December 1976): 335-50.

Describes an online search service offered by the University of Utah Library and presents the results of a user satisfaction survey conducted in April and May of 1975. Responses are statistically presented for each question asked. Patrons generally judged the service to be "very worthwhile" and indicated a willingness to pay for future searches.

438. Kidd, J. S. **"Toward Cost-Effective Procedures in On-Line Bibliographic Searches."** *College and Research Libraries* 38 (March 1977): 153-59.

Reports five professors' reactions to online searches at the Cranfield Institute of Technology. Unrequested searches based on descriptions of courses taught by the five professors were conducted, documents acquired, and a "packet of selected documents given to the professors." The typical reaction was "unenthusiastic." A reformatted, less selective bibliographic list was received more positively. Reasons for these reactions are postulated.

439. McCarthy, Susan E.; Shirley S. MacCabee; and Cyril C. H. Feng. **"Evaluation of MEDLINE Service by User Survey."** *Bulletin of the Medical Library Association* 62 (October 1974): 367-73.

Reports the responses to a questionnaire given to 350 patrons who had conducted MEDLINE searches at the Calder Memorial Library of the University of Miami School of Medicine in 1973. Responses were highly favorable and users typically indicated a willingness to pay for such searches in the future. The questionnaire is appended and responses to each question are statistically given in tables.

440. Magnenat-Thalmann, Nadia; Daniel Thalmann; and Philippe Bergeron. **"A Computer Graphical Tool for Analyzing the User Reaction to Videotex Systems."** *Online Review* 6 (April 1982): 135-45.

Notes the dramatic increase predicted for videotex systems and the necessity of using graphic forms to communicate visual information quickly and clearly. The INVIDO system (Systeme d INformations VIsuelles a DOmicile), a graphical device designed to determine user reactions to videotex systems, is described in some detail. Results of preliminary tests indicate that "people generally find traditional presentations the clearest, but not the most attractive."

441. Tagliacozzo, Renata. **"Estimating the Satisfaction of Information Users."** *Bulletin of the Medical Library Association* 65 (April 1977): 243-49.

Identifies various areas which must be considered in attempting to determine user satisfaction with an online search. Results of a follow-up questionnaire sent to MEDLINE users are presented and analyzed. Because of contradictory responses and difficulty in distinguishing between "helpfulness" and "usefulness," caution should be used in any evaluation of user satisfaction.

442. Tessier, Judith A.; Wayne W. Crouch; and Pauline Atherton. **"New Measures of User Satisfaction with Computer-Based Literature Searching."** *Special Libraries* 68 (November 1977): 383-89.

Discusses how to measure user satisfaction with computerized information searches. Notes that the user evaluates four specific areas of the process: 1) the result; 2) the interaction with the searcher; 3) the policies of the services; and 4) the entire library operation. User satisfaction is shown to be directly affected by expectations, needs, and compromises necessitated. Stresses the need to attempt to measure all aspects of user satisfaction.

443. Warden, Carolyn L. **"User Evaluation of a Corporate Library Online Search Service."** *Special Libraries* 72 (April 1981): 113-17.

Reports the results of a user survey given primarily to first-time or remote-site users of an online search service available in a corporate library. Users indicated satisfaction with the results received and generally noted the cost-effectiveness of the service. Results confirmed the theory that, for best results, patrons should be present when the search is run. Increased productivity and time saved were the two benefits noted most frequently. Actual questionnaire is appended.

USER FEES

The financing of online search services is a controversial issue, but in many cases some type of user fee is assessed when a search is conducted. Philosophical and practical arguments for and against user fees have been presented. The effects of user fees have also been noted and alternative sources of funding suggested.

Related sections in this bibliography include:

Economics of Online Searching (Entries 94-112)
Impact of Online Searching (Entries 208-221)
Setting Up and Managing an Online Search Service (Entries 345-367)

444.   Blake, Fay M. and Edith L. Perlmutter. **"The Rush to User Fees: Alternative Proposals."** *Library Journal* 102 (October 1, 1977): 2005-2008.

Argues against user fees in libraries and proposes various alternatives. Notes that the current "rush to user fees" is caused by the "online onslaught." However, other technological advances affecting the library will soon require funding. Regards user fees as a "delusion" and emphasizes the need for political action on behalf of libraries. Federal help is suggested as a possible short-term solution, but any long-term answer will involve radical changes in public tax policies.

445.   Cooper, Michael. **"Charging Users for Library Services."** *Information Processing and Management* 14 (1978): 419-27.

Considers various philosophical and practical arguments for and against charging for library services. The issue of charging for online bibliographic searching is specifically investigated. Concludes that, since information must be considered a "merit good," instead of a "private good," such services should be provided, within set limits, free of charge.

446.   Cooper, Michael D. and Nancy A. DeWath. **"The Effect of User Fees on the Cost of On-Line Searching in Libraries."** *Journal of Library Automation* 10 (December 1977): 304-319.

Investigates the costs of online searching and, using data compiled in the DIALIB project during the period August 1974 through May 1976, compares the costs involved when the service was free and when a user fee was required. Findings reveal that cost and time needed to conduct an online search were always less when the patron was paying for the service. This suggests, but does not prove, that libraries "are more efficient in providing on-line searching services when the user pays a fee."

447.   Crawford, Paula J. and Judith A. Thompson. **"Free Online Searches Are Feasible."** *Library Journal* 104 (April 1, 1979): 793-95.

Advocates the use of online searching as simply "an alternative reference tool" and, therefore, considers charging for such a service inappropriate and unnecessary. Searches are provided free for students and faculty at the Library at California State College, Stanislaus. Stresses the need for professional judgment in selecting topics for searches to guarantee cost-effective information retrieval.

448.   Huston, Mary M. **"Fee or Free: The Effect of Charging on Information Demand."** *Library Journal* 104 (September 15, 1979): 1811-14.

Stresses the need for libraries to provide "equitable access to information," even if this means not charging users for online searching of bibliographic databases. Notes that such fees have been established without any research into their effects and with few attempts to find other means of funding online services. Grants and reallocation of library funds are suggested as alternatives. Libraries must continue "actively and imaginatively seeking alternatives to direct user fees."

449.   Knapp, Sara D. **"Beyond Fee or Free."** Guest editor of "Online Services." Edited by Danuta Nitecki. *RQ* 20 (Winter 1980): 117-20.
Presents statements by librarians from three different academic libraries on the issue of user fees for online searching. Procedures, reasons for their fee structure, and patron reactions are discussed for each library. Institutions represented are Pennsylvania State University, California State University, Chico, and California State College, Stanislaus. No conclusions or direct comparisons are drawn.

450.   Kranich, Nancy. **"Fees for Library Service: They Are Not Inevitable!"** *Library Journal* 105 (May 1, 1980): 1048-51.
Argues against charging patrons for use of various library services, especially online searching. While user fees might make it easier initially to begin offering new automated services, the long-term problems would be substantial. Options to user fees include cooperative agreements among libraries and seeking to diversify revenue sources. Concludes that "imposing fees may force us to contradict the very purpose for which the public library exists."

451.   Lehman, Lois J. and M. Sandra Wood. **"Effect of Fees on an Information Service for Physicians."** *Bulletin of the Medical Library Association* 66 (January 1978): 58-61.
Examines the effect of user fees required for either literature searches or document delivery provided for physicians by the Milton S. Hershey Medical Center in Pennsylvania. Only doctors not associated with the medical center were charged. Services had initially been free until 1975, when fees were initiated. Charging reduced the number of requests by one-third, and remaining users were primarily from rural areas.

452.   **"Pay Libraries and User Charges."** *Library Journal* 100 (February 15, 1975): 363-67.
Analyzes the growing debate over the funding of libraries in the future. The costs of online searching have made this a very immediate and "emotionally and politically charged" issue. Reviews "disturbing trends, issues, and attitudes" and advocates moderation from both publishers and librarians. The costs involved in online searching are briefly summarized.

453.   Rettig, James. **"Rights, Resolutions, Fees, and Reality."** *Library Journal* 106 (February 1, 1981): 301-304.
Argues that user fees for online searches "are here and are probably here to stay" and suggests that librarians concentrate on providing these services in an otherwise nondiscriminatory manner. Notes other discriminatory limits on library use (e.g., no interlibrary loan requests for undergraduates) and concludes that in the real world "neither wishes nor resolutions will eliminate fees."

454.   Teitelbaum-Kronish, Pricilla. **"Online Services in Academic Libraries: Fee or Free?"** *Science & Technology Libraries* 1 (Fall 1980): 51-56.
Proposes that an online search service in an academic library should be supported both by some sort of user fees and through the library budget. Factors in determining the

actual costs of online searching are analyzed and justifications for both user fees and library support are presented. The experiences of New York University in implementing a search service are described. The need for promotion of the service is also briefly stressed.

USERS GROUPS

Search analysts have been forming local online users groups since the early beginnings of online searching. These groups hold regular meetings to discuss search techniques and other related topics of interest. In many cases, a database producer is willing to provide a free demonstration of its databases at such meetings. Users groups have become well established in many regions of the country.

Related sections in this bibliography include:

Search Analysts (Entries 296-308)
Search Strategies and Techniques (Entries 321-340)
Training and Education of Search Analysts (Entries 400-435)

455. Berger, Mary **"Berger Bytes."** See issues of *Online* beginning with volume 2, #4 and ending with volume 4, #3.

Publicizes activities of online user groups and discusses various issues related to organizing and promoting such groups. (See also #459.)

456. Berger, Mary. **"Online Usage and Database Preference. Some Current Statistics from the Cleveland Online User's Group."** *Online* 1 (July 1977): 66-72.

Presents follow-up statistics to an earlier article (see #457) concerning the origins of the Cleveland Area Online Users' Group. Membership statistics and a list of the most heavily used databases as of April 1976 are given. Online time per month is also summarized for the various types of users represented.

457. Berger, Mary C. **"Starting Up an Online User's Group — A Case History."** *Online* 1 (April 1977): 32-44.

Depicts the establishment of the Cleveland Area Online Users' Group in 1975-1976. A list of "Do's and Don'ts" for implementing an online users group is given. First-year activities are described, and the availability of database seminars presented by database producers is stressed. Benefits of conducting a local survey to identify both searchers and databases used are also noted. (See also #256.)

458. Cornick, Donna P. and John A. Erlandson. **"Planning a User Group Workshop."** *Online* 4 (January 1980): 48-54.

Outlines the planning necessary to organize and present an online users group conference. Overall planning is discussed, and the decision not to have small group presentations is justified. Publicity and funding are also considered. An agenda and evaluation form used at a workshop arranged by the North Carolina Online User Group are appended. A list of "Do's and Don'ts" is also included.

459. Gonzalez, Rebecca. **"Circuit News."** See issues of *Online* beginning with volume 4, #4.

Covers the activities of online users groups. Continues an earlier column by Mary Berger (see #455).

460.   Lawrence, Gerri G. **"Online User Forum."** See issues of *Online Review* beginning with volume 3, #1.

Deals with the activities of online users groups. Issues, problems, program topics, and other areas of interest to searchers and online users groups are discussed in this regular column in *Online Review.*

461.   **"Online User Group Directory."** See issues of *Online* beginning with volume 3, #1.

Lists active online users groups. Groups are organized by MEDLARS regional geographic divisions and include name, address, and telephone number of a contact person.

462.   **"Online User Groups."** *Online Review* 2 (June 1978): 151-53.

Presents a list of online users groups in existence as of June 1980. Arranged by regions, the address of a contact person is given for each users group listed.

463.   Pemberton, Jenny C. **"Online User Group Clearinghouse."** See issues of *Online* beginning with volume 2, #3.

Represents a national online users group newsletter. Articles dealing with establishing and maintaining an active online users group are included. Periodically lists active groups and provides address and name of a contact person. (See also #460.)

464.   Thiriet, B. and M. Ch. Langlois. **"Aims of a French On-Line Users Group."** *Serials Librarian* 2 (Summer 1978): 411-12.

Details the activities and objectives of a French online users group established in 1975 by the Association Francquis de Documentation Automatique en Chimie (AFDAC). Policy and technical objectives of the group are explained. The impact of EURONET, a European online searching service is also briefly noted.

Journal Articles

Part II
SPECIALIZED SUBJECT AREAS AND
DATABASES OF ONLINE SEARCHING

AGRICULTURE, FOOD SCIENCE, AND NUTRITION

Databases are available that cover the literature of agriculture and forestry. These include AGRICOLA, formerly known as CAIN and produced by the National Library of Agriculture; CAB, produced by the Commonwealth Agricultural Bureaux; and BIOSIS, the online version of the major publications of BioSciences Information Service. Two major databases are accessible which specialize in the coverage of food science and nutrition: FSTA (*Food Science and Technology Abstracts*) and FOODS ADLIBRA. Other databases in medicine, the life sciences, or chemistry are also often searched for topics in these areas.

Related sections in this bibliography include:

Chemistry (Entries 509-539)
Medicine and Life Sciences (Entries 602-644)

465. Brooks, Kritina. **"A Comparison of the Coverage of Agricultural and Forestry Literature on AGRICOLA, BIOSIS, CAB, and SCISEARCH."** *Database* 3 (March 1980): 38-49.
Studies four databases—AGRICOLA, BIOSIS, CAB, and SCISEARCH—which cover the literature of agriculture and forestry. Investigates the advantages and disadvantages of searching each for various topics. Currency, access points, and searching capabilities are discussed. The extent of overlap is also presented. While no one database is identified as the best, certain distinctions are made. For example, AGRICOLA is often searched first because it is the least expensive, but CAB may be searched if abstracts are essential. Tables comparing citations retrieved are appended.

466. Burton, H. D. **"Computerized Bibliographic Service for USDA Research."** *Journal of Forestry* 76 (February 1978): 93-96.
Describes various online services developed for researchers by the Agricultural Research Service of the U.S. Department of Agriculture. The Current Awareness Literature Service (CALS) is presented in some detail. Notes the relevance of this service to scientists in the Forest Service or related forestry areas. Development of user profiles and problems in document delivery are also discussed.

467. Burton, Hilary D. **"Computer-Based Literature Searching at the USDA/ARS."** *Food Technology* 30 (May 1976): 70-72.

Describes the services and databases made available to researchers by the U.S. Department of Agriculture's Agricultural Research Service. Primarily an SDI service. The need for both batch and online capabilities are noted. Problems of providing hardcopy document backup and manipulating large personal data files are also discussed. Databases available in the area of food science are listed.

468. Burton, Hilary D. **"Multi-Data Base Searching in Agriculture. A Cooperative, Computerized Service."** *Special Libraries* 69 (July 1978): 244-49.

Analyzes results of a one-year study of an SDI service provided to three groups of agricultural scientists by the National Agricultural Library and the Agricultural Research Service. Items retrieved and comments of users were analyzed to determine the best databases in the area of sorghum research. Concludes that no one database is comprehensive enough, but that BIOSIS and CAB are the most productive.

469. Caponio, Joseph F. and Leila Moran. **"CAIN: A Computerized Literature System for the Agricultural Sciences."** *Journal of Chemical Information and Computer Science* 15 (August 1975): 158-61.

Describes the document locator and bibliographic control system developed by the National Agriculture Library. Known as CAIN in 1975, this database provides online access to the collection of the National Agricultural Library. Both online services and printed products are discussed. A sample search strategy and resulting printout are included. Evaluation studies are reported, with most users emphasizing the amount of time saved by an online search.

470. Cittadino, Mary L.; Ronald L. Giese; and Jerry V. Caswell. **"Three Computer-Based Bibliographic Retrieval Systems for Scientific Literature."** *Bioscience* 27 (November 1977): 739-42.

Compares three databases (AGRICOLA, BIOSIS, and CAB) used to research the effect various environmental factors have on the development of gypsy moths. All searches were run on DIALOG in 1977. Results are statistically compared with regard to cost, currency, comprehensiveness, and "cleanness" (lack of duplication). Advantages of each database are noted, but unique information was also found in each.

471. Cohen, Elinor and Joan Federman. **"Food and Science Technology Abstracts."** *Database* 2 (December 1979): 34-45.

Describes the background, scope, and coverage of the *Food Science and Technology Abstracts* (FSTA) database. Abstracts are indexed using a KWOC index and are also assigned to one of nineteen specific catagories. Difficulties in using the printed thesaurus are detailed and the advantages of using free text searching are emphasized. Comparisons are made between searching FSTA on DIALOG and SDC. Concludes that while FSTA provides "unique coverage" of many food science journals, it is generally necessary to search other related databases for comprehensive coverage. "Searchguides" and "Database Specifications" are appended.

472. Cronin, Blaise. **"CAB Abstracts: A Global View."** *Aslib Proceedings* 32 (November/December 1980): 425-37.

Reports the results of a survey conducted to ascertain user satisfaction with the various print and online abstracting services produced by the Commonwealth Agricultural Bureau (CAB). Survey design and objectives are briefly noted and then the results are generally analyzed. Survey results indicate that CAB provides an "efficient, reliable and selectively comprehensive information service tailored to the sectoral needs of its multi-disciplinary user population."

473. Cuadra, Carlos A. and Harry Boyle. **"Online Information for Food Science and Technology."** *Food Technology* 30 (May 1976): 60-63.

Describes the advantages of searching for information on food science and technology on databases made available by SDC. Brief background of SDC is presented. CHEMCON is discussed as a major source of information in this field. Other available SDC databases are briefly noted.

474. Fisk, Dorothy A. and Todd D. Weiss. **"Data Base Development: Federal Programs."** *Special Libraries* 71 (April 1980): 217-21.

Describes a prototype database of food, agriculture, and nutrition programs developed by the U.S. General Accounting Office. Designed to aid in budget and appropriation development, the database design of the Food, Agriculture, and Nutrition Inventory (FANI) is described in detail. Uses of the database and proposed improvements are also discussed.

475. Gilreath, Charles L. **"AGRICOLA: Multipurpose Data Base for Agricultural and Life Sciences Libraries."** *Serials Librarian* 3 (Fall 1978): 89-95.

Describes various uses of the AGRICOLA database, besides normal bibliographic searching. Points out that it can be used for preorder and precataloging searching, in interlibrary loan verification, and in collection development. Examples of the types of bibliometric studies that can be conducted online in AGRICOLA are presented. Procedures are identified only as "possibilities" and actual testing is urged.

476. Hopper, Paul F. **"Information Systems in Industry."** *Food Technology* 30 (May 1976): 74-76.

Analyzes the online sources of information in the food industry. Notes that food companies need three types of information: 1) technical material; 2) safety data; and 3) international governmental regulations. Printed sources are compared to online databases available in 1976. Stresses the benefits to be gained by utilizing online searching.

477. Johnson, B. K. **"A Comparison of Online Databases in Relation to Agricultural Research and Development."** *Online Review* 5 (December 1981): 469-79.

Compares 11 databases which cover various aspects of agriculture, especially agrochemicals. Two test questions were searched to examine overlap between the various files. The large biological databases (e.g., BIOSIS and CAB) and CA CONDENSATES retrieved the most relevant citations. Found "surprisingly little overlap between the agricultural files." Search results are statistically analyzed and presented in numerous tables.

478. Johnston, Susan M. **"Choosing between Manual and On-Line Searching — Practical Experience in the Ministry of Agriculture, Fisheries and Food."** *Aslib Proceedings* 30 (October-November 1978): 383-93.

Compares manual and online searches of the same topics. Seventy-five requests for information received by the British Ministry of Agriculture, Fisheries, and Food were searched both manually and online and the results compared. While costs were similar and online searchings much quicker, the most significant difference was the variation in references retrieved. Differences between the printed and machine-searchable forms are investigated. A series of questions to ask when selecting a method of searching is also given.

479. Kreilkamp, Hermes D. **"The National Agricultural Library's Data Base: AGRICOLA."** *College and Research Libraries* 38 (July 1977): 298-303.

Traces the historical development of AGRICOLA. Various evaluations of the database are cited and their conclusions summarized in this bibliographic essay. General conclusions are drawn based on the studies cited. Suggests that such large databases are feasible, automatic indexing has a "definite future," and trained searchers are very important.

480. Longo, Rose Mary Juliano and Uboldino Dantas Machado. **"Characterization of Databases in the Agricultural Sciences."** *Journal of the American Society for Information Science* 32 (March 1981): 83-91.

Compares three databases (AGRICOLA, AGRIS, and CAB) which cover the agricultural sciences. Journals indexed by each were analyzed and no significant duplication of titles was discovered. Geographical coverage, primarily by continents, was also considered. CAB is judged the best single database because of its internationally broad coverage. AGRICOLA is considered the best database to use for most topics after CAB has been searched.

481. McCann, Anne and Jonathan G. Burgess. **"Procurement of Literature Searching Services."** *Online* 3 (January 1979): 36-47.

Covers the planning and executing of comprehensive online searches, undertaken by the Food and Drug Administration's Bureau of Foods' Technical Operations Staff, on the safety of food additives. Details the entire process from planning for the literature search to defining the topic to evaluating offline results. Evaluation criteria and price considerations are also discussed.

482. Mayer, William J. and Joel T. Komp. **"Foods Adlibra—A Highly Current Database for the Food Industry."** *Database* 2 (September 1979): 10-23.

Describes the FOODS ADLIBRA database. Three major categories of information are included in the file: 1) new products/product marketing; 2) marketing information; and 3) research information. Search options and file organization are discussed. Advantages include its currency and coverage of publications not indexed by any other abstracting service. Six sample questions and their online answers are included. Concludes that FOODS ADLIBRA is a "unique source of information references to food industry developments." "Database specifications" are appended.

483. Metcalfe, John R. **"CAB World Agriculture Information Service."** *Aslib Proceedings* 31 (March 1979): 110-17.

Describes the coverage of international agricultural literature. Users of such information and their needs are first identified and details of the CAB service provided. Both the machine-readable and hardcopy products of CAB are discussed. Stresses that the aim of CAB is to provide information, not simply access to information. Backup services available and future developments of CAB services are noted.

484. Newton, John. **"Commonwealth Agricultural Bureaux' World Agricultural Information Service."** *Special Libraries* 69 (July 1978): 250-54.

Describes the organization and products of the Commonwealth Agricultural Bureaux in covering international agricultural information. Publications and services, including online services through DIALOG, are summarized. Other services, such as the Commonwealth Institute of Biological Control, are briefly described.

485. Peters, Jeffrey R. **"AGRICOLA."** *Database* 4 (March 1981): 13-27.
Describes the development and coverage of AGRICOLA, the agricultural database, which represents the recent collections of the National Agricultural Library. AGRICOLA is directly compared to CAB, its British equivalent produced by the Commonwealth Agricultural Bureaux. An additional database, USDA/CRIS, which represents the Department of Agriculture's Current Research Information Service, is also described. Various search techniques are explained and sample searches included. Concludes that the absence of abstracts for most items in AGRICOLA reduces false drops, but may limit retrieval of some relevant documents.

486. Roe, Keith E.; Vladimir Micuda; and Robert S. Seeds. **"Literature Searching with the CAIN On-Line Bibliographic Data Base."** *Bioscience* 25 (December 1975): 796-97.
Describes the CAIN database as it was searchable in 1974-1975. General impressions and suggestions of users are presented. Notes the relative value of title and author searching and the impressive number of foreign references. Although more current than printed indexes, online databases are not seen as a replacement for traditional journal scanning by researchers. Dependence on search services to make the database available is lamented.

487. Stadelman, W. J. **"Information Systems in the University."** *Food Technology* 30 (May 1976): 78.
Analyzes the needs of academic researchers in the field of food science. Distinguishes between undergraduate, graduate, and professor usage of literature in this field. Briefly notes the advantages of online searching. Expresses the hope that students and researchers do not become "totally dependent on data banks."

488. Sze, Melanie C. **"Computer-Based Information Retrieval for the Food Industry."** *Food Technology* 34 (June 1980): 64-70.
Discusses the coverage of the various aspects of the food industry by online databases. Twenty-three databases are summarized in a chart which indicates years of coverage, subject coverage, and availability. The following areas are presented in detail: packaging, nutrition and health, patents, research and development, and marketing. Benefits of online searching are also enumerated.

489. Sze, Melanie C. **"Online Information Resources for Human Nutrition."** *Online* 5 (April 1981): 11-19.
Uses two hypothetical questions to examine the online coverage of human nutrition. One question deals with basic research (effects of dietary potassium of aldosterone") and the other is more practical ("sources of vitamin A"). Searches for each topic are conducted on the following six databases: CHEMICAL ABSTRACTS, BIOSIS, EXCERPTA MEDICA, MEDLINE, CAB, and FSTA. General comparisons are made.

490. Tchobanoff, James B. **"The Database of Food — A Survey of What Works Best ... and When."** *Online* 4 (January 1980): 20-25.
Deals with online searching to retrieve technical or patent information on food science and technology issues. FSTA (*Food Science and Technology Abstracts*) is the primary database for all food searching. Results are supplemented by searching other files, most

notably the Chemical Abstract databases. Patent searching is best done on the CLAIMS and Derwant files. Other secondary and specialized databases are briefly discussed.

491.   Walton, Ronald J. **"The National Agricultural Library Data Base."** *Bulletin of the American Society for Information Science* 3 (February 1977): 21-22.

Describes the content and coverage of AGRICOLA. Distinguishes between CAIN and AGRICOLA and explains the various print and machine-readable products of the National Library of Agriculture (NAL). Presents the availability of AGRICOLA through various commercial search services. Notes that while AGRICOLA cannot meet all agricultural research needs, it is a "very valuable tool at NAL in handling its increasing collection of food and agricultural literature."

492.   White, Linda M. **"Forestry Literature Access through Computer Systems."** *Journal of Forestry* 76 (February 1978): 84-88.

Describes the use of online searching to locate references in forestry literature. Nine relevant databases and systems are individually described. Numerous other applicable databases are noted, but concludes that no one database is generally sufficient. Searches in either AGRICOLA or CAB are suggested for current references to general topics. Advantages and limitations to using computer searches to retrieve forestry information are summarized.

493.   Wood, David E.; Brian K. Johnson; John Turton; and John Newton. **"CAB Abstracts on DIALOG."** *Database* 1 (December 1978): 68-79.

Describes the 24 abstract journals which compose the online CAB database. Produced by the Commonwealth Agriculture Bureaux, CAB offers worldwide coverage for researchers of information relating to agricultural sciences. A list of the subfiles and corresponding abstract journals is given. The high quality of the indexing and the abstracts is stressed. One problem involves duplicate records in the various subfiles. A "Searchguide" and "Database Specifications" are appended.

BUSINESS

Databases are heavily used to retrieve business information, and both bibliographic and nonbibliographic files are available from the major commercial search services. Online searches allow the basic data retrieved to be sorted or restricted to fit the needs of the requester, e.g., retrieve only those companies with at least 500 employees and sales of over $5 million located in New York. Major databases available in business include: ABI/INFORM, DISCLOSURE, EIS NONMANUFACTURING ESTABLISHMENTS, EIS PLANTS, MANAGEMENT CONTENTS, and PTS (Predicasts Terminal System).

Related sections in this bibliography include:

Law (Entries 584-601)
News and Current Events (Entries 650-670)

494.   Bayer, Mark P. **"Database Description: Disclosure II."** *Online* 6 (March 1982): 34-39.

Presents a detailed description of DISCLOSURE II which totally replaced the earlier DISCLOSURE database (see #495). System enhancements and additional features are briefly noted. A sample record and "Database Specifications" are appended. Emphasizes the expanded access to company profiles and financial data.

495. Bayer, Mark P. **"Disclosure Online (Database Description)."** *Online* 4 (April 1980): 51-55.
Describes the DISCLOSURE database produced by Disclosure, Inc. under a contract with the U.S. Securities and Exchange Commission. Briefly gives content and structure of the file. The availability of document delivery is also noted. A sample DISCLOSURE record is included and "Database Specifications" are appended. (See #494.)

496. Burylo, Michelle A. **"Database Review: EIS Plants."** *Online* 1 (July 1977): 53-58.
Summarizes uses for the EIS PLANTS database and outlines basic search techniques. Coverage in 1977 was restricted to American manufacturing and mining industries. An "EIS Application Chart" details coverage of the database. A sample record is annotated and an example of an actual search is presented. "Database Specifications" are included.

497. Donati, Robert. **"Decision Analysis for Selecting Online Databases to Answer Business Questions. A Guide for Beginning Business Searchers and Non-Business Intermediaries."** *Database* 4 (December 1981): 49-63.
Focuses on the decisions made in selecting which databases to search for different types of business information. Two major "key decision points" are presented: 1) "Is information on a specific item of general interest?" and 2) "Is information on a specific item needed?" Subcategories are then given for each and appropriate databases suggested based on the identified subject nature of the request. Sample records from 19 DIALOG databases which include relevant business information are included.

498. Gould, Jay M. **"Instant Summaries of State and County Industry Shipments."** *Online* 3 (July 1979): 31-33.
Describes a new online service, Economic Business Information Service, produced jointly by Control Data Corporation and Economic Information Systems, Inc., which provides statistical summaries of current industry shipments restricted geographically. Notes the ability of the end user to manipulate the data directly. An example is provided which demonstrates how sales can be forecast.

499. Gould, Jay M. **"On the Accuracy of the EIS Estimate of Sales."** *Online* 1 (October 1977): 65-67.
Details how the estimate of a plant's sales volume and its corresponding market share figure is compiled in the EIS PLANTS database. EIS procedures are summarized and an estimate of accuracy given. Notes the utility of using the database to compile lists limited to specific industries or sizes. Presents statistical calculations of the impact of errors based on a 25% standard of error estimate.

500. Gould, Jay M. **"Share of Market Data ... from the EIS Corporate Database."** *Online* 3 (January 1979): 22-25.
Distinguishes between the EIS PLANTS database available on DIALOG and the database offered by the TRW Business Credit Services Division. Although both focus on business establishments, additional market information is available on the latter. Search capabilities are described, and sample online reports generated by the Control Data/EIS Service are provided.

501.   Keck, Bruce L. **"An Investigation of Recall in the ABI/INFORM Database When Selecting by Journal."** *Online Review* 5 (October 1981): 395-98.

Compares retrieval in ABI/INFORM when four valid fields—Journal Code (JC), Journal Title (JN), Coden (CO), and ISSN (SN)—are used to search for the same journal titles. Results are statistically compared and error rates calculated. The recommended search technique is to use the assigned journal codes. It is necessary to expand JN to check for title variations. Variant spellings and missing information are the most common reasons for not retrieving a journal.

502.   Kuranz, John D. and Saresta J. Rosenberg. **"Database Review: Management Contents. A Brand New File for Business and Public Administration."** *Online* 1 (July 1977): 30-34.

Previews a file newly available on SDC in 1977, MANAGEMENT CONTENTS. Major bibliographic elements are identified and methods of searching them demonstrated. A sample unit record is analyzed and examples from the Management Contents Thesaurus are provided. Background and coverage of the database is briefly noted. "Database Specifications" are provided.

503.   Popvich, Charles J., ed. **"Business Data Bases: The Policies and Practices of Indexing."** *RQ* 18 (Fall 1978): 5-15.

Summarizes presentations made at a program at the ALA 1977 Annual Conference sponsored by the Business Reference Services Committee of the Reference and Adult Services Division. Representatives of three business database producers (Management Contents, ABI/INFORM, and Predicasts) described the features of their companies' databases. A reactor panel of business librarians added comments and made suggestions to improve the various databases.

504.   Sharp, Geoffrey. **"Online Business Information."** *Online* 2 (January 1978): 33-40.

Differentiates between various types of business databases available on DIALOG in 1977. ABI/INFORM and MANAGEMENT CONTENTS are individually described and compared. The databases available from PTS (Predicasts Terminal System) are also discussed and the uses of the various PTS thesauri are noted. Other business and related nonbusiness databases are briefly identified.

505.   Trubkin, Loene. **"Auto-Indexing of the 1971-77 ABI/INFORM Database."** *Database* 2 (June 1979): 56-61.

Describes how items included in the ABI/INFORM file from 1971 to 1977 were assigned index terms in 1978 using an automatic computerized process known as "auto-indexing." Details the process and the resulting problems (e.g., false drops and errors of omissions). Since 1978 index terms have been assigned by the editorial staff, and by 1980, 40% of the file will have been indexed by the editorial staff. Concludes that searchers of the post-1978 portion of the file will find high precision and comprehensive retrieval. Written by the president of Data Courier, the supplier of ABI/INFORM.

506.   Wagers, Robert. **"ABI/INFORM and Management Contents on DIALOG."** *Database* 3 (March 1980): 12-36.

Compares and contrasts ABI/INFORM and MANAGEMENT CONTENTS as they were available on DIALOG in late 1979. The following aspects of both databases are described: 1) journal and article selection; 2) indexing; 3) producer support materials and services; and 4) record unit. Comparisons are made on their coverage of financial journals and on numerous specific search topics. Finds relatively little overlap and concludes that this results from differences in indexing practices and thesauri structure and from the "idiosyncratic" nature of human indexing. Specific recommendations are made concerning searching both databases. Sample searches and "Database Specifications" are appended.

507.   Wagers, Robert. *"Search Inform and Learn Inform: A Review." Database* 5 (June 1982): 51-53.

Reviews two search aids available from Data Courier. Improvements in their *User Guide to ABI INFORM* are noted and various uses described. LEARN INFORM, a training supplement using both a loose-leaf notebook and an audio tape, is also reviewed. Problems in presenting materials useful to both beginning and experienced searchers are noted. Both search aids are recommended "to all students of online searching."

508.   Wolpert, Samuel A. **"Use and Implications of Online Information Retrieval for Management."** *Journal of Chemical Information & Computer Sciences* 16 (August 1976): 150-51.

Describes the wide variety of information available through the Predicasts Terminal System (PTS) files. Sample searches from one PTS database, MARKET ABSTRACTS, are presented to demonstrate the potential uses of online searches for decision makers. General history and future potential of such databases are briefly given.

CHEMISTRY

The various databases produced by the Chemical Abstracts Service (CAS), e.g., CHEMCON or CHEMNAME, and made available through the major commercial search services represent the primary sources for online chemical information. Online chemical dictionaries are available, and the CAS Registry Number is widely used to standardize references to chemical compounds. Similar CAS files are made available under different names from the three major commercial search services.

Related sections in this bibliography include:

Medicine and Life Sciences (Entries 602-644)
Technology, Engineering, and Science (Entries 700-722)

509.   Antony, Arthur. **"Searching the Chemistry Files for Synthetic Organic Chemistry."** *Database* 1 (September 1978): 82-86.

Examines various searches dealing with some aspect of the synthesis of organic compounds performed on CA CONDENSATES and CASIA on DIALOG. Difficulties in finding registry numbers are described, as are possible sources for these numbers. Advantages and disadvantages of searching both files are discussed. Actual searches are used as examples in explaining various search techniques.

510.   Baker, Dale E.; Jean W. Horiszny; and Wladyslaw V. Metanomski. **"History of Abstracting at Chemical Abstracts Service."** *Journal of Chemical Information and Computer Sciences* 20 (November 1980): 193-201.

Describes the historical development of the abstracting procedures for *Chemical Abstracts* from 1907 to 1980. The exponential growth of chemical literature is documented and the changes from volunteer abstractors to in-house document analysts to computer processing are presented. Actual preparation of the various publications and databases of Chemical Abstracts Service is also discussed.

511. Barker, Frances H. **"Chemical Abstracts Material On-Line."** *Aslib Proceedings* 31 (December 1979): 538-50.

Summarizes the availability of the various Chemical Abstracts Service (CAS) files on six commercial search services. Numerous "service features" for each service are described as they relate to the CAS databases. Cost factors are also analyzed. Suggests ways to determine which service to use first, but no conclusions are drawn.

512. Bawden, David. **"Chemical Toxicology Searching."** *Database* 2 (June 1979): 11-18.

Describes methods of using online bibliographic databases to retrieve information on the toxic and harmful effects of various chemical substances. Major databases (e.g., CHEMICAL ABSTRACTS, BIOSIS, TOXLINE, MEDLINE, EXCERPTA MEDICA, and SCISEARCH) are discussed in detail. Examples and suggestions for searching both chemical structures and toxic effects are presented for each database. Coverage, indexing procedures, user aids, and searching hints are also given for each database. Summary tables of searching features are provided.

513. Bernstein, Herbert and Lawrence Andrews. **"The NIH-EPA Chemical Information System."** *Database* 2 (March 1979): 35-49.

Describes the NIH-EPA Chemical Information System developed jointly by the National Institute of Health and the U.S. Environmental Protection Agency. It is designed to aid in the "characterization and identification of chemical substances in industrial, academic, regulatory, and emergency response environments." Brief historical background and generalized search philosophy are given. Four subsystems are described in some detail: 1) Mass Spectral Search System; 2) Structure and Nomenclature Search System; 3) Oil and Hazardous Materials Technical Assistance Data Systems; and 4) X-ray Crystallographic Search System. Numerous examples are appended.

514. Blair, John. **"Cross-Database Searching a Chemical Compound: Comparing Lockheed, SDC, BRS, and NLM."** *Online* 5 (April 1981): 46-61.

Compares the mechanics of executing a multiple-file search using the same search strategy on BRS, NLM, DIALOG, and SDC. Difficulties in formulating a strategy that can be used in various files are identified. Use of the "searchsave" and "cross-file search" techniques, as they are available from the four major commercial search services, are explained. Extensive examples of searching for chemical compounds are given.

515. Blair, John C., Jr. **"Enzyme Searching: Easing the 'ASE' Out of Compounds."** *Database* 4 (June 1981): 48-57.

Provides specific examples of searching for enzymes in various databases. Four search approaches (segmentation, Enzyme Commission numbers, registry numbers, and acronyms) are presented for four files (BIOSIS, CA SEARCH, EXCERPTA MEDICA, and MEDLARS). Practically, a combination of approaches and files is typically required. Examples are given from the major commercial search services. Stresses that searching for enzymes can be more complicated than searching for other chemical compounds.

516. Buntrock, Robert. **"Chemcorner."** See issues of *Online* volumes 1 and 2. See issues of *Database* beginning with volume 2, #1.

Discusses various aspects of online searching of chemistry-related databases. Many of these regular columns, initially in *Online* and now in *Database*, deal with specific search techniques or applications in retrieving chemical information online.

517.   Buntrock, Robert E. **"Searching Chemical Abstracts versus CA Condensates."** *Journal of Chemical Information & Computer Sciences* 15 (August 1975): 174-76.

Compares *Chemical Abstracts* with its online version, CHEMCON, available from SDC. Search examples are presented involving corporate author, personal author, compound, and reaction class searches. Searching for specific compounds is best done manually, but in most other cases CHEMCON can be considered the best searching method. Combined searches of both *Chemical Abstracts* and CHEMCON are recommended.

518.   Callahan, M. V. and P. F. Rusch. **"Online Implementation of the CA SEARCH File and the CAS Registry Nomenclature File."** *Online Review* 5 (October 1981): 377-93.

Examines the availability of CA SEARCH files and CHEMNAME on DIALOG. The DIALOG Chemical Information System is outlined and a distinction made between questions dealing with subject areas and questions concerning retrieval of specific chemical substances. Segmentation of certain search terms and the use of CAS Registry Numbers in CA SEARCH files are explained. Access points and techniques used in searching CHEMNAME are also described. Advantages of online searches over manual searches of corresponding print indexes are noted.

519.   Dayton, David L. et al. **"CASSI: File for Document Access."** *Special Libraries* 69 (September 1978): 337-47.

Describes both the publications included in Chemical Abstracts Service Source Index (CASSI) and how it can be used as a union list. The scope of CASSI is summarized and statistically analyzed. Various uses, both manual and online, of CASSI are presented and examples given. Future uses are also envisioned.

520.   Dayton, D. L. et al. **"Comparison of the Retrieval Effectiveness of Chemical Abstracts Condensates and Chemical Abstracts Subject Index Alert (CASIA)."** *Journal of Chemical Information & Computer Sciences* 17 (February 1977): 20-28.

Compares the relative effectiveness of CA CONDENSATES and CASIA (CA Subject Index Alert) for retrieving chemical information. Database characteristics of each file are presented, and two methods of comparing potential retrieval — vocabulary study and text search study — are explained and applied to CASIA and CA CONDENSATES. Differences in substantive word content are noted between the files. Notes that CASIA may achieve better results then CA CONDENSATES for substance-oriented topics.

521.   Dessy, R. E. and M. K. Starling. **"Information Retrieval and Laboratory Data Management."** *Analytical Chemistry* 51 (August 1979): 924-48.

Reports on current-awareness and retrospective search capabilities available for chemists. Search techniques, costs, batch versus online, and typical access points are described. A selected list of available databases is given. Considers numeric databases and laboratory applications of data management. Record management systems are also discussed. Future developments in both hardware and software are predicted.

522.   Drum, C. A. and N. F. Pope. **"Online Databases in Chemistry Literature Education."** *Journal of Chemical Education* 56 (September 1979): 591-92.

Details how section on online searching was introduced into a course in Chemical Literature offered by the Chemistry Department at the University of Florida. Rationale for the inclusion of computerized information retrieval is presented and the outline of the mini-course described. Classroom lectures and demonstrations are combined with individualized searches conducted for each student by the chemistry librarian. Concludes it fostered a "positive student-teacher-librarian relationship."

523.   Farmer, Nick A. and Michael P. O'Hara. **"CAS Online: A New Source of Substance Information from Chemical Abstracts Service."** *Database* 3 (December 1980): 10-25.

Describes CAS ONLINE, an online system developed and produced by Chemical Abstracts Service. File features, as available in 1980 and planned enhancements scheduled for late 1981, are detailed. Since this system is not available through any of the commercial search services, unique search features, cost factors, equipment and training needs, and other aspects of acquiring CAS ONLINE are given in some detail. Types of screens, system commands, structure input, system architecture, and numerous sample searches are also included.

524.   Heller, Stephen R. and George W. A. Milne. **"Linking Scientific Databases — The NIH/EPA Chemical Information System."** *Online* 4 (October 1980): 45-57.

Presents an annotated printout of the online demonstration session used to explain the NIH/EPA Chemical Information System. Four main parts of the system are identified: 1) numerical databases; 2) data analysis software; 3) structure and nomenclature search system; and 4) database referral. Notes that these various parts are linked together through the use of CAS registry numbers. Availability of the system is briefly explained.

525.   Huleatt, Richard S. **"Online Use of Chemical Abstracts: A Primer for Beginning Chemical Searchers."** *Database* 2 (December 1979): 11-21.

Attempts to simplify the use of *Chemical Abstracts* online by searchers who do not have substantial chemistry backgrounds. The online versions of *Chemical Abstract* indexes produced by the Chemical Abstracts Service are examined as they are available in 1979 from DIALOG, SDC, BRS, and NLM. Other related files are briefly mentioned. Discusses differences in access points, print formats, and other search techniques between the commercial search services used. Summarized list of standard data elements and search tools is appended. Sample searches are also included.

526.   Johnson, Susan W. and Ronald A. Rader. **"Information Retrieval for the Safety Evaluation of Cosmetic Products."** *Special Libraries* 69 (May/June 1978): 206-214.

Demonstrates how online searching can greatly facilitate the investigation of the toxicity or safety of chemicals or products used in the production of various cosmetics. Manual sources and procedures are also summarized. Types of searches (e.g., biological aspects or medical factors) and appropriate databases (e.g., MEDLINE or CHEMLINE) are described.

527.   Kaback, S. M. **"Chemical Structure Searching in Derwent's World Patents Index."** *Journal of Chemical Information & Computer Sciences* 20 (February 1980): 1-6.

Discusses search techniques used to retrieve information on chemicals from Derwent's World Patent Index (WPI). Coverage by WPI of chemical products and compounds is analyzed. Notes future developments which may significantly enhance the coverage of chemical patent information by WPI. Examples of various search techniques are provided.

528.   Kasperko, Jean. **"Online Chemical Dictionaries: A Comparison."** *Database* 2 (September 1979): 24-35.

Describes three major online chemical dictionaries (CHEMNAME, CHEMDEX, and CHEMLINE) as they were available in 1979. Strengths and weaknesses of each are demonstrated with specific examples. Different types of questions and the best database to use are presented. Stresses that the printed *Chemical Abstracts* greatly enhances the usefulness of the online dictionaries. Distinguishing characteristics and access points are summarized in a lengthy table for each of the three files.

529. Kremin, Michael. **"Chemical Search Reference Tools."** *Database* 2 (March 1979): 50-53.

Lists 10 reference tools judged to be valuable for online chemistry searching. Items were selected for their utility, availability, coverage, and cost. Bibliographic citation, price, and abstract are provided for each title. Items selected include: 1) *Clinical Toxicology of Commercial Products*; 2) *The Condensed Chemical Dictionary*; 3) *Glossary of Chemical Terms*; 4) *Glossary of Clinical Chemistry Terms*; 5) *Handbook of Chemistry and Physics*; 6) *The Merck Index*; 7) *Chemical Synonyms and Trade Names*; 8) *Organic Chemistry*; 9) *Registry of Toxic Effects of Chemical Substances*; and 10) CHEMLINE.

530. Marguat, R. Gary et al. **"The NIH/EPA CIS Federal Register Notices Search System."** *Online* 4 (January 1980): 45-49.

Describes the NIH/EPA Chemical Information System, a collection of databases and computer programs used to search for chemicals cited in official U.S. publications (specifically, the *Federal Register* and the *Code of Federal Regulations*). Ten main categories of search parameters are identified: 1) substance identification; 2) general descriptors; 3) actions; 4) EPA/Pesticides codes; 5) EPA pollution regulations; 6) FDA codes; 7) FDA drug dosage codes; 8) Government Department/Agency; 9) Acts of Congress; and 10) Data codes.

531. O'Dette, Ralph E. **"Chemical Abstracts Service Database."** *Pure and Applied Chemistry* 49 (1977): 1781-92.

Provides an overview of print and machine-readable publications and services provided by Chemical Abstracts Service (CAS). The selection, content, structure, and management of the various CAS databases are outlined. The CAS Chemical Registry System is discussed and the value of various user aids produced by CAS noted.

532. Oppenheim, Charles. **"Methods for Chemical Substance Searching Online. 1: The Basics."** *Online Review* 3 (December 1979): 381-87.

Explains various methods for searching chemical databases to retrieve specific chemical compounds. Notes that an "ideal chemical database" would encode chemical compounds in a unique and unambiguous fashion and allow for substructure searching. Seven methods of representing chemical compounds are described and their applicability to online retrieval noted.

533. Pothier, Patricia E. **"Substructure Searching in CHEMLINE."** *Online* 1 (April 1977): 23-25.

Demonstrates how experienced searchers can use the ring information in CHEMLINE even if they are not professional chemists. The ring information in CHEMLINE is described, and search techniques using name fragments, formula fragments, and ring structure information to retrieve classes of compounds are explained. Notes that the inclusion of ring information has made generic searching in CHEMLINE much easier.

534. Ross, Johanna C. **"Searching the Chemical Literature via Three On-Line Vendors: A Comparison."** *Journal of the American Society for Information Science* 30 (March 1979): 103-106.

Compares online searching of *Chemical Abstracts Condensates* on the three major commercial search services (SDC, BRS, and DIALOG). A series of searches were performed on the three systems and the results analyzed in terms of relevancy, recall, and cost. Results of general topic searches varied only in terms of cost. BRS is identified as the least expensive system, although it may not contain the most recent information. The CASIA database, available only on DIALOG in 1978, is the best source for information on specific chemicals.

535. Schultheisz, Robert J. and Donald F. Walker. **"Design and Implementation of an On-Line Chemical Dictionary (CHEMLINE)."** *Journal of the American Society for Information Science* 29 (July 1978): 173-79.

Describes the design and development of CHEMLINE, the chemical nomenclature file used with TOXLINE. Difficulties in implementing CHEMLINE on existing retrieval systems are examined. Techniques needed to create inverted file terms for chemical names, molecular formula, ring information, and Wissesser Line Notations are also discussed. Hardware configurations are briefly noted.

536. Smith, Roger Grant; Louise P. Anderson; and Susan K. Jackson. **"On-Line Retrieval of Chemical Patent Information. An Overview and a Brief Comparison of Three Major Files."** *Journal of Chemical Information & Computer Sciences* 17 (August 1977): 148-57.

Surveys various databases which offer access to patent information. The coverage and retrieval capabilities of three databases (CHEMCON, CLAIMS, and WPI) are investigated in detail. Similar searches conducted on all files demonstrate that no database is clearly superior. Concludes that the more comprehensive you need to be, the more databases you must search. Other databases containing at least 5% patent information are listed and briefly described.

537. Stevens, B. A. **"Online Searching Techniques: Retrieving Every Metallic Element Using Registry Numbers."** *Online* 2 (July 1978): 67.

Details how to use the Chemical Abstracts service registry numbers to retrieve all metallic elements. Demonstrates the effective use of truncation to restrict results to certain registry numbers. DIALOG files which include registry numbers as access points are identified.

538. Tate, F. A. **"Techniques for the Retrieval of Chemical Information; Dreams vs. Nightmares."** *Pure and Applied Chemistry* 49 (1977): 1897-1900.

Notes that chemical databases available in 1977 are "very immature" and cannot be used for comprehensive literature searches. Dislikes the necessity of trusting intermediaries to perform the actual search and doubts their ability to understand many topics. Concludes that printed copies of *Chemical Abstracts* will not "die out in the next couple of decades."

539. Weisgerber, David W. **"CASIA – The Precise Way to Search CA CONDENSATES."** *Online* 1 (January 1977): 52-56.

Distinguishes between CA CONDENSATES, CHEMNAME, and CASIA. CASIA (Chemical Abstracts Subject Index Alert) is described in detail and its uses in conjunction with other Chemical Abstracts Service files are presented. Notes that the biggest advantages of CASIA are its use of controlled vocabulary and highly controlled indexing of chemical substances. Search aids available and "Database Specifications" are also included.

EDUCATION AND LIBRARY SCIENCE

ERIC, the preeminent database in the field of education, has been discussed and examined in many articles. However, many other educational indexes are now available online, especially in the areas of special education and audiovisual materials. LISA is available as an online source of library and information science.

Related sections in this bibliography include:

Social Sciences (Entries 681-699)

540.   Antony, Arthur; Sally Weimer; and Veronica Eden. **"An Examination of Search Strategy and an On-Line Bibliographic System Pertaining to Library and Information Sciences."** *Special Libraries* 70 (March 1979): 127-34.
Analyzes the coverage in ERIC of comparative studies of online bibliographic searching and databases. Presents statistical results of searches using only controlled vocabulary and similar searches using both controlled and uncontrolled terms. This latter approach is recommended for greater coverage. This review of the literature indicates that formal evaluation of online databases is only in the beginning stages.

541.   Booth, Barbara. **" A 'New' ERIC Thesaurus, Fine-Tuned for Searching."** *Online* 3 (July 1979): 20-29.
Reports on two projects being conducted by the Educational Resources Information Center (ERIC) to improve searching in the ERIC file. The Identifier Cleanup Project involved standardizing and weeding over 48,000 unique identifiers which had been used in the first 12 years of ERIC. The Vocabulary Improvement Project was a complex intellectual effort which sought to totally update and revise the *Thesaurus of ERIC Descriptors*. It involved two phases: 1) thesaurus evaluation and 2) production and implementation of changes. Significantly, both projects involved retrospective changes and reindexing of the entire database.

542.   Clay, Katherine. **"Searching ERIC on DIALOG: The Times They Are a'Changing."** *Database* 2 (September 1979): 46-67.
Provides historical background on the ERIC database, details the degree of overlap with other files, and discusses various search techniques as they relate to ERIC on the DIALOG system. A list of "Search Tips" is given and sample searches are also provided. ERIC's weaknesses (e.g., some inconsistent indexing) and strengths (e.g., low cost) are enumerated. Several lengthy charts and "Database Specifications" are appended.

543.   Erickson, Donald K. **"Exceptional Child Information Resources. One-of-a-Kind Database."** *Illinois Libraries* 59 (September 1977): 519-23.
Identifies the unique features of the *Exceptional Child Education Resources* (ECER) database and compares its coverage to other educational databases. ECER is produced by the Council for Exceptional Children (CEC) and is concerned with the education of all exceptional children—both gifted and handicapped. Provides background information on the services provided by CEC and explains their acquisition policies and procedures for the index and database.

544.   Folke, Carolyn Winters. **"Getting Something Extra Out of ERIC.... "** *Database* 5 (June 1982): 62-65.

Describes how online searches of ERIC can be used to locate curriculum materials for teachers and public school administrators. Various options considered by the Wisconsin Dissemination Project are discussed and the advantages of using ERIC are enumerated. Search strategies for retrieving curriculum materials are also presented.

545. Gavryck, Jacquelyn A. **"Teaching Concept Identification through the Use of the** *Thesaurus of ERIC Descriptors.***"** *Online* 4 (January 1980): 31-34.

Elaborates on the use of the *Thesaurus of ERIC Descriptors* to teach concept identification, informational interview techniques, and search strategy formulation in an online reference course taught at the SUNY/Albany School of Library and Information Science. Both extensive interviewing practice and a basic understanding of indexing conventions of each database are viewed as essential elements of completing a successful search. Describes how exercises in using the *Thesaurus* help students become better interviewers and searchers.

546. Harper, Laura G. **"ECER on BRS."** *Database* 2 (June 1979): 37-55.

Describes the *Exceptional Child Education Resources* (ECER) database produced by the Council for Exceptional Children (CEC). Limitations include: 1) delay in indexing; 2) difficulty in avoiding duplications when searching both ERIC and ECER; 3) lack of both major and minor descriptors before 1976. Advantages are: 1) depth of indexing; 2) option of free text searching; and 3) economical price. ECER is compared to other related files (e.g., PSYCHOLOGICAL ABSTRACTS) and print indexes (e.g., *Deafness, Speech, and Hearing Abstracts*). Examples of search techniques and strategies are demonstrated using ECER on BRS in early 1979. A "Searchguide" and "Database Specifications" are appended.

547. Hawkins, Donald T. and Betty Miller. **"On-line Data Base Coverage of the On-line Information-Retrieval Literature."** *Online Review* (March 1977): 59-64.

Analyzes the coverage of the literature of online retrieval systems by eight major databases available in 1977. Results are ranked and compared. Almost 400 unique references were retrieved. Concludes that at least six databases need to be searched to obtain a relatively comprehensive bibliography. These six databases, listed in order of productivity, are INSPEC, CA CONDENSATES, SOCIAL SCISEARCH, ERIC, MEDLINE, and BIOSIS. Stresses the need for an online database in library and information science.

548. Knapp, Sara D. and Maria L. Zych. **"The ERIC Data Base and the Literature of Library and Information Science."** *RQ* 16 (Spring 1977): 209-212.

Analyzes the coverage of library and information science in the ERIC database in 1974 and 1975. Full indexing for more of the journals and the inclusion of more dissertations are strongly recommended. Concludes that ERIC provides good coverage on current topics in the field, but does not extensively cover more ephemeral items or foreign journals. Statistical analysis of ERIC distribution by publication type is also provided.

549. LaBorie, Tim and Michael Halperin. **"The ERIC and LISA Databases: How the Sources of Library Science Literature Compare."** *Database* 4 (September 1981): 32-37.

Compares two databases (ERIC and LISA) which cover the field of library and information science. Subject searches were performed on both databases and the results were evaluated against bibliographies manually prepared by students in Drexel University's School of Library and Information Science. Findings include: 1) many items found by the students were not retrieved by searching ERIC and LISA: 2) there is much overlap between the two databases; and 3) ERIC is the "preferred" database when a comprehensive search is not necessary. Reasons for these findings are examined.

550.   Schippleck, Suzanne. **"Impossible Indexing, or Looking at ERIC."** *RQ* 11 (Summer 1972): 352-55.

Criticizes the indexing system used by ERIC in 1972. Major complaints about the *Thesaurus of ERIC Descriptors* include: 1) too many synonymous descriptors; 2) inconsistent use of descriptors; 3) failure to index under both a broad and specific subject term; and 4) inability to restrict searches by geographical location. Stresses the importance of proper vocabulary control when assigning index terms.

551.   Slusser, Margaret G. **"NICEM, the Non-Print Database."** *Database* 3 (September 1980): 63-67.

Traces the origin and development of the NICEM database. Produced by the National Information Center for Educational Media, it contains over 500,000 entries for all types of nonprint media (films, filmstrips, 8mm film cartridges, transparencies, audio tapes, video tapes, records, and slides). Bibliographic elements, searchable indexes, and examples of searches are provided. Brief bibliography is appended.

552.   Sward, Andrea J. **"CIJE—Searching for the Answers to Two Questions: Do You Need Supplementary Education Index Searches? Can You Save Money by Skipping Full Format Output?"** *Database* 2 (December 1979): 22-27.

Evaluates the need for both online ERIC and manual *Education Index* searching for the same topic. Concludes: 1) *Education Index* is typically more current and covers earlier years (1929-1968) and 2) abstracts in *CIJE* are valuable and should be printed in most cases. Other differences (e.g., selective or comprehensive article selection) between the two educational indexes are discussed. Cites six circumstances when a supplementary manual search of *Education Index* is recommended.

553.   Yarbough, Judith. **"A Novice's Guide to ERIC—The Database of Education."** *Online* 1 (July 1977): 24-29.

Outlines the process of conducting a computer search on ERIC. Deciding on an online search and choosing which database to search are important initial considerations. Defining the problem and selecting ERIC descriptors and identifiers are then undertaken. ERIC indexing rules are summarized and four basic indexing concepts are identified: 1) population concepts; 2) action or material concepts; 3) curriculum concepts; and 4) document type concepts. Major search steps are summarized.

ENERGY, ENVIRONMENT, AND EARTH SCIENCES

While there is a great deal of overlap in the coverage of the environmental, energy, and earth science areas, the following topics and specialized databases can be identified:

1)   Energy
      Major databases include APILIT and APIPAT (American Petroleum Institute; published literature and patents), EBIB (Energy Bibliography and Index), ENERGYLINE, FEDEX (Federal Energy Data Index), P/E NEWS, and TULSA.

2) Oceanography and Water Resources
   Major databases include OCEANIC ABSTRACTS and WATER RESOURCES ABSTRACTS.

3) Geosciences
   Major databases include GEOARCHIVE and GEOREF.

4) Environmental Health and Pollution
   Major databases include ENVIROLINE, EPB (Environmental Periodicals Bibliography), and POLLUTION ABSTRACTS.

Many multidisciplinary databases, e.g., NTIS or CONFERENCE PAPERS INDEX, might also be searched for information in any of these areas.
Related sections in this bibliography include:

Agriculture, Food Science, and Nutrition (Entries 465-493)
Technology, Engineering, and Science (Entries 700-722)

554.   Adams, Gary and Robert R. Walter. **"Aquatic Sciences and Fisheries Abstracts (ASFA)."** *Database* 4 (March 1981): 37-53.
Describes the scope and subject coverage of the Aquatic Sciences and Fisheries Abstracts (ASFA) database as it was searchable on DIALOG in early 1981. ASFA indexes the international literature on "Marine, brackish, and freshwater environments." It is compared to *Oceanic Abstracts* and found to include at least twice as many citations for most major subject categories. Uses of the various fields in the basic index (e.g., geographic descriptions) are described in some detail, and the additional indexes are also mentioned. An annotated list of search aids is included. Search samples and "database specifications" are appended.

555.   Bridges, Kitty. **"Environmental Health and Toxicology: An Introduction for the Online Searcher."** *Online* 5 (January 1981): 27-34.
Outlines search techniques and vocabulary problems encountered by experienced online searchers who do not have a background in environmental health and toxicology, but must occasionally search for information in these areas. The need to know technical, as well as popular, terms is stressed. The following bibliographic databases are individually described: 1) APTIC; 2) BIOSIS; 3) CHEMICAL ABSTRACTS; 4) MEDLINE; and 5) NTIS. Nonbibliographic databases and databases containing government regulations are also discussed.

556.   Burk, Cornelius F., Jr. **"A Worldwide List of Source and Reference Databases in the Geosciences."** *Database* 5 (June 1982): 11-21.
Lists 128 databases which provide coverage in the geosciences. Eighty-two are defined as "source databases," e.g., they provide information directly, and the remaining forty-two are considered "reference databases," e.g., they direct users to sources of information. Databases are grouped by subject coverage and the following information provided for each: name, producer, country of origin, public availability, and comments. Articles describing specific databases are identified and included in an extensive bibliography.

557.   Fears, Charles B. and Marjorie M. K. Hlava. **"Search Corner—Coal Information: How to Find It."** *Online Review* 4 (September 1980): 290-93.

Emphasizes the need to conduct both manual and online searches to retrieve comprehensive information about coal and the coal industry. Traditional print sources, including relevant indexes and journals, are described. Available online databases, e.g., GEOREF, are also discussed. Print sources are best when the search must cover many years or when legal information is required. Online searches can economically survey current literature.

558.   Ford, Shelley and Eulalie Brown. **"Federal Energy Data Index on BRS."** *Database* 4 (March 1981): 28-35.

Details the uses of the Federal Energy Data Index (FEDEX) database on BRS. Not only are standard bibliographic citations provided for relevant items, but statistical tables, graphs, and other data presentations are also separately indexed to a high level of specificity. Demonstrates how it is also possible to restrict a search by data date, data sources, data aggregate, and information level. Searchable fields and the type of data presentation on BRS are described. FEDEX is briefly compared to other related databases. Differences in accessing FEDEX on BRS and on DOE/RECON are also considered.

559.   Kaback, Stuart M.; Karen Landsberg; and Anne Girard. **"APILIT and APIPAT: Petroleum Information Online."** *Database* 1 (December 1978): 46-67.

Describes the two technical information files produced by the American Petroleum Institute (API) — APILIT (published literature) and APIPAT (patents). Recent substantial changes in coverage are indicated and other databases dealing with the oil industry are mentioned. General search techniques are given, but searching for patents and chemicals is emphasized. Importance of hierarchical relationships in the *API Thesaurus* are stressed. Highly specialized search techniques (e.g., use of roles and links) are discussed in some detail. "Searchguides" and "Database Specifications" are appended.

560.   Leigh, B. **"Online Searching of Bibliographic Geological Databases and Their Use at the Science Reference Library."** *Journal of the Geological Society* 138 (September 1981): 589-97.

Highlights the use of geological databases at the British Library Reference Divisions Science Reference Library. A brief overview of online searching is provided and then three major geological databases (GEOREF, GEOARCHIVE, and the earth science subfile of PASCAL) are individually examined. Costs of searches are presented and the operation of the Science Reference Library briefly noted.

561.   Luedtke, John R. and Richard D. Walker. **"Water Resources Abstracts Database."** *Database* 3 (June 1980): 11-17.

Describes the WATER RESOURCES ABSTRACTS database, the online version of *Selected Water Resources Abstracts*. It is available on the DOE/RECON system. Brief historical background is presented and the coverage of the database is detailed. Various parts of the unit record are dealt with individually. The 60 subject classifications used are listed and explained. Sources of input into the database ("Centers of Competence") are also described. Basic search hints are presented. A list of different types of vocabulary used in the database is also included.

562.   McCuaig, Helen. **"Navigating Your Way through Oceanic Abstracts Database."** *Database* 1 (September 1978): 26-41.

Describes the scope and coverage of OCEANIC ABSTRACTS. Detailed lists of appropriate subject areas are provided. Although OCEANIC ABSTRACTS' coverage of oceanography is very comprehensive, eight other related databases are described. A typical search is presented to demonstrate various search techniques. Notes certain weaknesses, but concludes that OCEANIC ABSTRACTS is an excellent database for its subject. A "Searchguide," "Database Specifications," and a lengthy list of abbreviations used are appended.

563. Mellor, D. G. **"Information Service for Maritime Industry."** *Special Libraries* 70 (April 1979): 170-72.

Describes the services and publications concerning the maritime industry which are available through the Maritime Research Information Service. Online retrieval of this information is available through DIALOG in 1979. Brief description of the contents of the database is presented. An appendix indicates the 24 subject classifications used.

564. Miller, Betty. **"Energy Information Online."** *Online* 2 (January 1978): 27-32.

Identifies various databases which cover energy information and groups them into various fields (e.g., patents, oil, engineering, etc.). The following seven files are individually described: APILIT, APIPAT, PIE NEWS, TULSA, NTIS, CA CONDENSATES, and ENERGYLINE. Results of sample searches are presented. Concludes that several files must be searched for comprehensive coverage.

565. Miller, Betty. **"Overlap among Environmental Databases."** *Online Review* 5 (October 1981): 403-404.

Compares the coverage of environmental information by three databases available on DIALOG: 1) POLLUTION ABSTRACTS; 2) ENVIRONLINE; and 3) EPB (Environmental Periodicals Bibliography). Results of eight sample searches are statistically presented in tables. Concludes that there is a "low overlap among the three files and reaffirms the need to search more than one file for a comprehensive search."

566. Mulvihill, John G. **"Additional Searches Submitted by the American Geological Institute."** *Database* 3 (December 1980): 47-48.

Presents alternative search strategies to those used in a preceding article (see #567) which evaluated the GEOREF database. Written by the director of the American Geological Institute, the producer of GEOREF. Consists of search strategies for the same six topics used in the accompanying article. Suggests that searchers of GEOREF should: 1) use truncation; 2) search in the basic index; 3) exclude items by using the general categories; and 4) prepare thoroughly.

567. Oppenheim, C. and S. Perryman. **"GeoRef/GeoArchive."** *Database* 3 (December 1980): 41-46.

Details a comparative evaluation of two geoscience databases conducted in the summer of 1979. GEOREF, produced by the American Geological Institute and available on SDC, and GEOARCHIVE, a product of Geosystems and available online through DIALOG, are briefly described and then compared on the basis of 12 searches executed on both files. While both are judged to be very useful databases, GEOREF is recommended as the "first choice for geological searches." This conclusion is drawn because GEOREF is found to be easier to use and has better coverage of pre-1974 materials (See also #566.)

568. Rholes, Julia M. **"The Energy Bibliography and Index Database—A Small, Specialized File with Some Unique Contents."** *Database* 5 (June 1982): 38-46.

Describes the background and content of the EBIB database available on SDC. EBIB corresponds to the printed *Energy Bibliography and Index*, which covers the energy-related materials in the Texas A&M University Library. Emphasizes the EBIB is a specialized database and is best used to retrieve unique types of documents (e.g., maps or German documents) and identify older materials. Subject coverage, access points, and indexing procedures are also discussed.

569. Robinson, Jo and Margaret Hu. **"DOE's Energy Database (EDB) versus Other Energy Related Databases: A Comparative Analysis."** *Database* 4 (December 1981): 10-27.

Uses three sample search topics to compare the Department of Energy's (DOE) Energy Data Base (EDB) with other related energy databases. Search strategies and results are analyzed for each topic. Problems are also indicated for each search. Found that EDB has "very good, but not complete coverage" of energy information. EDB typically yielded a high number of citations, including many unique and foreign items. Concludes that EDB should be searched first on any energy or energy-related subject. Tables are appended which statistically compare the databases used.

570. Rogalski, Leonore. **"Online Searching of the American Petroleum Institute's Databases."** *Journal of Chemical Information and Computer Sciences* 18 (February 1978): 9-12.

Discusses the three databases produced by the Central Abstracting and Indexing Service of the American Petroleum Institute. The databases cover the petroleum and chemical fields and include APILIT (which covers bibliographic references), APIPAT (which lists patents), and PIE NEWS (which covers current news items from five specialized publications in the field). Online search features and examples are given for each database.

571. Shatz, Sharon. **"Database Review: ENVIROLINE."** *Online* 1 (January 1977): 20-23 + .

Describes ENVIRONLINE, a database devoted solely to environmental information, produced by the Environment Information Center. Disadvantages of using ENVIRONLINE on RECON are given and its availability on DIALOG is noted. Concludes that the database is easy to use, and the availability of documents retrieved on microfiche is lauded. An example of using ENVIRONLINE for an "impossible" request is given. "Database Specifications" are also listed.

572. Starr, Susan S. **"Databases in the Marine Sciences."** *Online Review* 6 (April 1982): 109-125.

Investigates the overlap in both subject coverage and serials indexed of four databases which deal with sources in marine biology. Statistical comparisons are presented and certain overall conclusions reached: 1) BIOSIS has the most references to marine biology, but GEOREF provides the best coverage of marine geology; 2) ASFA, GEOREF, and OCEANIC ABSTRACTS do overlap considerably in their indexing of the major serials in the field; and 3) BIOSIS offers the best system of taxonomic indexing. Notes that "databases never overlap completely."

573. Walker, Richard D. **"Database Review: GEOREF (Plus Other Geoscience Databases)."** *Online* 1 (April 1977): 74-78.

Describes the background and coverage of the GEOREF database, produced by the American Geological Institute. Search features and access points are described and corresponding printed bibliographies and indexes identified. Notes that GEOREF is designed for use by "professional geoscientists." Availability of documents retrieved and other related geoscience database are briefly discussed. "Database Specifications" are included.

574. Walker, Richard D. **"Geoarchive: A Brief Review."** *Online* 2 (October 1978): 40-43.

Describes the GEOARCHIVE database produced by Lea Associates Limited of London, Geosystems Division. Its coverage and availability on DIALOG are discussed. Access points and level of indexing are also considered. GEOARCHIVE is tentatively compared with GEOREF and the two databases are found to be "very complementary."

575. Walker, Richard D. **"GeoArchive Online."** *Database* 1 (December 1978): 34-45.

Details the searching of GEOARCHIVE on DIALOG in 1978. GEOARCHIVE is a comprehensive database covering all areas of "geoscience." A list of topics and subject areas indexed is given. Examples of search techniques using standard DIALOG prefix and suffix codes are provided. Concludes that certain limitations (e.g., only being able to search online since 1974) are present, but that these are more of an inconvenience than a serious limitation. The "Classification of Geoscience" and "Database Specifications" are appended.

576. Walker, Richard D. and Kurt F. Wendt. **"DOE/RECON and the Energy Files; Some Files That May Soon 'Go Public.' "** *Database* 2 (December 1979): 54-67.

Describes the DOE/RECON search system and the 23 databases available through it in late 1979. Originally developed by Lockheed and the U.S. Atomic Energy Commission, RECON (REmote CONsole) is currently produced under the authority of the Department of Energy. Similarities between DOE/RECON and DIALOG are briefly mentioned. Problems of the system are summarized. Searching on two files is described in detail: 1) DOE ENERGY DATABASE and 2) GENERAL AND PRACTICAL DATABASE. Urges that all of the databases in DOE/RECON be made more available through commercial search services.

577. Weiner, Anthony and Gilbert Cintra. **"P/E News."** *Database* 4 (June 1981): 58-67.

Describes the content of P/E News and offers suggestions for effectively searching the database. Indexing of the seven core journals (*Middle East Economic Survey, National Petroleum News, The Oil Daily, The Oil and Gas Journal, The Petroleum Economist, Petroleum Intelligence Weekly*, and *Platt's Oilgram News*) is explained, as is coverage of other supplementary journals. Two search aids available from the American Petroleum Institute (Index Guide and Keyword Frequency List) are explained. Specific search tips and precautions are enumerated. Plans to expand coverage and add abstracts for some items are mentioned.

HUMANITIES AND FINE ARTS

The humanities were the last discipline to be affected by online searching, but coverage is rapidly expanding. Specific databases are now available in literature (MLA BIBLIOGRAPHY), art (ART MODERN), philosophy (PHILOSOPHER'S INDEX), music (RILM ABSTRACTS), and religion (ATLA RELIGION). In addition, many multidisciplinary databases, e.g., COMPREHENSIVE DISSERTATIONS INDEX or MAGAZINE INDEX, can often be used to retrieve references in the humanities.

Related sections in this bibliography include:

News and Current Events (Entries 650-670)

578.   Anderson, James D. **"Structure in Database Indexing."** *The Indexer* 12 (April 1980): 3-13.

Describes the project undertaken by the Modern Language Association to design a prototype indexing system for the *MLA International Bibliography*. The structure of the database index is explained and the use of the highly structured CIFT system (Contextual Indexing and Faceted Taxonomic Access System) is discussed.

579.   Brady, Darlene and William Serban. **"Searching the Visual Arts: An Analysis of Online Information Access."** *Online* 5 (October 1981): 12-32.

Investigates the online coverage of the visual arts, as exemplified by references retrieved related to stained glass. Searches were conducted on DIALOG's DIALINDEX file, and 54 databases are identified as containing some relevant references. Different aspects of the topic (e.g., artistic trends and materials science) were searched. Cites needs for online access to other arts-related indexes and more retrospective coverage. Search strategies and the number of items retrieved are given for each database listed.

580.   Hoffman, Herbert H. and Alice B. Grigsby. **"Online Access to the Embedded Literature of 'Literature.'"** *Database* 4 (March 1981): 55-63.

Considers five databases that appear to provide online access to literature. Three files (LIBCON, BOOKINFO, and DISSERTATION ABSTRACTS) are considered too "analytic" and are not discussed in detail. Test searches are run against the two databases (MAGAZINE INDEX and MLA BIBLIOGRAPHY) judged to provide coverage of the "embedded literature of literature—literary texts and critiques." Difficulties in literary searching are detailed, and the need to distinguish between subject descriptors and genre descriptors is stressed. Concludes that online access to embedded literary works is "rudimentary, at best."

581.   Mackesy, Eileen M. **"MLA Bibliography Online Provides Access to Language, Literature, and Folklore."** *Database* 2 (September 1979): 36-43.

Details the history and development of the online version of the *MLA International Bibliography*. Scope and methods of compiling the bibliography are briefly discussed. A comparison of print and online access is also presented. Due to the classified arrangement in the printed *MLA Bibliography*, an online search offers many more points of access, which is a significant advantage. Search fields, as available on DIALOG in 1979, are mentioned. Future plans for the database are described and "Database Specifications" are appended.

582.   Sheng, Katharine K. **"ART MODERN/DIALOG."** *Database* 2 (June 1979): 19-33.

Presents a review of ARTBIBLIOGRAPHIES MODERN, the online version of *ARTbibliographies MODERN*. Scope and coverage ("almost all aspects of modern art and design") are stated briefly. Access points are discussed and examples given for six searchable fields: 1) basic index; 2) author index; 3) document type; 4) gallery index; 5) journal index; and 6) update. Limitations include: 1) small size (only 20,000 + citations in 1978); 2) limited coverage (art and design since 1800); and 3) delays in updating the file and other technical difficulties. General suggestions for a search interview are given. A "Searchguide" and "Database Specifications" are appended.

583.   Sievert, Mary Ellen. **"The Philosopher's Index."** *Database* 3 (March 1980): 50-61.

Examines how PHILOSOPHER'S INDEX is searched on DIALOG. Policies behind coverage, journal selection, and indexing are discussed. Nine searchable fields are individually explained. Stresses the importance of searching the Named Person field.

Concludes free text searching of the basic index should be sufficient in most cases. Other possibly related databases (e.g., SOCIAL SCISEARCH) are briefly noted. Search examples and a "Searchguide" are appended. Database is produced by the Philosophy Documentation Center in Bowling Green, Ohio.

LAW

WESTLAW and LEXIS are the two main online legal resources. Much has been written about their impact on the legal profession and law students. Complementary databases which cover various types of legal information are also available on the major commercial search services.

Related sections in this bibliography include:

News and Current Events (Entries 650-670)
Political Science, History and Government (Entries 671-680)

584. Appenzellar, Terry. **"Non-Legal Databases: Informing Clientele of the Existence and Application of Online Services."** *Law Library Journal* 73 (February 1980): 867-71.

Suggests how law librarians can make lawyers and other patrons aware of nonlegal databases and how they can be useful to them. Before marketing the service it is first necessary to "judge your audience" and determine how much information about the service needs to be disseminated. Online demonstrations are considered the best form of publicity but other methods are described. Stresses the value in having "educated clients."

585. Bull, Gillian. **"A Brief Survey of Developments in Computerized Legal Information Retrieval."** *Program: Automated Library and Information Systems* 15 (July 1981): 109-119.

Reviews the general characteristics of legal literature and the criteria for a successful computer-based retrieval system. Summarizes the international developments in this area, with special emphasis on American and Canadian activity. The two systems available in the United Kingdom (LEXIS and EUROLEX) are described and British projects are also noted.

586. Dee, Mathew F. and Ruth M. Kessler. **"The Impact of Computerized Methods on Legal Research Courses: A Survey of LEXIS Experience and Some Probable Effects of WESTLAW."** *Law Library Journal* 69 (May 1976): 164-84.

Investigates the effect of requiring law students to use either LEXIS or WESTLAW in their legal research courses. Presents results of a survey of LEXIS use by law schools in 1976. WESTLAW was not available in any law school at that time, but predictions are made based on the use of LEXIS. Concludes that online research systems "can enjoy a future in the legal research methodology," but realizes that costs may prevent immediate widespread use in law schools.

587. Greguras, Fred M. and Larry L. Carlile. **"Databases of the Legal Profession: A Survey of Speciality, Legal Files and Legal Information in Bibliographic Databases."** *Database* 3 (June 1980): 46-50.

Identifies databases available in early 1980 in the field of law and legal research. WESTLAW, produced by the West Publishing Company, and Mead Data Control's LEXIS are described and contrasted. Complementary databases available on DIALOG and ORBIT are also described and these search services are compared with WESTLAW and LEXIS. Examples of "innovative problem solving" using computer-assisted legal research (CALR) services are given. Concludes that technological advances (e.g., optical character scanning) will greatly affect online legal databases in the future.

588.   Hambleton, James E. **"JURIS: Legal Information in the Department of Justice."** *Law Library Journal* 69 (May 1976): 199-202.

Describes JURIS, an online legal information system developed by the U.S. Department of Justice. A historical overview is provided and developments in the system described in chronological order. Coverage of memoranda, briefs, and other legal work produced within the department are emphasized. Results of an evaluation project conducted in May 1975 are briefly discussed. Future plans for JURIS are also noted.

589.   Harrison, Nicolas. **"LEXIS: A Radical Approach to Computer-Assisted Legal Research."** *Program: Automated Library and Information Systems* 15 (July 1981): 120-31.

Discusses generally legal research and traditional sources of the law. The need for a computer-based system to provide better access to various areas of legal research is emphasized. The LEXIS system is then described. Demonstrates searching on LEXIS with various examples and explains the file structure and system logic. Points out that LEXIS is organized in a form familiar to lawyers.

590.   Larson, Signe. **"Online Systems for Legal Research."** *Online* 1 (July 1977): 10-14.

Reports the results of a survey conducted by the Federal Judicial Center in 1975 and 1976 that showed "online systems superior" to manual research. The three online systems used (LEXIS, WESTLAW, and AUTO-CITE) are then described and compared. Concludes that computer-assisted legal research can complement manual searching, but that economic factors make it a very "expensive alternative." Advantages and disadvantages of full text systems are also briefly discussed.

591.   Laurence, R. **"Introducing Students to LEXIS: A Model Self-Teaching Exercise."** *Law Library Journal* 71 (August 1978): 467-70.

Presents a model self-teaching exercise to be used to introduce law students and other users to LEXIS. Brief introduction is followed by the complete exercise used by first-year law students at the University of Illinois College of Law. Designed to be completed in 15 minutes, the exercise can also easily be adapted by the instructor to fit a specific type of legal problem. It can also be used by professional librarians, library science students, and legal secretaries.

592.   Munro, Robert J.; J. A. Bolanos; and Jan May. **"LEXIS vs. WESTLAW: An Analysis of Automated Education."** *Law Library Journal* 71 (August 1978): 471-76.

Compares the scope and content of WESTLAW and LEXIS. Discusses both the organization of documents within the system and the organization of data within the documents. Search techniques, online commands, and system services are also compared. WESTLAW has advantages of full text coverage of all 50 states, while LEXIS special libraries in tax, trade, security law, and the *U.S. Code* are very beneficial. Concludes that the two systems are "nearly equivalent in strengths and weaknesses."

593.   Myers, Mindy J. **"Impact of LEXIS on the Law Firm Library: A Survey."** *Law Library Journal* 71 (February 1978): 158-69.

Presents the results of a questionnaire sent to Lexis subscribers in four cities (Cleveland, Chicago, New York, and Washington, DC). The following points were investigated: 1) usage of LEXIS, and library staff size; 2) subscription to the National Reporters; 3) role of the law librarian in conducting searches; 4) full text or citation-only retrieval systems and the use of other bibliographic databases. Results are statistically presented and discussed. The actual questionnaire is appended.

594. **"Online Information Retrieval for the Legal Profession: A User's Perspective — A Panel."** *Law Library Journal* 70 (November 1977): 522-49.

Reports the presentations and discussions of a panel at the Seventieth Annual Meeting of the American Association of Law Libraries. Speakers addressed the following issues: 1) how to select a system; 2) how to improve use of a system; and 3) how to initiate improvements in currently available systems. Comparisons were generally made between LEXIS, WESTLAW, and JURIS. Emphasis was on "practical suggestions for managing the use of online legal information retrieval systems."

595. Rust, Ronald A. **"Automated Legal Research and Litigation Support: Comparisons and Contrasts."** *Online* 4 (July 1980): 12-15.

Distinguishes between automated litigation support and automated legal research. Descriptions of both types of services are presented and uses of LEXIS and WESTLAW in legal research are summarized. Comparisons of legal research and litigation support are made in the following areas: 1) database content; 2) size of the database; 3) potential users; 4) life expectancy of the database; 5) security; 6) volatility of the database; 7) report requirements; and 8) computer software.

596. Schulte, Linda. **"Survey of Computerized Legislative Information Systems."** *Law Library Journal* 72 (Winter 1979): 99-129.

Presents a state-of-the-art review of statutory and legislative information systems that are available to facilitate legislative research. Historical developments and suggestions for a future national system are discussed. Describes systems providing statutory retrieval (e.g., LEXIS) and bill status reporting systems. Profiles of existing state and commercial systems are provided in an appendix.

597. Seba, Douglas B. **"Online in Court: Some Novel Uses of Computerized Databases."** *Online* 1 (October 1977): 24-27.

Examines the usefulness of online databases in adversary actions, administrative hearings, and related regulatory actions of the United States Environmental Protection Agency. Finds that the impact of online searching is substantial. Actual examples are presented. Uses of online searching in preparing cases, improving cross-examinations, and verifying witnesses' statements are described. Notes, however, that in most cases, items retrieved by online searches supplemented information obtained elsewhere.

598. Sprowl, James A. **"Computer-Assisted Legal Research: Westlaw and Lexis."** *American Bar Association Journal* 62 (March 1976): 320-23.

Compares two legal research services — LEXIS of Mead Data Corporation and WESTLAW of West Publishing Company. Similarities in coverage and search techniques are noted. Tables are included which list legal sources available in each and also present sample search requests. Noting that the two systems have major differences, no comparative conclusions are drawn.

599. Sprowl, James A. **"WESTLAW vs LEXIS: Computer-Assisted Legal Research Comes of Age."** *Program: Automated Library and Information Systems* 15 (July 1981): 132-41.

Describes WESTLAW and LEXIS. Examples are presented for both systems to demonstrate how they can be used to conduct legal research. Search techniques, access points, and coverage are explained for each. Specific comparisons are made between the two for the following: data input, text editing, indexing procedures and text enhancements, updating, and hardcopy support. Despite differences identified, concludes that the "customer will find it difficult to choose between them."

600.   Welsh, Eric L. **"WESTLAW: A Database Review and Searching Primer."** *Online* 4 (July 1980): 16-23.

Summarizes the content and applications of WESTLAW, an online legal research service produced by the West Publishing Company. Searchable fields are identified and explained. Actual search examples are used to demonstrate specific search techniques and strategies. Specialized searches, e.g., statute or topic keynumber, are also presented with appropriate sample strategies given. Also discusses when to use WESTLAW and why it is not more heavily used.

601.   Zick, K. A. **"Developing and Implementing a Law School Westlaw Orientation Program."** *Law Library Journal* 72 (Spring 1979): 260-75.

Describes an instructional program used at the Wake Forest University Law Library to expose law students to WESTLAW. Development of the program and its objectives are summarized. The actual manual used by the law students is reproduced. It serves as an introduction to computerized legal research and guides the student through various searches on WESTLAW.

MEDICINE AND LIFE SCIENCES

MEDLINE, one of the MEDLARS databases produced by the National Library of Medicine, is the most well-known medical database. However, there are other databases available which cover all aspects of medicine and the life sciences. Other MEDLARS databases include AVLINE, BIOETHICS, CANCERLIT, POPLINE, and TOXLINE. EXCERPTA MEDICA is one of the leading international sources of biomedical information. BIOSIS is the major source of information in the life sciences. Medical information can be found in a wide variety of other databases, ranging from SCISEARCH to DRUGDOC, and multiple file searches are often required.

Related sections in this bibliography include:

Multiple Database Searching (Entries 242-249)
Chemistry (Entries 509-539)

602.   Adams, S. **"The Way of the Innovator: Notes toward the Prehistory of Medlars."** *Bulletin of the Medical Library Association* 60 (October 1972): 523-33.

Presents a chronological history of the development of MEDLARS prior to 1961. Factors which influenced the basic design and rationale behind MEDLARS include the need for a machine-readable medical index, the Welch Medical Indexing Research Project, the need to develop standardized medical indexing, and the initial Index Mechanization Project. Notes the success of the original planning for the entire MEDLARS project.

603.   Bac, Robert. **"A Comparative Study by the PDR of Toxicology Information Retrieval from Online Literature Databases."** *Online* 4 (April 1980): 29-33.

Reports the results of a study conducted by members of the Toxicity Data Committee of the Pharma Documentation Ring PDR from April 1977-February 1979 to investigate the coverage of toxicology information by online databases. Four search topics were performed on six databases (RINGDOC, CA CONDENSATES, TOXLINE, MEDLINE, EXCERPTA MEDICA, and BIOSIS) and the results statistically compared. Stresses the need to search more than one database for reasonably comprehensive coverage.

604.   Bawden, D. and T. K. Devon. **"RINGDOC: The Database of Pharmaceutical Literature."** *Database* 3 (September 1980): 29-39.

Describes the Derwent RINGDOC pharmaceutical database. RINGDOC is a highly specialized database designed to meet the needs of the pharmaceutical industry. It is available only by subscription with Derwent and only on SDC. Outlines the coding system used and provides specific search examples to demonstrate the various search features discussed. The use of "Codeless Scanning" access points is also explained. Stresses that RINGDOC is too complex to be adequately explained in a journal article and notes that over 20 user manuals are available to aid in searching the database.

605.   Blair, John C., Jr. **"Online Drug Literature Searching: EXCERPTA MEDICA."** *Online* 4 (October 1980): 13-23.

Outlines the coverage of the pharmaceutical literature by EXCERPTA MEDICA. Search techniques and access points applicable to the database, as available on DIALOG, are discussed in detail. Four main approaches to the drug literature are identified and explained: 1) adverse reactions; 2) drug dependence; 3) clinical applications; and 4) toxicology. Concludes that "EXCERPTA MEDICA is probably unexcelled in its coverage of drugs used in clinical settings."

606.   Bowen, Ada M. **"On-Line Literature Retrieval as a Continuing Medical Education Course."** *Bulletin of the Medical Library Association* 65 (July 1977): 384-86.

Describes a two-hour continuing education course, "Patient Management/ Computerized Information Resources Used in Patient Care," sponsored and conducted by the Medical Center Library of the University of South Florida. Course content and publicity are discussed. A small enrollment was a negative factor, but the course was judged a success and will be offered again.

607.   Bridgman, Charles F. and Emanuel Suter. **"Searching AVLINE for Curriculum-Related Audiovisual Instructional Materials."** *Journal of Medical Education* 54 (March 1979): 236-37.

Discusses how AVLINE can be searched online to retrieve audiovisual instructional materials for use in medical schools. Content of the database is described and typical search strategies identified. Suggests that items retrieved be evaluated with regard to their currency, comments contained in the abstract, and their sponsorship. Difficulties in obtaining the actual material are noted.

608.   Burrows, Suzetta and Sylvia Kyle. **"Searching the MEDLARS File on NLM and BRS. A Comparative Study."** *Bulletin of the Medical Library Association* 67 (January 1979): 15-24.

Notes differences and similarities of the MEDLARS database as it is available from BRS and NLM. Comparisons of citation elements and system features are presented. Lengthy tables provide summarized comparisons of these items. Concludes that, while the coverage is identical on both commercial search services, "significant capability differences" exist between searching MEDLARS on BRS and NLM.

609. Crampon, Jean E. **"Introducing the Laboratory Animal Data Bank."** *Database* 4 (September 1981): 12-29.

Describes the Laboratory Animal Data Bank (LADB) developed by the National Library of Medicine and operated by the Battelle Columbus Laboratories. Details what LADB is, how and when it can be used, and from where the information contained in the file originates. Both clinical observations and reference information of control animals are included. LADB facilitates comparative studies because it indexes by species, source, age, sex, the type of feed, and other husbandry variables. Nineteen tables are included which present numerous sample searches on the database.

610. Curtis, Dade T. **"On-line Retrieval as an Information Source for Bench Bioscientists."** *Online Review* 1 (December 1977): 279-88.

Reports the results of a survey conducted in 1977 to determine the extent to which research bioscientists use online searching. Ranking of sources used by respondents indicates that it is not a major source. Profiles of searchers, potential searchers, and nonsearchers are presented and compared. Causes of low search usage include communication problems between bioscientists and information specialists, inadequate training of users and intermediaries, and ineffective marketing of online databases.

611. Egeland, J. **"SUNY Biomedical Communication Network: Six Years of Progress in Online Bibliographic Control."** *Bulletin of the Medical Library Association* 63 (April 1975): 189-94.

Summarizes the development and expansion of the SUNY Biomedical Communication Network from 1968 to 1974. Available databases are listed and the SUNY Network membership is described. Information gained about the following aspects of regional networks is also discussed: 1) monographic indexing and retrieval; 2) shared cataloging; 3) user education; and 4) administration of networks. Concludes that high-quality online search services can be provided at a reasonable cost through regional networks.

612. Eger, Arthur J. **"Looking for Information on Carcinogenic Properties of Chemicals."** *Database* 5 (June 1982): 55-61.

Analyzes various sources which can be used to retrieve information on the carcinogenic activity of a specific compound. Bibliographic and nonbibliographic databases are listed and briefly individually described. Ten print sources are also given. Stresses that searchers must become more familiar with the various databases because "multiple database searches must be carried out" in most cases.

613. Eisenberg, Laura J.; Roy A. Standing; Charles S. Tidball; and Joseph Leiter. **"*MEDLEARN*: A Computer-Assisted Instruction (CAI) Program for MEDLARS."** *Bulletin of the Medical Library Association* 66 (January 1978): 6-13.

Describes *MEDLEARN*, a second-generation computer-assisted information program designed to train users of MEDLINE. *MEDLEARN* uses online tutorial dialogues, practice drills, testing, and simulation to expose users to the MEDLINE database. Arrangement of *MEDLEARN* in three distinct levels of search operations is explained. Benefits and limitations are also noted, as is the availability of *MEDLEARN*.

614. Fisher, Douglas A. **"Keeping Current through Computer Information Services: Bioscience Information Service."** *Food Technology* 30 (May 1976): 66-68.

Describes the preparation and indexing involved in producing BIOSIS. General background of online searching is provided and then BIOSIS is discussed in some detail. Cooperative efforts between database producers concerning overlap of coverage are also noted. Medical aspects related to food technology are stressed.

615. Foreman, Gertrude; Margaret Allen; and Donna Johnson. **"A User Study of Manual and MEDLINE Literature Searches in the Hospital Library."** *Bulletin of the Medical Library Association* 62 (October 1974): 385-87.

Evaluates the receptibility of health practitioners to online searches. Requests for searches were performed both manually and online on MEDLINE, and both sets of results were given to the patron. A user survey indicated acceptance of online searching, but a preference for a manual search. Results were affected by the provision of copies of relevant articles from the manual search, but not of articles retrieved by MEDLINE. Concludes that medical librarians should regard MEDLINE as a "valuable supplement to the manual search."

616. Green, Ellen Wilson. **"Searching the MEDLARS File for Information on the Elderly."** *Bulletin of the Medical Library Association* 69 (October 1981): 359-67.

Describes search strategies and techniques that can be used to search MEDLARS databases for information on the elderly. General terms used in geriatric studies are identified and defined. Sample search topics are presented and actual online results given. Provides an overview of the coverage of geriatrics by the following MEDLARS databases: AVLINE, BIOETHICS, CANCERLIT, CATLINE, HEALTH, MEDLINE, POPLINE, and TOXLINE. Concludes that while MEDLARS is "extensive in scope, it is by no means exhaustive."

617. Greenberg, Bette; Robert Breedlove; and Wendy Berger. **"MEDLINE Demand Profiles: An Analysis of Requests for Clinical and Research Information."** *Bulletin of the Medical Library Association* 65 (January 1977): 22-30.

Presents a statistical analysis of the professional use of MEDLINE at the Yale Medical Library. Results are analyzed with regard to rank and department affiliation, age, grant support and frequency of use. Findings include: 1) broad searches are requested more often; 2) requests are primarily research-oriented; 3) associate and assistant professors use MEDLINE the most; 4) highest percentage of use is by junior faculty; and 5) frequency of use correlates with faculty rank and years in the profession.

618. Hafner, Arthur; Laural A. Haycock; and Diane J. Caroll. **"Searching the MEDLARS Special List Catagories."** *Online* 1 (July 1977): 73-81.

Clarifies the use of the Special List categories when searching MEDLINE. Emphasis is given to the Special List Nursing, and search examples were performed on MEDLINE through the National Library of Medicine. Sample searches are used to demonstrate how the Special List Nursing can be used to limit retrieval and generally increase effectiveness. Stresses that searchers must be aware of constantly changing indexing procedures.

619. Hoover, Ryan E. **"RINGDOC—The Database for Pharmaceutical Manufacturers and Researchers."** *Online Review* 5 (December 1981): 453-68.

Provides an overview of the RINGDOC database of Derwent Publications Ltd. RINGDOC's coverage of pharmaceutical literature is summarized and the structure of the database described. Two indexing systems are explained: 1) codeless scanning, a system of searching by keywords and 2) Ring Code System, a technique unique to RINGDOC for searching chemical compounds and biological activities. Numerous examples of search techniques and RINGDOC records are presented.

620. Johnson, Jenny A. **"Appraisal of Educational Materials for Avline: An Educational Materials Project in Health Education."** *Audiovisual Instruction* 21 (January 1976): 22-27.

Details the development of the National Library of Medicine's AVLINE (AudioVisual Catalog Online). An "expert-review" type of evaluation is used to select and review nonprint materials for the file. In many cases, the critique of an expert reviewer is added to the record in AVLINE. Notes that evaluations and modifications of the project are expected in 1976.

621. Jones, Norbert A.; August Swanson; and Jenny Johnson. **"Educational Materials Reviewed for Avline."** *Journal of Medical Education* 51 (April 1976): 299-304.

Describes the development of AVLINE and its expanding role in providing access to nontextbook educational materials for medical educators. Identification of items to be considered for inclusion in the database is discussed, as is the formal review process. Three main reasons for not recommending an item for AVLINE are presented — content quality, instructional design, and technical quality.

622. Katter, Robert V. and Karl M. Pearson, Jr. **"MEDLARS II: A Third Generation Bibliographic Production System."** *Journal of Library Automation* 8 (June 1975): 87-97.

Describes MEDLARS II and points out the new technologies and advances in information retrieval which are incorporated in this new version of the MEDLARS system. System design and major features of MEDLARS II are summarized. Six subsystems are discussed: 1) specification maintenance; 2) input and release; 3) file maintenance; 4) retrieval; 5) publication production; and 6) management reporting. Examines various reasons for the success of MEDLARS II.

623. Lorent, Jean-Pierre. **"Online Literature Retrieval in Poison Control."** *Clinical Toxicology* 14 (1979): 115-21.

Assesses the coverage of information relating to the toxic effects of drugs and chemicals by online databases. Three main files are described and compared: TOXLINE, SCISEARCH, and EXCERPT MEDICA. Results of 12 searches run of these three databases are presented and statistically analyzed. The results show a "remarkable predominance of TOXLINE."

624. McCarn, Davis B. **"MEDLINE: An Introduction to Online Searching."** *Journal of the American Society for Information Science* 31 (May 1980): 181-92.

Considers MEDLINE a "prototype for on-line bibliographic search systems" and describes its historical development. Indexing procedures and file organization are also discussed. Special search techniques are identified and demonstrated through sample searches. Briefly describes the development of a document delivery system by the National Library of Medicine to complement MEDLINE.

625. McGee, Jenny L. **"A MEDLINE Feasibility Study."** *Bulletin of the Medical Library Association* 68 (July 1980): 278-87.

Reports the results of a MEDLINE feasibility study conducted by the Northeastern Consortium for Health Information (NECHI) to determine and promote MEDLINE use in hospital libraries. The study investigated the use of shared service to provide online access to MEDLINE and included demonstrations to all appropriate health care personnel. Notes that utilization improved with publicity and when the service was available within the requester's institution. The study demonstrated sufficient use to justify continued use of MEDLINE in NECHI.

626. Moll, Wilhelm. **"MEDLINE Evaluation Study."** *Bulletin of the Medical Library Association* 62 (January 1974): 1-14.

Reports the results of a survey of MEDLINE users conducted in 1973 at the University of Virginia Medical Library. Over 93% of the surveyed users labeled MEDLINE a "substantial improvement" over traditional print indexes, and three-quarters replied that they would be willing to pay for such a service in the future. Notes that such user fees may limit the use of MEDLINE by medical students and professionals.

627. Norman, Margaret. **"Continuing Education within a Hospital Library MEDLINE Consortium."** *Bulletin of the Medical Library Association* 67 (April 1979): 255-57.

Describes a continuing education group established by the Cincinnati MEDLINE Consortium to reinforce search skills and to provide a means of communication and consultation among area MEDLINE searchers. Monthly meetings include both business and instructional sessions. Program topics are described. Concludes that the continuing education group "has proven effective in providing high-quality MEDLINE services."

628. Powell, James R. **"Evaluation of Excerpta Medica On-Line."** *Special Libraries* 67 (March 1976): 153-57.

Analyzes the coverage of biomedical literature by EXCERPTA MEDICA. EXCERPTA MEDICA was compared with MEDLINE and TOXLINE. Search characteristics and results are described in some detail. Notes that EXCERPTA MEDICA is especially good in covering the drug literature. Suggestions for improving the database are presented. Concludes that EXCERPTA MEDICA has "considerable potential" and can serve as a supplement to the other medical databases.

629. Powell, James R., Jr. **"Excerpta Medica (EMBASE) Online — A Reacquaintance."** *Online* 4 (January 1980): 36-41.

Examines the background and major features of Excerpta Medica online (EMBASE). The 50 subject sections are listed and a sample DIALOG record is annotated. The use of the controlled thesaurus, *Malimet* (Master List of Medical Indexing Terms), is discussed. Results of sample searches are analyzed and cost figures given. Annotated references to available search aids are also included.

630. Russell, T. E. **"Medline: An Efficient, Inexpensive Way to Search Implant Literature."** *Journal of Oral Implantology* 8 (1978): 83-97.

Alerts implantologists to the availability of MEDLINE. Stresses the need for oral implantologists to be aware of recent advances in their field and suggests that MEDLINE is "probably the most useful aid available to the implantologist in his or her attempt to stay current." Other relevant databases available from the National Library of Medicine are briefly described.

631. Schirner, Hedi and Jean-Pierre Lorent. **"An Attempt to Compare EMCS with Toxline."** *Online Review* 2 (June 1978): 155-62.

Compares TOXLINE and EMCS (Excerpta Medica Computer System). Sixteen topics on various aspects of toxicology were searched on both databases. TOXLINE retrieved 559 unique citations, while EMCS yielded 247. Overlap varied from 6% to 50%. Expresses surprise that EMCS retrieved 31% of the unique references and concludes that it can be used to supplement searches on TOXLINE.

632. Schoolman, Harold M. **"Retrieving Information on Clinical Trial Methodology."** *Clinical Pharmacology and Therapeutics* 25 (May 1979): 758-60.

Examines the possibility of using online MEDLINE searches to identify articles which deal with the methodologies of clinical trials. Results indicate this can be done successfully, but that few detailed studies of any specific clnical trial have been published. Suggestions to improve both publication and retrieval of items published are also presented.

633. Schultheisz, Robert J. **"TOXLINE: Evolution of an Online Interactive Bibliographic Database."** *Journal of the American Society for Information Science* 32 (November 1981): 421-29.

Describes the development and content of TOXLINE, an online interactive bibliographic database of biomedical toxicology information available since 1972. Preparation of the file is described in some detail, and difficulties encountered in standardizing formats and data elements received from 11 different sources are noted. The development of algorithms for creating inverted file terms is also presented.

634. Simkins, M. A. **"Comparisons of Data Bases for Retrieving References to the Literature on Drugs."** *Information Processing and Management* 13 (1977): 141-54.

Compares the coverage of drug literature by six major databases (ASCA, RINGDOC, DRUGDOC, BIOSIS, CA CONDENSATES, and MEDLARS). Results of searches are analyzed with regard to coverage by the databases, retrieval by nonproprietary names, and currency. Results are statistically presented in charts. Greatest differences are in coverage of conference abstracts and indexing of general articles. The cost aspect was not considered.

635. Soben, Phyllis and Charles S. Tidball. **"***MEDLEARN***: Orientation to MEDLINE."** *Bulletin of the Medical Library Association* 62 (April 1974): 92-94.

Describes the ***MEDLEARN*** training file developed to aid users in learning to use MEDLINE. Development of ***MEDLEARN*** is summarized and its features explained. An interactive online presentation is used in conjunction with a printed manual. Ability of users to choose their own sequence of instruction from 40 available sections is noted. Evaluations of ***MEDLEARN*** at various medical schools are summarized.

636. Sparks, Susan M. **"AVLINE for Nursing Education and Research."** *Nursing Outlook* 27 (November 1979): 733-37.

Summarizes the educational and research uses of AVLINE (Audiovisuals On-line). Coverage of the AVLINE database is described and selection processes noted. Two categories of items are included—audiovisual instructional packages and references to scheduled educational events. Specific educational and research applications are presented. The availability of AVLINE is also given.

637. Tancredi, Samuel A.; Richard H. Amacher; and John H. Schneider. **"CANCERLINE: A New NLM/NCI Data Base."** *Journal of Chemical Information & Computer Sciences* 16 (August 1976): 128-30.

Describes the development of CANCERLINE by the National Cancer Institute and the National Library of Medicine. General characteristics and search features of the database are presented. Proposed costs and methods of making it available to users are also presented. Future improvements planned for the database are noted.

638. Thueson, Judy. **"Online Searches Net Data for Administrators."** *Hospitals* 53 (June 16, 1979): 103-108.

Describes the HEALTH PLANNING AND ADMINISTRATION database which is produced by the National Library of Medicine. Specific examples are presented to demonstrate the utility of the database. The option of hospital libraries providing online access to this and other NLM databases is presented and costs and other considerations briefly discussed.

639. Tousignaut, Dwight R. and Fran Spigai. **"Search 'Pharmacy' Databases: Nomenclature Problems and Inconsistencies."** *Database* 5 (February 1982): 23-29.

Begins by listing nine sample questions which can be searched on the International Pharmaceutical Abstracts (IPA) database. Distinguishes between medical, pharmacy, and pharmaceutical literature. IPA's strengths are: 1) international coverage of pharmaceutical literature; 2) coverage of pharmaceutical items in clinical medical journals; and 3) coverage of pharmacy trade literature. The problem of inaccurate literature, especially in the listing of drugs, is a significant one which should be pointed out to searchers. Answers to the nine questions are provided and search strategies explained.

640. Van Camp, Ann. **"Health Science Audiovisuals in Online Databases."** *Database* 3 (September 1980): 17-27.

Examines 14 databases which can be used to identify audiovisual materials available in all areas of the health sciences. Each database is described individually and the following points are given: 1) search services on which the file is available; 2) database producer information; 3) subject content; 4) start date and update frequency; 5) search aids; 6) printed equivalents; 7) abstracts; 8) document delivery; and 9) comments and search hints. The following databases are included: 1) AGRICOLA; 2) AVLINE; 3) AVMARC; 4) BIOETHICSLINE; 5) CATLINE; 6) CHILD ABUSE AND NEGLECT; 7) DRUG INFO; 8) ERIC; 9) EXCEPTIONAL CHILD EDUCATION RESOURCES; 10) LIBCON; 11) NICEM; 12) NICSEM/NIMIS; 13) NIMH; and 14) OCLC.

641. Van Camp, Ann J. and Gertrude Foreman. **"BIOSIS Previews and Medlars—A Biomedical Team."** *Online* 1 (January 1977): 24-31.

Notes how the MEDLARS and BIOSIS files can be used to complement each other in providing information to academic users. Actual search examples where one database is used to supplement the other are presented. A sidebar article describes the coverage and indexing of both files. A "Search Guide" for using BIOSIS and DIALOG is included. Software differences are also noted.

642. Watkins, Steven. **"*BIOSIS Search Guide*: A Review."** *Database* 5 (June 1982): 34-37.

Reviews the 1981 revised edition of the *BIOSIS Search Guide*. Describes the arrangement of both the database and the *Search Guide*. Five sections are identified and summarized: 1) Master Index; 2) Concept Codes; 3) Biosystematic Codes; 4) Content Guide; and 5) Profile Guide. Additional BIOSIS search aids are also noted. Concludes that the *Search Guide* is "highly recommended for all regular searchers of BIOSIS Previews."

643. Watkins, Steven G. **"The IRL Life Science Collection and BIOSIS: A Comparison of Online Access to the Literature of Biology."** *Database* 4 (September 1981): 39-59.

Compares the IRL LIFE SCIENCES COLLECTION database with BIOSIS. Both databases are individually described and then various features (e.g., depth of indexing) are evaluated. Search aids and indexing practices for both databases are also discussed. Sample searches are presented which demonstrate effective search techniques and show how the two files differ. The degree of overlap is also investigated. Concludes that BIOSIS "remains the single strongest database in the field of the life sciences." IRL should, however, be searched to obtain comprehensive coverage and when the topic is directly covered by the database. Sample searches and tables comparing results are appended.

644. Werner, Gloria. **"Use of On-Line Bibliographic Retrieval Services in Health Sciences Libraries in the United States and Canada."** *Bulletin of the Medical Library Association* 67 (January 1979): 1-14.

Presents the results of a questionnaire sent to 708 U.S. and Canadian users of MEDLINE in November 1977. Statistics were compiled for the following: 1) type of institution and current serial subscriptions; 2) use of NLM databases; 3) use of non-NLM databases; 4) operational service patterns; 5) staffing; and 6) fees for the service. Perception of the impact of such services on the library or institution is also investigated. General trends are noted, but no actual conclusions are drawn.

MULTIDISCIPLINARY

Many databases cover a wide range of topics and deal with more than one identifiable subject area. These multidisciplinary databases can be considered as possible files to be searched for most topics. Representative multidisciplinary databases include ASI, COMPREHENSIVE DISSERTATIONS INDEX, CONFERENCE PAPERS INDEX, FOUNDATION DIRECTORY, FOUNDATION GRANTS DIRECTORY, GRANTS, and PAIS.

Related sections in this bibliography include:

Multiple Database Searching (Entries 242-249)

645. Green, Lynn A. **"Database Review: American Statistics Index (ASI)."** *Online* 2 (April 1978): 36-40.

Describes both the print and online versions of the American Statistics Index (ASI). The multidisciplinary nature of the index is emphasized. Combining both controlled and free text searching is suggested, and other valuable search techniques (e.g., STRING SEARCH) are noted. Includes "Database Specifications."

646. Kulin, Joseph. **"Philanthropy at Your Fingertips: The Foundation Directory and Foundation Grants Index."** *Online* 1 (January 1977): 67-72.

Distinguishes between the FOUNDATION DIRECTORY and FOUNDATION GRANTS INDEX databases and describes how they both can be searched on DIALOG. Retrieval tips and an explanation of the natural language index are presented. Stresses that neither database is bibliographic, but both contain a brief, factual summary of a specific grant or foundation. Databases are compared to their print counterpoints. "Database Specifications" for each are included.

647. Provenzano, Dominic. **"PAIS International."** *Online* 5 (January 1981): 11-25.

Describes both the print and online versions of PAIS. Subjects covered, languages included, and document types represented in the database are outlined. Detailed examples are provided which demonstrate how PAIS is searched on DIALOG. The various online access points are individually presented. Overlap with other major social science and multidisciplinary databases is found to be insignificant. Concludes that PAIS "is a straightforward database to search."

648.   Snelson, Pamela. **"Online Access to Dissertations."** *Database* 5 (June 1982): 22-33.
Describes searching the COMPREHENSIVE DISSERTATION INDEX database on DIALOG. General background and file content are presented. Numerous DIALOG search techniques are demonstrated and illustrated with actual examples. Notes the lack of in-depth subject indexing and stresses the need to search the title field. Other online sources of dissertations are briefly noted. Two search examples are also presented.

649.   Unruh, Betty. **"Database Description. Conference Papers Index."** *Online* 2 (July 1978): 54-60.
Describes both the print and online versions of the CONFERENCE PAPERS INDEX. Ease of use and variety of access points are cited as advantages to using the online database. Searchable fields are listed and examples provided for each. "Database Specifications" are included.

NEWS AND CURRENT EVENTS

The New York Times INFORMATION BANK was one of the first databases to offer current access to a major newspaper index. Competition has come from NATIONAL NEWSPAPER INDEX, available on DIALOG, and NDEX, SDC's Newspaper Index. In addition, other current news services, like the Dow Jones News/Retrieval Service (DJNR), are now readily available. References to current popular magazine articles can be retrieved from MAGAZINE INDEX.
Related sections in this bibliography include:

References Uses of Online Searching (Entries 279-285)
Political Science, History and Government (Entries 671-680)

650.   Aveney, Brian. **"Competition in News Databases."** *Online* 3 (April 1979): 36-38.
Describes the NATIONAL NEWSPAPER INDEX and the New York Times INFORMATION BANK and compares them. Significant differences in coverage and selection policies are noted. Other online competitors (e.g., SDC's NEWSPAPER INDEX and the Dow Jones News/Retrieval Service) are also discussed. The intent of NATIONAL NEWSPAPER INDEX to offer "quicker, cheaper and easier access to news" is stressed.

651.   Bement, James H. **"DJNR. What Is It? How to Use It!"** *Online* 2 (July 1978): 39-40.
Presents an actual search requiring immediate access to current economic forecasts to demonstrate the value of the Dow Jones News/Retrieval Service (DJNR). DJNR is briefly described and its coverage discussed. Difficulties and limitations (e.g., no Boolean logic and no full text searchers) are noted and suggestions for improvement given.

652.   Cebula, Theodore R. **"On-Line Literature Searches: What Milwaukee Learned from the New York Times Information Bank."** *Wisconsin Library Bulletin* 73 (May-June 1977): 107-108.
Describes the implementation of online searching of the New York Times INFORMATION BANK by the Milwaukee Public Library in 1976. Main emphasis of the

project was staff development and education. Certain qualities needed by those trained to be searchers are identified. Types of requests received are analyzed and the cost factor briefly considered.

653. Dolan, Donna. **"Subject Searching of the New York Times Information Bank."** *Online* 2 (April 1978): 26-30.
Offers assistance to users of the New York times INFORMATION BANK in selecting subject terms and makes suggestions to improve the vocabulary used. Problems are identified in four areas: 1) currency; 2) multiconcept terms; 3) generic descriptors; and 4) verbosity. Hints and specific search techniques are given and illustrated with appropriate examples.

654. Garoogian, Rhoda. **"Library Use of the New York Times Information Bank: A Preliminary Survey."** *RQ* 15 (Fall 1976): 59-64.
Summarizes the results of a survey of 10 libraries using the New York Times INFORMATION BANK in 1975. Respondents were asked to indicate reasons for subscribing, who performs the searches, hours of operation, types of users, types of questions, and general use statistics. Difficulties encountered in using the system and general levels of satisfaction were also identified. Concludes that the New York Times INFORMATION BANK is "making inroads into libraries."

655. Greengrass, A. R. **"Information Center Profile. The New York Times Information Bank."** *Information Part-1* 6 (January 1974): 29-30.
Describes the development of the New York Times INFORMATION BANK. Coverage and indexing practices are noted. The process of indexing the daily newspaper is chronologically presented and the hardware used is briefly discussed. The potential of marketing the database to commercial users and other future plans are also mentioned.

656. Hogan, Thomas H. **"News Retrieval Services — Growing but Where Are They Headed?"** *Online Review* 3 (September 1979): 247-52.
Describes the differences and similarities between four online services providing access to newspaper and other news media: 1) New York Times INFORMATION BANK; 2) NATIONAL NEWSPAPER INDEX (on DIALOG); 3) NEWSPAPER INDEX (on SDC); and 4) Mead Data Control. Questions the need for extensive general news retrieval services. Problems involving full text searching and using intermediaries are also discussed.

657. **"The Information Bank Picture Story."** *Online* 4 (July 1980): 49-54.
Provides an overview of the operations of the New York Times Information Service. A tour of the facility in Parsippany, New York, is presented through pictures and brief descriptive comments. Mentions the various online databases produced by the New York Times Information Service, but aspects of the New York Times INFORMATION BANK are emphasized.

658. Moulton, James C. **"Dow Jones News/Retrieval."** *Database* 2 (March 1979): 54-65.
Defines the scope and development of the Dow Jones NEWS/RETRIEVAL (DJNR) database. Describes refinements (e.g., geographic categories for foreign news) added to the system by early 1979. The extreme currency (e.g., within 90 seconds after it appears on the Dow Jones wire service) is cited as a significant advantage over other databases. Numerous limitations are described and specific search hints are explained. DJNR is compared with the INFORMATION BANK and Predicasts databases and found to be

more current and to offer more citations. Sample searches are included. A "Searchguide" and "Database Specifications" are appended.

659.   Nash, Mary M. **"Globe and Mail Database: A Canadian First."** *Online Review* 3 (December 1979): 367-71.
    Highlights the development of the Toronto GLOBE AND MAIL database. This is the first database to become publicly available that includes the full text of a major newspaper. The file is generally described and the searchable fields and access points discussed in some detail. Examples of search strategies are provided.

660.   Oliver, Dennis and Jennifer Arbuckle. **"New York Times Information Bank in the North York Public Library."** *Canadian Library Journal* 34 (February 1977): 17-22.
    Details the experimental introduction of the New York Times INFORMATION BANK in a branch of the North York (Ontario) Public Library in 1974. Differences between the INFORMATION BANK and standard print reference tools are noted. Results and costs are analyzed and the impact of the new service on reference and other library areas is discussed. Searches were offered free. Concludes that the INFORMATION BANK can be an "important and valuable reference tool."

661.   **"Online Visits Dow Jones."** *Online* 3 (January 1979): 68-71.
    Presents a brief overview of the Dow Jones News/Retrieval Service and includes pictures of operations at Dow Jones headquarters in New York city. Various staff members are pictured and identified.

662.   Provenzano, Dominic. **"NEXIS."** *Database* 4 (December 1981): 30-41.
    Describes NEXIS, the database produced by Mead Data General which offers access to the full text of wire services, magazines, and newspapers. The coverage of the various wire services is described in some detail. Search keys, costs, logical connectors, and other search factors are generally described. Suggestions for improvement in the database are noted and planned enhancements described.

663.   Rhydwen, David A. **"Computerized Storage and Retrieval of Newspaper Stories at the Globe and Mail Library, Toronto, Canada."** *Special Libraries* 68 (February 1977): 57-61.
    Describes a computerized information storage and retrieval system designed and implemented at *The Globe and Mail*, a Toronto newspaper. Methods of retrieval, search modes, and special features are explained. Advantages of this system over traditional manual clipping files are also enumerated. Brief background of the system is also provided.

664.   Roblee, Martha. **"NY Times Information Bank Provided Quick, Easy Reference."** *Library Occurrent* 26 (May 1978): 59-62.
    Presents a general discussion of the implementation and use of the New York Times INFORMATION BANK in the mid-1970s by the Reference and Loan Division of the Indiana State Library. Statistics are given for costs, number of searches requested and performed, and types of libraries which requested searches. Coverage and search techniques are briefly discussed.

665.   Rothman, John. **"The New York Times Information Bank."** *Special Libraries* 63 (March 1972): 111-15.
    Describes the New York Times INFORMATION BANK as it was about to become operational in 1972. Brief background and problems faced in compiling such a database

are briefly discussed. Input features and search capabilities are also generally presented. Projected future developments are also enumerated.

666.   Rothman, John. **"The Times Information Bank on Campus."** *Educom: Bulletin of the Interuniversity Communications Council* 8 (Fall 1973): 14-19.
Describes the use of the New York Times INFORMATION BANK at the University of Pittsburgh in 1973. The INFORMATION BANK is generally outlined and then topics actually researched online are analyzed. Costs of providing access to the INFORMATION BANK are also detailed. Benefits to students, professors, and libraries are noted.

667.   Seulowitz, Lois. **"All the News That's Fit to Print."** *Online* 1 (January 1977): 57-60.
Analyzes the coverage and practical uses of the New York Times INFORMATION BANK in 1976. Examples of searches taking anywhere from 3 to 20 minutes are provided. Cost figures are presented and disadvantages and advantages of the system noted. The total dependence on a controlled vocabulary is criticized.

668.   Slade, Rod. *"Magazine Index*: **Popular Literature Online."** *Online* 2 (July 1978): 26-30.
Describes the MAGAZINE INDEX database available on DIALOG and finds it to be "complementary" with the New York Times INFORMATION BANK. Access points and coverage are defined. Uses of the "Named Person" and "Product Name" fields are examined. The low cost and general availability of the items indexed are cited as advantages to this database.

669.   Slade, Rod and Alex M. Kelly. **"Source of Popular Literature Online: New York Times Information Bank and the Magazine Index."** *Database* 2 (March 1979): 70-83.
Compares the INFORMATION BANK, a subsidiary of the New York Times Company, and MAGAZINE INDEX (as they were searchable in early 1979). Although both are commonly used as sources of popular literature, there are actually few similarities between the two. Significant differences in focus, indexing procedures, vocabulary used, online uses, and offline results are noted. Business and government users are directed to the INFORMATION BANK, and MAGAZINE INDEX is suggested for more general and academic uses. Concludes that: "The question determines the database to be used." "Searchguides" are appended for each file.

670.   Walsh, John. **"New York Times: All the News That's Fit to Printout."** *Science* 181 (August 17, 1973): 640-42.
Provides an early description of the New York Times INFORMATION BANK. The expense and problems encountered in designing the system are noted. Coverage and basic search techniques are demonstrated. Concludes that the INFORMATION BANK is not "at the forefront of technology," but is a pioneering effort in the field of information retrieval.

POLITICAL SCIENCE, HISTORY, AND GOVERNMENT

A wide variety of databases are available that cover the areas of political science, history, and government. The two primary databases in historical research are AMERICA: HISTORY AND LIFE and HISTORICAL ABSTRACTS. Political science and the related area of criminal justice are covered by USPSD (United States Political Science Documents) and NCJRS (National Criminal Justice Research Service). Congressional sources are indexed in many databases, including CRECORD, CIS, and FEDREG. The GPO MONTHLY CATALOG is the source of actual government publications.

Related sections in this bibliography include:

Law (Entries 584-601)
News and Current Events (Entries 650-670)
Social Sciences (Entries 681-699)

671. Conger, Lucinda D. **"Codes and Context in the CIS Database."** *Database* 1 (September 1978): 42-49.

Acknowledges that the online version of the Congressional Information Service's *Index to Congressional Information* is very complex, and entry formats and content terms can be extremely complicated to search because of specialized codes. Specific examples are given in searching by: 1) committee code; 2) document type; 3) date; and 4) bill numbers. A selective list of terms which can be used to limit results by various special characteristics (e.g., only those with statistical data) is also provided.

672. **"Database Visits Congressional Information Service."** *Database* 2 (March 1979): 66-69.

Presents a pictorial overview of the staff and services of Congressional Index Service. Brief histories of the development of ASI (*American Statistics Index*) and CIS (Congressional Information Service) are given. Recent expansions and future objectives are also discussed.

673. Dolan, Donna R. and Carol E. Heron. **"Criminal Justice Coverage in Online Databases."** *Database* 2 (March 1979): 10-32.

Provides an overview of databases which cover some aspect of criminology. NCJRS (National Criminal Justice Reference Service) database is judged to be the only "pure" file in this subject area, although not available from any of the major commercial search services in 1978. Representative "Hot Topic" searches and certain general search strategies were executed in 45 databases available in 1978 from DIALOG, SDC, National Library of Medicine, and the INFORMATION BANK. Results are presented and analyzed. Database selection is discussed and recommended databases for various aspects of criminal justice are listed. Descriptions of and descriptors used in various databases are also appended.

674. Falk, Joyce Duncan. **"Computer-Assisted Production of Bibliographic Databases in History."** *The Indexer* 12 (April 1981): 131-39.

Explains the editing and indexing procedures used to produce both the print and online versions of *Historical Abstracts* and *America: History and Life*. The American Bibliographical Center's Subject Profile Index (SPIndex) is described and the entire processing system detailed. Sample indexing and abstracts are presented and the production procedure diagrammed.

675. Green, Lynn A. **"Database Review: CIS Index."** *Online* 1 (January 1977): 47-51.

Provides an overview of the CIS index and database as it was available on SDC in 1976. Content and the thesaurus used to index congressional publications are described. The complexity of the unit record is discussed and briefly explained. Search aids available and the accessibility of microfiche copies of items retrieved are also noted. Concludes that searches on CIS often lead to "hidden wellsprings of scientific and technical data." "Database specifications" are included.

676. Gregory, N. **"The U.S. Congress: Online Users as Policymakers."** *Online Review* 3 (December 1979): 355-60.

Describes various internal online systems used by members of the U.S. Congress. Congressmen and their staffs are labeled the "world's largest concentration of policymakers using online systems." Congressional office use, electronic voting, and correspondence control are cited as examples of increased online use by national legislators. The availability of various sources of information retrieval, especially from the Library of Congress, are noted. Policy implications are also discussed.

677. Hunt, Deborah S. **"Accessing Federal Government Documents Online."** *Database* 5 (February 1981): 10-17.

Examines databases that can be used to retrieve federal documents online. Considers only those files that are currently publicly available and in which over half of the indexed items are federal documents. Databases are briefly described in the following categories: 1) general information; 2) congressional information; 3) business information; 4) U.S. government procurement; 5) medical information; 6) legal information; 7) criminal justice information; 8) technical reports; and 9) statistical information. A chart is appended which summarizes the databases listed under the nine broad categories.

678. Pilachowski, David M. **"United States Political Science Documents — USPSD."** *Database* 2 (December 1979): 68-77.

Enumerates the goals and access points of the United States Political Science Documents (USPSD) database. Comparisons are made between the loading of USPSD by DIALOG and SDC. Notes a time lag in updating when the article was written in July 1979. Suggests that some foreign periodicals be included in the coverage of the database. Sample records, examples of geographic searching, advantages and disadvantages of searching USPSD, and "Searchguides" are included.

679. Price, James R. and John Kaldahl. **"*The Congressional Record* Abstract File of Capitol Services, Inc."** *Online* 1 (July 1977): 36-41.

Describes the *Congressional Record* database, prepared by Capitol Services, Inc., as it is available on SDC as CRECORD and through the Library of Congress' SCORPIO information retrieval system. Similarities in citations are noted and differences in searchable fields are identified. The four sections of the *Congressional Record* are summarized. Technical hardware aspects are briefly noted. "Database Specifications" are included.

680. Usdane, Bernice S. **"U.S. Government Publications: Their Value, Online Accessibility and Availability for International Information Needs."** *Online Review* 4 (June 1980): 143-51.

Describes databases available on SDC and DIALOG which offer access to U.S. government publications. Emphasis is on databases which primarily include only federal publications. Both private and government databases are presented and compared in a chart which considers availability, coverage, cost, document delivery, and percent of federal publications. CIS, ASI, CRECORD, FEDREG, and GPO MONTHLY CATALOG databases are examined in detail.

SOCIAL SCIENCES

The social sciences typically cover a wide range of subjects and, consequently, multiple database searches are often required. The major databases in the social sciences are PSYCINFO, SOCIAL SCISEARCH, and SOCIOLOGICAL ABSTRACTS. NIMH (National Institute for Mental Health) competes with PSYCINFO and other specialized databases, e.g., CHILD ABUSE AND NEGLECT, are available from many of the major commercial search services.

Related sections in this bibliography include:

Multiple Database Searching (Entries 242-249)
Law (Entries 584-601)
Political Science and Government (Entries 671-680)

681. Angier, Jennifer J. **"Online Searching in Mental Health: The National Institute of Mental Health Database."** *Database* 4 (December 1981): 73-78.

Describes the National Institute of Mental Health (NIMH) database. Since federal funding was abolished in October 1981, continuation and updating of the database is in doubt. Coverage and background of NIMH is discussed and it is compared with PSYCINFO, MEDLINE, SOCIAL SCISEARCH, and other related databases. Concludes that NIMH is an "excellent, low cost single source."

682. Baranowski, George V. **"A Comparison of the Psychological Abstracts and National Institute of Mental Health Databases."** *Behavioral and Social Sciences Librarian* 2 (Fall 1980/1981): 13-24.

Compares the similarities, differences, and overlap between the PSYCINFO and NIMH (National Institute of Mental Health) databases. Analyzes the following points: journal coverage, degree of overlap, indexing procedures, and subject coverage. There was almost a 50% overlap in citation coverage, but concludes that the two databases are "complementary, not competitive." Searchers are urged to search both for comprehensive retrieval.

683. Black, John B. **"Social Science Database and Databanks in the United States and Canada."** *Inspel* 14 (1979): 40-45.

Discusses the availability and use of social science databases in the United States and Canada. General definitions of "social science" and "databases" are presented. Emphasizes bibliographic databases, but does note the increasing number of numeric and statistical databases in the social sciences. The following trends are identified: 1) growth in databaes, availability, and use; 2) increased competition between commercial search services; 3) improvements in telecommunications; and 4) technological advances. An appendix lists examples of social science databases available in 1979.

684. Bonnelly, Claude and Gaëtan Drolet. **"Searching the Social Sciences Literature Online: Social SciSearch."** *Database* 1 (December 1978): 10-25.

Describes the coverage and content of SOCIAL SCISEARCH, the online version of the *Social Science Citation Index*. Types of journals indexed, document types, languages represented, and relations with other files are briefly discussed. Various searchable fields are explained, but emphasis is placed on searching the basic index and the citation index. One problem is short or general article titles. Advantages include: 1) currency; 2) coverage of "core" journals; and 3) multidisciplinary coverage. A "Searchguide" and "Database Specifications" are appended.

685.   Caldwell , Jane and Celia Ellingson. **"A Comparison of OVERLAP: ERIC and Psychological Abstracts."** *Database* 2 (June 1979): 62-67.
Examines the degree of overlap between two highly used databases, ERIC and PSYCHOLOGICAL ABSTRACTS in 1979. Difficulties in determining actual overlap are discussed. For example, while only 21% of the over 1,000 journals indexed by *Psychological Abstracts* are also indexed by *Current Index to Journals in Education*, differences in selectivity of coverage, topics, and size of abstracts mask the true degree of overlap. Sample searches are provided and their results contrasted. Suggestions are given to aid searchers in choosing between ERIC and PSYCHOLOGICAL ABSTRACTS.

686.   Conger, Lucinda D. **"International Resources Online in the Social Sciences: The Holes in the Swiss Cheese."** *Behavioral and Social Sciences Librarian* 1 (Summer 1980): 275-79.
Investigates the online coverage of international relations and diplomacy. Databases in the social sciences are evaluated and found to be generally lacking in their coverage of this specialized area. Difficulties in searching the available databases are also discussed. Coverage of international law and business is judged to be very good and relevant databases are identified. Laments the lack of a specialized database dealing with diplomacy.

687.   Dolan, Donna. **"Psychological Abstracts/BRS."** *Database* 1 (September 1978): 9-25.
Describes the overall scope and historical development of the PSYCHOLOGICAL ABSTRACTS database. Problems which have resulted from the indexing policies of the American Psychological Association and the handling of the database by BRS are also detailed. The free text search capability can compensate for problems in searching the second edition of the *Thesaurus of Psychological Index Terms*. A list of search hints is provided, as are numerous examples of searches conducted on BRS. A "SearchGuide" for PSYCHOLOGICAL ABSTRACTS on BRS is also appended.

688.   Donati, Robert. **"Scanning the Social Sciences and Humanities through DIALOG."** *Online* Part I, 1 (October 1977): 48-57; Part II, 2 (January 1978): 41-52.
Summarizes the databases available on DIALOG which cover the social sciences and humanities in 1977. Ten primary databases, ranging from SOCIAL SCISEARCH to CHILD ABUSE AND NEGLECT, are individually described and briefly compared. Charts and tables provide comparative information and coverage of selected databases. General DIALOG search techniques are detailed, and specialized methods relevant to the social sciences and humanities databases are also discussed. Examples are presented in 20 figures.

689.   Donati, Robert. **"Selective Survey of Online Access to Social Science Data Bases."** *Special Libraries* 68 (November 1977): 396-406.
Provides an overview of the databases available in the social sciences on DIALOG in 1977. Databases are briefly described and coverage of selected social science topics is investigated. Charts and tables statistically compare the databases. Uses of the various thesauri available and the SEARCHSAVE feature on DIALOG are discussed. Cost figures are also presented and compared.

690.   Feinberg, Richard A.; David Drews; and David Eynman. **"Positive Side Effects of Online Information Retrieval."** *Teaching of Psychology* 8 (February 1981): 51-52.

Reports the results of an experiment to determine the effects that access to online searching has on undergraduate students enrolled in psychology courses. Students were assigned to prepare a literature review either manually or by having an online search conducted. Students who utilized online retrieval received higher grades on the project and felt more positive toward the library. Concludes that online searching "not only leads to better performance but had the unintended consequence of improving feelings and attitudes toward the library and the literature review process."

691.   Gerke, Ray. **"An Examination of the National Institute of Mental Health (NIMH) Database for Education-Related Information."** *Reference Services Review* 9 (October-December 1981): 61-66.

Summarizes uses of the NIMH databases in retrieving education-related materials. A brief description of the National Institute of Mental Health is provided. Compares NIMH to both PSYCINFO and ERIC. Results of sample single-term searches on all three databases are presented and analyzed. Because of the higher cost of PSYCINFO, NIMH is suggested as a logical "secondary database" in education after ERIC has been searched.

692.   Janke, Richard V. **"Searching the Social Sciences Citation Index on BRS."** *Database* 3 (June 1980): 19-45.

Concentrates on those aspects of the SOCIAL SCISEARCH database which are unique because of the way they are handled by BRS in 1979. General characteristics and coverage are not discussed. Four major features of SSCI on BRS are examined: 1) limiting search results by language, number of cited references, and year of publication; 2) splitting the database into two files, current years online and back years offline; 3) using assigned subject codes to refine search results; and 4) saving searches on an inexpensive file and executing them on SOCIAL SCISEARCH. Seventeen examples are presented in the text and five sample searches are also appended. A "Searchguide" and "Database Specifications" are also supplied.

693.   Kerbel, Sandra Sandor. **"Searching Sociological Abstracts."** *Database* 4 (June 1981): 30-44.

Evaluates the SOCIOLOGICAL ABSTRACTS database. The online file is briefly compared to the print version. Strengths of the database include: 1) only comprehensive file in sociology; 2) coverage from 1963; 3) indexing of conference papers; 4) numerous access points; 5) an authority file for personal names. Weaknesses are: 1) problems with broad indexing terms; 2) use of primarily single-term descriptors; 3) weak authority file; 4) delays in updating the online file; and 5) problems in indexing of conference papers. Suggests that searchers should use both free text capabilities and the broad descriptors. Concludes that SOCIOLOGICAL ABSTRACTS does "not easily lend itself to information retrieval." A "Searchguide" is appended.

694.   Knapp, Sara D. **"Online Searching in the Behavioral and Social Sciences."** *Behavioral and Social Sciences Libraries* 1 (Fall 1979): 23-36.

Describes 48 databases which provide online access to information in the behavioral and social sciences. A list is presented which gives the following for each database: producer, print equivalent, scope, availability, years, update frequency, and thesaurus. Limitations of online searches are noted and the importance of keeping up to data is emphasized. A selective bibliography is included.

695.   Parr, Virginia H. **"Online Information Retrieval and the Undergraduate."** *Teaching of Psychology* 6 (February 1979): 61-62.

Stresses the value of online searching of PSYCINFO and other social science databases for undergraduate students of psychology. Describes a typical informational interview with a student and the resulting search. Examples of undergraduate term papers researched online are presented. Students in psychology benefit because of the large number of relevant databases available.

696.   Rawles, R. E. **"The Function of the Library in a Computerized Information System for Psychologists."** *Education Libraries Bulletin* 21 (Spring 1978): 32-43.

Reports the responses of 15 psychology professors at the University of London to the availability of online searches of PSYCHOLOGICAL ABSTRACTS. Free searches were provided and a questionnaire used to evaluate satisfaction. Actual comments are quoted to indicate reactions to various aspects of the service. Overall comments were very favorable, but the possibility exists that the professors were biased because they were previously very active users of the library.

697.   Steiner, Roberta. **"Selected Computerized Search Services in Areas Related to the Behavioral Sciences."** *Special Libraries* 65 (August 1974): 319-25.

Provides a selective list of databases available in 1974 covering the behavioral sciences. Source of input, time coverage, turnaround time, availability, and cost are given for each database listed. Twenty databases or services are included. No qualitative comparisons or judgments are made.

698.   Wheeler, T. J. and A. J. Foster. **"Computerized Information Searching in Psychology."** *British Psychological Society. Bulletin* 30 (1977): 315-17.

Considers the various databases available in psychology as of January 1977. Basic search procedures are summarized and seven relevant databases briefly described. Advantages of online searches include thoroughness, speed, currency, and increased productivity. Limitations cited concern problems of relevance and recall. The "serendipity" of psychologists is also noted.

699.   Williams, Martha E. and Elaine Tisch Dunatov. **"Databases for Coping with Human Needs."** *Drexel Library Quarterly* 12 (January-April 1976): 110-38.

Lists commercially available databases and selected information and referral services which can serve as sources of information on "coping with human needs." General information and referral services are discussed and the need for national standards emphasized. A selective bibliography of coping literature is included.

TECHNOLOGY, ENGINEERING, AND SCIENCE

Many highly technical and scientific databases are available from the major commercial search services. Some are general in their coverage of these areas, e.g., INSPEC covers all areas of physics, electrical engineering, and computer science and COMPENDEX indexes the engineering literature. Other databases deal with a much more specialized subject, e.g., METADEX deals only with metals and WORLD ALUMINUM ABSTRACTS covers only items relevant to aluminum research or manufacture. SCISEARCH is the largest and most comprehensive source for information from many of the technical and scientific publications.

Related sections in this bibliography include:

Chemistry (Entries 509-539)

700.   Almond, J. R. and C. H. Nelson. **"Improvements in Cost Effectiveness in Online Searching. II. File Structure, Searchable Fields, and Software Contributions to Cost Effectiveness in Searching Commercial Databases for U.S. Patents."** *Journal of Chemical Information and Computer Sciences* 19 (November 1979): 222-27.

Considers the advantages and disadvantages of searching for U.S. patent information on three databases (CA CONDENSATES, CLAIMS, and WPI). Differences which affect search results and cost include: 1) file organization; 2) variety of access points; 3) assignee designation; 4) classification system usage; 5) free text capabilities; 6) equivalents; 7) software factors; and 8) relevance of the database to the specific topic. Concludes that selection of one database for a search depends on the individual topic to be researched.

701.   Antony, Arthur; Robert Sivers; Virginia Weiser; and Alfred Hodina. **"An Online Component in an Interdisciplinary Course on Information Resources for Science and Engineering Students."** *Online Review* 2 (December 1978): 337-44.

Describes a course for university students in science and engineering at the University of California which incorporates a section on practical applications of online searching. Students individually perform a search and explain the results to the class. Problems are discussed and student reactions noted. Stresses the need for such online exposure to students in these fields.

702.   Archer, Mary Ann E. **"Database Review. INSPEC."** *Online* 1 (October 1977): 42-45.

Examines the coverage and content of INSPEC (International Services for the Physics and Engineering Communities). Both the print and online versions produced by the British Institute of Electrical Engineers are briefly described. Difficulties in manual searching and advantages to online retrieval are emphasized. Emphasizes the usefulness of the subject classification codes and the various user aids. "Database Specifications" and a "Search Guide" are included.

703.   Byrne, J. R. **"Relative Effectiveness of Titles, Abstracts and Subject Headings for Machine Retrieval from the Compendex Services."** *Journal for the American Society for Information Science* 26 (July-August 1975): 223-29.

Investigates the effectiveness of searching for engineering information in COMPENDEX by searching on titles, subject headings, abstracts, free text terms, and combinations of these fields. Titles in engineering literature are found to be too general, and it is normally necessary to search both titles and abstracts. For comprehensive retrieval all data elements should be searched. A possible compromise is to search titles and subject headings with the same free text terms.

704.   Crawford, S. Y. and A. M. Rees, ed. **"Perspectives on On-Line Systems in Science and Technology."** *Journal of the American Society for Information Science* 31 (May 1980): 153-200.

Introduces a series of five articles (see also #190, 200, 260, 624, 718) which present an overview of the uses of online searching in science technology libraries. The following questions are considered in all of the articles: 1) What are online systems and what is the basic technology involved? and 2) How did they develop and how will they affect information retrieval in science and technology?

705. Dow, Richard F. **"INSPEC on BRS."** *Database* 1 (September 1978): 70-81.

Describes the coverage of INSPEC (International Services for the Physics and Engineering Communities). INSPEC is the online version of three print abstracting journals: *Physics Abstracts, Electrical and Electronics Abstracts*, and *Computer and Control Abstracts*. Subject search techniques are discussed and it is suggested that searchers use the Category and Treatment Codes assigned by INSPEC to all documents. Some minor problems are mentioned and advantages to using INSPEC on BRS are presented. A "Searchguide" and "Database Specifications" are appended.

706. Ellison, Sallie H. and Barbara K. Kunkel. **"Transportation and Vehicular Engineering: Online Literature Searching."** *Database* 3 (September 1980): 41-60.

Compares several databases which can be used to retrieve transportation literature, especially automotive engineering. The files used most often at the General Motors Research Laboratories Library are individually described. These include: 1) NTIS; 2) COMPENDEX; 3) ISMEC; 4) METADEX; 5) INSPEC; 6) SAE ABSTRACTS; 7) HIGHWAY SAFETY LITERATURE; and 8) TRIS (Transportation Research Information Service). Three sample searches are presented and the extent of overlap and relevancy of retrieved citations are analyzed. Stresses the need to search a wide variety of databases to cover the transportation field adequately.

707. Firschein, Oscar. **"Online Reference Searching."** *IEEE Spectrum* 12 (October 1975): 68-71.

Describes the general benefits to researchers and engineers in utilizing online searching. Sample questions from the engineering field and databases which can provide information on them are presented. Stresses that computer searches do not normally provide direct answers, but only yield bibliographic citations to relevant articles. Typical search examples are included.

708. Huleatt, Richard S. **"Product Safety Literature Searches."** *Database* 1 (December 1978): 26-33.

Summarizes a procedure used at the Armour Research Center to retrieve information on substances which are being considered for use in company products. Various databases available from the National Library of Medicine are used to identify potentially adverse effects or dangerous applications. A standardized search strategy is typically executed on a series of databases (e.g., CHEMLINE, RTECS [Registry of Toxic Effects of Chemical Substances], TOXICOLOGY DATA BANK Test File, TOXLINE, CANCERLIT, CANCERPROJ). Selection of databases and modifications of the standard search strategy are also described.

709. Iljon, Ariane. **"Scientific and Technical Data Bases in a Multilingual Society."** *Online Review* 1 (June 1977): 133-36.

Provides an overview of the use of different languages in databases, primarily scientific and technical, in 1977. Most databases are only searchable by using the English language. However, some databases have certain multilingual features (e.g., AGRICOLA displays both original and translated titles of foreign records). A few multilingual databases (e.g., TITUS) do exist. Concludes that this language problem must be faced, especially for European researchers.

710. Jerome, S. **"Comparative Study of the Coverage of Physics Journals by Two Computerized Data Bases—SPIN (Searchable and Physics Information Notes) and CAC**

(Chemical Abstracts Condensates)." *Information Storage and Retrieval* 9 (August 1973): 449-55.

Compares two databases (SPIN and CA CONDENSATES) which cover physics journals. Each database is briefly described. Both "qualitative evaluation" and "quantitative measurement of overlap" are considered. Concludes that the coverage in SPIN is "abnormally low" and that CA CONDENSATES is very comprehensive in some areas (e.g., nuclear physics), but poor in others (e.g., geophysics). Urges future cooperation between these two databases.

711. Kaback, Stuart M. **"Retrieving Patent Information Online."** *Online* 2 (January 1978): 16-25.

Provides an overview of databases and search techniques available to retrieve patent information online. Four sources of patent information are analyzed: 1) DERWENT WORLD PATENTS INDEX; 2) the Chemical Abstracts Services files; 3) IFI/Plenum CLAIMS files; and 4) American Petroleum Institute's APIPAT. Differences in timeliness, geographic coverage, access points, and spelling are discussed. The four files are found to have "large areas of overlap" and to be complementary.

712. Lavendale, Giuliana A. **"Computer in Research: A Real Time Partner."** *IEEE Spectrum* 15 (December 1978): 38-40.

Outlines the possible applications of online searching to electrical and electronic engineering. Generally describes the procedures and products of having a computer literature search performed. Engineering databases are identified and a chart indicates the appropriate database for various aspects of the electronics field.

713. Lerner, Rita G. **"SPIN."** *Online* 3 (October 1979): 23-26.

Presents an overview of SPIN (Searchable Physics Information Notices), produced by the American Institute of Physics. General background is provided and its coverage and unit record described. The use of international standards to classify each article is emphasized. Search aids and document delivery are briefly noted. "Database Specifications" are included.

714. Loader, J. M. **"Weldasearch—The Development of a Small Computerized Database."** *Aslib Proceedings* 30 (August 1978): 287-97.

Discusses the historical development and current capabilities of WELDASEARCH, a database produced by the Information Department of the Welding Institute. The need for SDI service and a thesaurus are examined. Retrospective file conversion and current file preparation are also described. Advantages of searching the file online are given.

715. Marsden, Tom and Barbara Laub. **"Databases for Computer Science and Electronics: COMPENDEX, ELCOM and INSPEC."** *Database* 4 (June 1981): 13-29.

Compares three databases (COMPENDEX, ELCOM, and INSPEC) which can be used to retrieve information in electronics and computer science. For general topics, all three files should be searched. Major characteristics of each database are described, as are their individual advantages and disadvantages. Concludes that: 1) INSPEC is the most current and yields the most comprehensive coverage; 2) ELCOM offers better coverage of trade literature; and 3) COMPENDEX has more foreign language items. Sample searches are demonstrated on both DIALOG and SDC. Comparisons and statistical analyses are also appended.

716. Murdock, Lindsay and Olivia Opello. **"Computer Literature Searches in the Physical Sciences."** *Special Libraries* 64 (October 1973): 442-45.

Lists databases available in 1973 which covered the physical sciences. Source of input, type of publications included, time coverage, availability, and cost are provided for each database given. Addresses are also provided for commercial search services which make the various databases available.

717. Nagle, Ellen. **"Sci-Tech Online."** See issues of *Science & Technology Libraries.*

Aims to "inform readers about the major developments in online searching relevant to sci-tech libraries." New databases are described and changes in files noted in this regular column in *Science & Technology Libraries.* Both bibliographic and nonbibliographic databases will be considered. Solicits the opinions and suggestions of the readers.

718. Regazzi, John J.; Bruce Bennion; and Susan Roberts. **"On-Line Systems of Disciplines and Specialty Areas in Science and Technology."** *Journal of the American Society for Information Science* 31 (May 1980): 161-70.

Lists and describes over 130 bibliographic databases available as of December 1979 which cover science and technology. Subject areas, source, commercial search service availability, and dates covered are given for each database included. Databases are further divided into two classifications: 1) discipline-wide, transdisciplinary, and multidisciplinary databases and 2) speciality or problem-oriented databases. Examples of larger databases in each category are individually discussed.

719. Savage, Gretchen S. and Jeffery K. Pemberton. **SciSearch on DIALOG."** *Database* 1 (September 1978): 50-67.

Provides a general overview of searching *SCISEARCH,* the online version of *Science Citation Index.* Subjects covered, journal indexes and companion citation indexes are briefly discussed. Suggests that two searches, one on the title index and one on the citation index, should typically be performed for comprehensive coverage. Search examples are provided for searching: 1) specific publications; 2) incomplete references; 3) expanding on author; 4) subject searching using a prominent author; 5) subject searching using keywords; and 6) limiting searches. A "Searchguide" is appended.

720. Spooner, Jane. **"The Use of Online Searching in the Field of Production Studies."** *Database* 2 (June 1979): 68-77.

Describes the use of online searching to retrieve information on production studies for students, faculty, and staff at the Cranfield Institute of Technology in England. Briefly provides background on the Institute and the information needs of the School of Production Studies. Search techniques for both general and production studies are examined. Most frequently used databases (e.g., COMPENDEX and NTIS) are listed and compared. Appendices include many actual searches.

721. Viesca, R. and A. Mendez. **Use of Online Terminals for Scientific Evaluation and Planning."** *Online Review* 2 (September 1978): 245-50.

Notes that online search services can be "new tools in the hands of scientific policy makers." Searches can be used to provide an objective evaluation of both earlier studies and the need for the proposed project. Three examples are presented in some detail. Notes that searches can even be used to identify journals which may report the results of a completed experiment.

722. Zundi, Pranas and John M. Gehl. **"Fire-Relevant Literature and Its Availability."** *Information Processing and Management* 12 (1976): 53-61.

Reports the coverage of fire-relevant literature in the various databases available in 1976. Databases produced by 37 different information centers were considered and their coverage of topics statistically analyzed. Found relevant items to be distributed over a wide assortment of databases. Eleven databases were selected as the best online sources of fire-relevant information. Fire literature is also shown to become rapidly out of date and to have a considerable time lag in processing by the database producers.

SOURCES OF ADDITIONAL INFORMATION

An attempt was made to select some of the significant books, directories, bibliographies, journals, and annuals and proceedings to supplement the journal articles previously annotated in the bibliography.

BOOKS

The following represent books which deal directly with online searching and would be valuable references for both experienced searchers and those librarians interested in this field. General books on information retrieval and books of a theoretical nature are not included. Since online searching is constantly changing, only the most current books are included.

723.   Atherton, Pauline and Roger W. Christian. **Librarians and Online Services.** White Plains, NY: Knowledge Industry Publications, 1977. 124p.
Provides an overview of online reference services. The impact on library staff and administrators and the startup considerations are analyzed. Financial procedures and costs involved, both directly and indirectly, in providing online searching are also considered. Of particular value are the many sample forms and checklists. Includes a brief bibliography.

724.   Chen, Ching-chih and Susanna Schweizer. **Online Bibliographic Searching: A Learning Manual.** New York: Neal-Schuman Publishers, 1981. 227p.
Serves as a self-instructional guide to online searching. The basics are well summarized and the following topics considered in detail:

1)   Question Negotiation;
2)   Searching for Database Indexes;
3)   Multi-database Searching;
4)   Major Commercial Search Services;
5)   Online Search Service Management; and
6)   Future of Online Searching.

Can also be used with the *DIALOG Lab Workbook* and provides answers to all of the online exercises. Includes many tables, figures, illustrations, and actual examples of searches.

725.   Henry, W. M.; J. A. Leigh; L. A. Tedd; and P. W. Williams. **Online Searching: An Introduction.** London: Butterworth and Company, Ltd., 1980. 209p.

Provides a brief historical introduction to online searching and then describes the hardware needed, the arrangement of information within a database, the types of services currently available, the role of the intermediary, and the need for education and training. Managerial aspects of providing online services are also emphasized. Appendices are included which provide information on BLAISE, ESA-IRS, INFOLINE, DIALOG, SDC, and EURONET.

726. Hoover, Ryan E., ed. **Library and Information Manager's Guide to Online Services.** White Plains, NY: Knowledge Industry Publications, 1980. 270p.

Designed as a guide for librarians and information managers who are initiating online search services. The following ten essays are included:

1) "Overview of Online Information Retrieval";
2) "Types of Data Bases Available";
3) "Producers and Vendors of Bibliographic Online Services";
4) "Management of an Online Information Retrieval Service";
5) "Measurement and Evaluation of Online Services";
6) "Promotion of Online Services";
7) "Training the Searchers";
8) "The Mechanics of Online Searching";
9) "Online User Groups"; and
10) "The Future of Online Services and Libraries."

A glossary of terms and a selected bibliography are also included.

727. Hoover, Ryan E., ed. **Online Search Strategies.** White Plains, NY: Knowledge Industry Publications, 1982. 345p.

Presents practical advice and search techniques for searching many of the bibliographic databases currently available from the major commercial search services. The book is organized by subject areas and each section is written by experienced searchers. Actual searches are reproduced and discussed. Intended for the experienced searcher.

728. Lynch, Mary Jo. **Financing Online Search Services in Publicly Supported Libraries: The Report of an ALA Survey.** Chicago: ALA, 1981. 55p.

Summarizes the results of a survey of publicly supported libraries which offer online searching to determine how such operations are financed. Over 70% of the libraries charge fees. Representative fee structures submitted by respondents are reproduced and analyzed. This brief book includes many tables which present detailed analysis of the responses to the survey. A bibliographic essay which reviews the financial aspects of online searching is also included.

729. Meadow, Charles T. and Pauline Cochrane. **Basics of Online Searching.** New York: John Wiley & Sons, 1981. 245p.

Outlines the basic theories and techniques involved in online searching. Designed to function as a textbook. Examples are drawn from the three major commercial search services, but the intent is to teach principles, not system specific techniques. Appendices include lists of databases available and examples of database descriptions and search aids.

730. Palmer, Roger C. **Online Reference and Information Retrieval.** Littleton, CO: Libraries Unlimited, 1983. 149p.

Introduces online searching as currently available from the three major commercial search services (BRS, DIALOG, and SDC). The book is divided into three parts: 1) overview of online information retrieval and database design; 2) separate chapters on searching procedures for the three major commercial search services; and 3) additional considerations. Designed to be used as a textbook, both individual and class assignments are included in each chapter, as are suggestions for supplemental reading.

DIRECTORIES

The major commercial search services readily provide lists of databases available on their systems. However, many more databases exist which are not accessible through these major services. Four directories are identified below which list and describe over one thousand databases currently available worldwide. In addition, a guide to terminals and microcomputers is included. Most of these publications are regularly updated, as noted.

731. **Directory of Online Databases.** Santa Monica, CA: Cuadra Associates. Published quarterly. 1979- .
Descibes a wide variety of databases publicly available. Access points include subject, database producer, database supplier, and commercial search service. Over 1,200 databases available from more than 190 online service organizations are included.

732. Hall, James L. and Marjorie J. Brown, eds. **Online Bibliographic Databases.** 2nd edition. London: Aslib, 1981. 213p. Distributed by Gale Research in the United States and Canada.
Provides detailed descriptions of 189 online bibliographic databases which are available from thirty-nine database suppliers or commercial search services. Information given includes name and acronym of the database, availability, subject coverage, file specifications, and costs involved.

733. Kruzas, Anthony J. and John Schmittroth, Jr. **Encyclopedia of Information Systems and Services.** 4th edition. Detroit: Gale Research, 1981. 933p.
Offers detailed descriptions of over 2,000 international organizations which produce, supply, make available, and/or use bibliographic and nonbibliographic databases. Individual databases are also extensively covered. Other aspects of the field of information technology, including videotex systems, software products, communications networks, and fee-based information services, are similarly described. Twenty-two different indexes provide easy access to the entries. Two periodical supplements (*New Information Systems and Services*) will be published between the fourth and fifth editions.

734. **Online Terminal/Microcomputer Guide & Directory, 1982-83.** 3rd edition. Weston, CT: Online Inc., 1982.
Includes both articles on choosing terminals and microcomputers and specifications on individual pieces of equipment. Over 60 print terminals and 70 video terminals are described, as are over 30 printers and 35 microcomputers. Two periodical supplements (November 1982 and November 1983) will update the information. Edited and compiled by the staff of *Online* and *Database*.

735. Williams, Martha E.; Laurence Lannom; and Carolyn G. Robins, eds. **Computer-Readable Databases: A Directory and Data Sourcebook.** White Plains, NY: Knowledge Industry Publications, 1982. Published for the American Society for Information Science. 1472p.

Includes more than 750 databases available worldwide. Each entry is described in detail and contains availability information, name of producer and supplier, size and growth, subject and chronological coverage, and much additional information. Indexes are provided for subject, database producer, database processor, and name.

BIBLIOGRAPHIES

Two bibliographies, one American and one British, have been published which provide extensive coverage of the field of online information retrieval. As well as journal articles, both include monographs, conference proceedings, reports, system documents, research studies, and other ephemeral publications. Because of the great number of items, annotations are either nonexistent or very brief.

736. Hall, J. L. **Online Information Retrieval Bibliography, 1965-1976.** London: Aslib, 1977. 267p. **Online Information Retrieval, 1976-1979.** Coauthored with A. Dewe. London: Aslib, 1980. 230p.

Provide international coverage of online bibliographic searching. Brief annotations are given for most entries. References come from books, conference and meeting proceedings, research reports, and journal articles. More than one thousand entries are included for the period 1976-1979. Author, Report Number, and Subject Indexes are provided.

737. Hawkins, Donald T. **Online Information Retrieval Bibliography, 1964-1979.** Marlton, NJ: Learned Information, Inc., 1980.

Covers online bibliographic, numeric, and other nonbibliographic databases and information retrieval systems. Citations to books, proceedings, research studies, journal articles, and other pertinent documents are included. The 1,784 unannotated entries are divided into the following seven sections:

1) Books, Reviews, Conferences;
2) Descriptions of Online Systems, Databases, and Services;
3) Man-Machine Studies, the User Interface and Attitudes, System Design and Evaluation;
4) Profile Development, Searching Techniques, Indexing;
5) Usage Studies, Economics, Promotion and Impact, Management;
6) User Education and Training; and
7) General, Miscellaneous.

This monograph is regularly updated by annual supplements in *Online Review* (See #171).)

PROCEEDINGS AND ANNUALS

The proceedings of the International Online Meeting sponsored annually by *Online Review* since 1977 are regularly published. Also listed are other general library science proceedings and annual reviews which are likely to include items of interest to online searching.

American Society for Information Science. **Proceedings of the ASIS Annual Meeting.** White Plains, NY: Knowledge Industry Publications, 1964- .

Annual Review of Information Science and Technology. Washington, DC: American Society for Information Science, 1966- .

Clinic on Library Applications of Data Processing. Proceedings. Urbana-Champaign, IL: University of Illinois, Graduate School of Library Science, 1963- .
Each volume is individually titled. The 1975 proceedings, *The Use of Computers in Literature Searching and Related Reference Activities in Libraries*, are of particular interest.

International Online Meeting. Proceedings. Oxford, England: Learned Information, 1977- .

JOURNALS

The major journals in the field of online searching are listed below. Three journals (*Database, Online*, and *Online Review*) are devoted almost exclusively to online searching.

Bulletin of the American Society for Information Science.

Bulletin of the Medical Library Association.

Database.

Information Technology and Libraries (formerly *Journal of Library Automation*).

Journal of the American Society for Information Science.

Online.

Online Review.

Special Libraries.

PERIODICALS CITED INDEX

All articles from *Database, Online*, and *Online Review* were included. A *de visu* examination of an additional seventeen journals (noted with an asterisk) was conducted for the period January 1970 through June 1982 and relevant items selected and annotated.

AUTHOR INDEX

Names have been standardized, e.g., items written by Danuta Nitecki and Danuta *A.* Nitecki are combined under one entry – Nitecki, Danuta A.

SUBJECT INDEX

Numbers in **bold type** should be regarded as primary sources.

Modern Management Accounting

A. TOM NELSON, PhD, CPA
PAUL B. W. MILLER, PhD, CPA

Professors of Accounting
University of Utah

Goodyear Publishing Company, Inc.
Santa Monica, California

Library of Congress Cataloging in Publication Data

Nelson, A. Thon as
  Modern management accounting.

  Includes index.
  1. Managerial accounting.   I. Miller, Paul B. W.,
joint author.   II. Title.
HF5635.N3973   658.1'552   76-12913
ISBN 0-87620-589-9

Copyright © 1977 by
Goodyear Publishing Company, Inc.
Santa Monica, California

Y-5899-3

Current printing (last digit):
10 9 8 7 6 5 4 3 2

Printed in the United States of America

Material from the Uniform CPA Examinations, copyright
© 1970, 1971, 1973, 1975 and 1976 by the American
Institute of Certified Public Accountants, Inc., is adopted
with permission.